WONDER WOMAN
UNBOUND

THE CURIOUS HISTORY OF THE WORLD'S MOST FAMOUS HEROINE

TIM HANLEY

CHICAGO
REVIEW
PRESS

An A Cappella Book

Copyright © 2014 by Tim Hanley
All rights reserved
Published by Chicago Review Press Incorporated
814 North Franklin Street
Chicago, IL 60610
ISBN 978-1-61374-909-8

Library of Congress Cataloging-in-Publication Data
Hanley, Tim.
    Wonder Woman Unbound : the Curious History of the World's Most Famous
Heroine / Tim Hanley.
        pages cm
    Summary: "With her golden lasso and her bullet-deflecting bracelets, Wonder
Woman is a beloved icon of female strength in a world of male superheroes. But
this close look at her history portrays a complicated heroine who is more than just
a female Superman. The original Wonder Woman was ahead of her time, advocating female superiority and the benefits of matriarchy in the 1940s. At the same
time, her creator filled the comics with titillating bondage imagery, and Wonder
Woman was tied up as often as she saved the world. In the 1950s, Wonder Woman
begrudgingly continued her superheroic mission, wishing she could settle down
with her boyfriend instead, all while continually hinting at hidden lesbian leanings. While other female characters stepped forward as women's lib took off in the
late 1960s, Wonder Woman fell backwards, losing her superpowers and flitting
from man to man. Ms. magazine and Lynda Carter restored Wonder Woman's
feminist strength in the 1970s, turning her into a powerful symbol as her checkered past was quickly forgotten. Exploring this lost history as well as her modern
incarnations adds new dimensions to the world's most beloved female character,
and Wonder Woman Unbound delves into her comic book and its spin-offs as well
as the myriad motivations of her creators to showcase the peculiar journey that led
to Wonder Woman's iconic status"— Provided by publisher.
    Includes bibliographical references and index.
    ISBN 978-1-61374-909-8 (pbk.)
    1. Wonder Woman (Fictitious character) 2. Women in literature. 3. Gender
identity in literature. 4. Comic books, strips, etc.—United States. 5. Literature
and society—United States. I. Title.

PN6728.W6H34 2014
741.5'973—dc23

                                2013045111

Unless otherwise indicated, all images are from the author's collection
Front cover design: Tim Hanley
Cover layout: Jonathan Hahn
Interior design: PerfecType, Nashville, TN

Printed in the United States of America
5 4 3 2 1

To my parents

Contents

Introduction

"**W**heeee! I'm a butterfly on the first day of spring!"

So exclaimed Diana Prince in *Wonder Woman* #182, her arms raised and her eyes closed, reveling in the joy of trying on expensive dresses in a trendy boutique in London. The year was 1969, and Wonder Woman had recently given up her superpowers, trading her bullet-deflecting bracelets and golden lasso for a normal life as her alter ego, Diana Prince.

Wonder Woman was a princess of the Amazons, the mythic race of warrior women, but when her sisters decided to leave for another dimension, Wonder Woman chose to stay behind with her boyfriend, Steve Trevor. Unfortunately, Steve died soon after she renounced her powers, and Diana set out on a quest to track down his killer. This brings us to London, where she took a hiatus from avenging Steve's death to go on a shopping spree with her new friend, Reginald Hyde-White. Reggie footed the bill for all of Diana's new mod fashions, and later that afternoon declared his love for her. Steve had just died three days before, and Diana had only met Reggie that morning, but our heroine was unable to resist his charms and kissed Reggie passionately. However, their love was short-lived: Reggie was employed

by Steve's killer, and he betrayed Diana later in the issue. Enraged, she attacked Reggie, nearly crippling him, and the story ended with a weeping and broken-hearted Diana running off into the night.

Wonder Woman is a recognizable figure: gold tiara, invisible jet, fights bad guys, looks like Lynda Carter. She's a role model for many, and the most famous female superhero in a genre dominated by males. She's also been a feminist icon since Gloria Steinem put her on the first cover of *Ms.* magazine in 1972. This gal, with no superpowers and no star-spangled outfit, cavorting with strange men, isn't the Wonder Woman that most people are familiar with.

Fans today tend to have a very iconic but generic concept of Wonder Woman, a combination of nostalgia for the 1970s TV show and vague associations with feminism. She is important and beloved as the most famous superheroine of all time, a bastion of female representation in a male-dominated genre, but she's a symbol more than a living, vibrant character. This is largely due to a lack of exposure; for the past thirty years, aside from her one sparsely read monthly comic, Wonder Woman has lacked the publication, television, and film presence of her fellow superheroes. The modern Wonder Woman is practically nonexistent outside of T-shirts and other memorabilia.

However, the early decades of Wonder Woman's history were incredibly bizarre, and these versions of the character fell by the wayside after Lynda Carter and *Ms.* magazine in the 1970s. Created in 1941 by a psychologist named William Moulton Marston, the original Wonder Woman looked and acted a lot like her modern-day counterpart, but she had an unusual background and some strange secrets. As years passed, new creators further convoluted the character, muddying her odd yet feminist origin. While American women grew from complacent housewives to protesters for women's liberation, gaining new strength and independence as they moved forward together, Wonder Woman fell backward.

Wonder Woman was created during the Golden Age of comics, before the temporary workplace gains of World War II, at a

time when women were told that their only place was in the home. An Amazon princess and the most powerful warrior of her race, Wonder Woman ignored these expectations. Her comics didn't just suggest equality of the sexes; they flat-out demonstrated that every woman had innate power and that Wonder Woman was superior to her male counterparts. By the 1950s, as the Silver Age of comics began, American women started to chafe under the limitations of their domestic lives just as Wonder Woman wanted to settle down. When women took to the streets in the late 1960s to demand their rights and Bronze Age heroines left behind the men who kept them down, a heartbroken Wonder Woman gave up her superpowers and sat out the women's liberation movement.

Wonder Woman grew opposite to the evolution of American women. But as it always is with Wonder Woman, there were further complications. Marston, the advocate of female power and strength, was also a kinky bondage enthusiast. The amazing Amazon who wished she could just be a housewife was labeled a man-hating lesbian by anti-comics crusaders. When not weeping over her lost love, our heroine flitted from man to man.

By rediscovering the forgotten history of Wonder Woman, we can both understand her journey to her current iconic status and flesh out Wonder Woman as a character and not just a symbol. Each of these early depictions of Wonder Woman was wrapped in contradictions, and none of them much resemble the contemporary Wonder Woman, but all of them together combine into the most peculiar and fascinating history of any comic book character.

★ PART 1 ★

The Golden Age

1

The Utopian Alternative

*O*rigin stories are an integral part of superhero comic books, repeated and referenced so often that they've become as iconic to the characters as the logos on their chests. Some origin stories have remained the same from the very beginning: in every telling of Batman's origin, Bruce Wayne witnesses the murder of his parents when he's a boy and dedicates his life to fighting crime. Other origin stories changed when new characters took on the mantle of an established hero: the original Golden Age Flash, Jay Garrick, gained superspeed by inhaling hard water vapors, while the Silver Age Flash, Barry Allen, gained the same powers from electrified chemicals.

Unlike the Flash, Wonder Woman remained the same character, but unlike Batman, each of her incarnations had its own distinct origin story.* Her first came from her creator, William Moulton

---

*Wonder Woman was relaunched in 1987 during DC Comic's companywide reboot following *Crisis on Infinite Earths*, an event meant to streamline fifty years of DC's continuity into one simple universe, and has been rebooted several times since.

Marston, a man whose lofty goals made him stand out among his fellow comic book creators in the early 1940s. He wanted to impart to his readers a specific message about female superiority. Most of the first superheroes had origins rooted in some sort of tragic event that motivated their crime-fighting career. Wonder Woman, on the other hand, was rooted in a feminist utopian vision. Her mission was not to resolve tragic personal issues but to help facilitate a coming matriarchy. Marston rejected the conventions of the burgeoning superhero genre and set up Wonder Woman as a new, unique brand of hero.

The Golden Age

The beginning of the comic book industry wasn't anything auspicious; publishers had a lot of paper and wanted to keep the presses running, so in the early 1930s they began reprinting newspaper comic strips as comic books. One of these new publishers was National Allied Publications, founded by Malcolm Wheeler-Nicholson in 1934. National's first series was *New Fun*, which premiered in February 1935. It was the first comic book to have only new material, most of which was written by Wheeler-Nicholson himself. National launched a second series with an even less imaginative title, *New Comics*, in December 1935. But Wheeler-Nicholson didn't have enough money to finance his third series, *Detective Comics*, so he turned to Harry Donenfeld, a publisher and distributor who headed the Independent News Company.

Donenfeld was a fierce businessman with a less than reputable history. His associations with gangsters and the mob dated back to the Prohibition Era, and in the early 1930s he published lurid, erotic pulp magazines. This new partnership with Wheeler-Nicholson led to the creation of Detective Comics Inc., and *Detective Comics* debuted in March 1937. Detective Comics Inc. was soon renamed National Comics when the crafty Donenfeld forced Wheeler-Nicholson out of

the company. Finding comics quite profitable, Donenfeld teamed up with another new publisher, Max Gaines, to form a sister company called All-American Publications in 1938.* Both companies used a logo based on the original partnership of Detective Comics Inc., the encircled initials "DC," and they were commonly known as DC Comics. *Detective Comics* did well, but it was National's new series, *Action Comics*, that changed the industry forever and marked the beginning of the Golden Age of comic books.

When comic books hit the newsstands in the early 1930s, two young men in Cleveland, Ohio, started submitting stories to every publisher they could find. The duo, writer Jerry Siegel and artist Joe Shuster, had a few scattered stories published, but they had one pitch that was continuously rejected for five years. In 1938, editor Vin Sullivan came across this pitch while trying to find a cover story for the first issue of *Action Comics*, and he hired Siegel and Shuster to do a story and provide the cover art.

Action Comics #1 premiered in June 1938. Its cover showed a strongman in blue tights and a red cape, with an S-shield emblazoned on his chest, lifting a car and smashing it onto a rock. The story identified this man as Superman, "champion of the oppressed, the physical marvel who had sworn to devote his existence to helping those in need," and the first superhero was born.

The character was an instant success; soon he was headlining *Action Comics* and his own eponymous series. His origin story, told briefly in *Action Comics* #1 and expanded upon in *Superman* #1, explained that Superman was actually Kal-L, a baby sent to Earth

---

*National and All-American Publications later formally merged and became National Periodical Publications in 1944. In the early days of comics, it was not uncommon for publishers to set up a new company for almost every book they published. The motivation behind this was that if a book failed, that company could be shut down easily without affecting the rest of the publishing line. Many comic book publishers were actually conglomerates of several smaller companies, housed in the same location and run by the same people.

in a rocket just before his home planet of Krypton was destroyed. Kal-L landed in Kansas, where he was found and later adopted by an elderly couple, the Kents, who named him Clark. Kryptonians had evolved to physical perfection, and because Earth was a smaller planet with weaker gravity, Clark developed superstrength and superspeed.* His adopted parents taught him to use his powers for good, and when they died he decided to become a hero and fight crime as Superman. As Clark Kent, he was a reporter at the *Daily Star*, alongside the ambitious Lois Lane, but whenever trouble came up he would duck out and Superman would shoot off to save the day. The enormous success of Superman made every comic book publisher want their own superhero, and they all told their editors to "get me a Superman."

National Comics won the race for the next big superhero, striking gold again with *Detective Comics* #27 in May 1939. The issue featured the Bat-Man (soon to be known as Batman), a vigilante in a bat-inspired costume with a dark cape and cowl. Created by Bill Finger and Bob Kane, Batman took to the streets to fight crime dressed like a bat because "criminals are a superstitious, cowardly lot, so my disguise must be able to strike terror into their hearts!"

Other superheroes soon followed, like Fawcett Publications' Captain Marvel in February 1940. Created by Bill Parker and C. C. Beck and first appearing in *Whiz Comics* #2, Captain Marvel was really a boy named Billy Batson who transformed into a powerful caped superhero when he said the name of the wizard Shazam.† Captain Marvel soon expanded into the Marvel Family with Mary Marvel and Captain Marvel Jr., and regularly outsold

---

*Later stories tweaked this origin slightly. Kal-L became Kal-El, and his powers came from Earth's yellow sun.
†Shazam is an acronym for the sources of Captain Marvel's powers: the wisdom of Solomon, the strength of Hercules, the stamina of Atlas, the power of Zeus, the courage of Achilles, and the speed of Mercury.

Superman.* Another "captain" continued the successful trend when Timely Comics published *Captain America Comics* #1 in March 1941. Created by Joe Simon and Jack Kirby, the comic featured the scrawny Steve Rogers, who volunteered to be a test subject for the army's super soldier serum and turned into the superpowered Captain America, the army's best weapon in World War II. The superhero craze continued for years, flooding the newsstands with new heroes every month.

Tragic Genesis and Violence

Superheroes in the Golden Age of comic books were somewhat maladjusted. A person would have to be powerfully motivated to dress up in a costume and fight crime, and for many of these heroes this motivation came from a tragic event.

Superman was the last of his race: his entire family, species, and planet were destroyed when Krypton exploded. His superpowers, and thus his ability to be a superhero, were tied to this destruction, and to the knowledge that he wasn't like other people. His adopted parents' deaths spurred him to become Superman, suggesting that he took up crime fighting as a way to deal with his loss.

Batman's origin story was told in *Detective Comics* #33: Bruce Wayne witnessed the death of his parents at the hands of an armed

---

*However, Captain Marvel resembled Superman to such a degree that DC Comics sued Fawcett for copyright infringement in 1941. After a decade of legal battling and facing a declining comic book market, Fawcett settled with DC in the early 1950s and shut down its comics division. Amusingly, DC licensed and later bought the rights to Captain Marvel and the whole Marvel family in the 1970s. DC still publishes Captain Marvel comics today, though he is now called "Shazam" to avoid conflict with Marvel Comics' Captain Marvel, originally an alien named Mar-Vell who first appeared in 1967. In current Marvel comics, the mantle of Captain Marvel has passed to Carol Danvers, who stars in a critically acclaimed eponymous series written by Kelly Sue DeConnick.

robber when he was a boy, and he pledged his life to avenging them and fighting a war on crime. Bruce used his family's wealth to become a master scientist and train his body to physical perfection.

Captain America's parents weren't part of his origin story, but Steve Rogers signed up for the super soldier program because he was deemed unfit to join the army. Steve Rogers's biological parents may not have been mentioned, but the man who was the "father" of Captain America, Dr. Josef Reinstein, was murdered by Nazis right at the hero's birth. Steve channeled his anger into patriotism.

Captain Marvel was yet another orphan. His uncle who was supposed to take care of him kicked him out and stole his inheritance. Lesser-known superheroes followed this tragic trend. Alan Scott became Green Lantern when a magical device allowed him to survive a train wreck that killed everyone else onboard. The Human Torch was an android buried away by his creator, manipulated by a racketeer, shot at by police officers, and exploited for financial gain by the first man to ever show him kindness—all over the course of just sixteen pages in his very first issue!

Several of these origin stories, including the very well-known tales of Superman and Batman, center on a character losing his parents at a very young age. The shock of this loss colors the rest of his life, and ultimately as a man he becomes a hero to resolve his feelings about this tragic event. This deep loss is at the core of his superhero identity, and while he can't get his own family back, he fights crime so that other families will be spared from tragedy.

When we look at the men who created the first generation of superheroes, this idea of dealing with tragic events becomes more pronounced. When Jerry Siegel was in junior high, his father died of a heart attack while his store was robbed. That he cocreated Superman, a hero powerful enough to stop any and every crime, seems appropriate.

World War II had a considerable influence on Jewish comic book creators as well. Many of the young creators in the early days of the industry were the sons of Jewish immigrants from Europe, or

immigrated themselves, including Jerry Siegel, Joe Shuster, Bill Finger, Bob Kane, Joe Simon, and Jack Kirby. All of these men created superheroes before the United States entered the war, and while the full extent of the Holocaust wouldn't be discovered until years later, the anti-Semitic beliefs of the Nazis were common knowledge in the late 1930s.

Superman was the first to deal with the war in Europe. The Man of Steel captured both Hitler and Stalin, scattered their troops, and delivered the two dictators to the League of Nations in a special two-page spread in the February 1940 issue of *Look* magazine. Captain America followed in March 1941, famously punching Hitler square on the jaw on the cover of the first issue of *Captain America Comics*, and then surprised a frightened Hitler by busting into a Nazi bunker on the cover of the series' second issue. America didn't even join the war until December 1941, so American comic book superheroes fought the war far before the nation's soldiers did, perhaps in their creators' stead.

For Golden Age comic book villains, there was only one way their felonious adventures could end: a superhero smashing through a wall or swinging through a window and rapidly dispatching a squad of goons before taking down the villain himself. Superheroes never calmly entered a room and politely informed the villain that he was under arrest. Violence was their only means of conflict resolution, and each character had his own particular methods.

Captain Marvel had a fondness for throwing people, for throwing things at people, and for swinging people around as if they were rag dolls, while Superman liked to mix in threats with his violence. In *Action Comics* #2, Superman confronted munitions magnate Emil Norvell and told him, "You see how effortlessly I crush this bar of iron in my hand?—That bar could just as easily be your neck!" Then after telling Norvell to leave town, Superman suggested that if Norvell decided to stay, "I swear I'll follow you to whatever hole you hide in, and tear out your cruel heart with my bare hands!"

Captain America's primary weapon was a shield, and he could simply hit bad guys with it, throw it, or use it as a battering ram to plough through goons. He also tended not to intervene when villains were about to kill themselves. When Dr. Reinstein's assassin, dazed by a mighty punch from Cap, stumbled toward dangerous lab equipment, Captain America did nothing, and after the assassin was electrocuted he noted that there was "nothing left of him but charred ashes . . . a fate he well deserved." Later in that issue, the Red Skull rolled onto his own poison-filled hypodermic needle and died. Captain America's sidekick, Bucky, was appalled and asked Cap why he didn't do anything to stop it, to which Cap replied, "I'm not talking, Bucky."

Batman tended to "accidentally" kill villains. A strong punch would "unintentionally" send a bad guy reeling backward through a railing and into a vat of acid. A defensive maneuver "just happened" to flip a goon over the edge of a roof. A strong kick to stop a gun-toting villain from taking a shot "inadvertently" broke his neck. A gas pellet thrown into the cockpit of a plane "unwittingly" resulted in a fatal crash.

In the years following the dawn of the Golden Age, violence toned down and most superheroes developed codes of conduct for humanely dealing with villains. But it was in the first few years of this brutal environment that Wonder Woman was created.

William Moulton Marston and the Origins of Wonder Woman

William Moulton Marston was most definitely not a typical comic book creator. The majority of Golden Age superhero writers were young men: Jerry Siegel was twenty-three when *Action Comics* #1 premiered, Bill Finger was twenty-five when *Detective Comics* #27 hit the stands, and Joe Simon was twenty-seven when *Captain America Comics* #1 was released. Marston was forty-eight years old when Wonder Woman first appeared in *All Star Comics* #8. Superman's Joe Shuster, Batman's Bob Kane, and Captain America's Jack Kirby

were all twenty-three when their respective heroes debuted, but H. G. Peter, the established cartoonist Marston handpicked to draw Wonder Woman, was nearly three times the age of his counterparts.

Many of these young creators worked in comics in hopes of parlaying their work into a "real" job, like advertising, but Marston already had a job. In fact, he had several. Marston was thrice a graduate of Harvard University, earning a BA in 1915, a law degree in 1918, and a PhD in psychology in 1921. He taught at several universities, published books, worked as an advisor for a film studio in Hollywood, and regularly wrote articles for magazines like the *Rotarian* and *Ladies Home Journal*.

Before Wonder Woman, Marston was best known for helping to invent the lie detector test, or polygraph, which was based on his research in systolic blood pressure. He was both an academic and a bit of a huckster, using his lie detector for noble purposes by assisting in criminal trials while also appearing in ads for Gillette razors to definitively prove they were the superior brand. Outside of the lie detector, Marston's psychological work had lasting effects as well, and his DISC theory on human behavior is still widely used as a template for personality assessment tests today.

Marston dabbled in many fields, but all of his work was connected through the common theme of his focus on the untapped potential of women. Less than a decade after women gained the right to vote, Marston argued that they were in fact psychologically superior to men. In the 1920s and 1930s, women made only slight gains in the workforce, and often in jobs with little opportunity for advancement. Although they could now vote, in many states women continued to fight for years for the rights of full citizenship, like serving on a jury. Those interested in higher education often faced oppressive caps that severely limited the number of women allowed in postgraduate studies.* Nonetheless, in a 1937 interview

---

*For instance, many medical schools capped female enrollment at a ridiculously low 5 percent of students.

in the *New York Times*, Marston declared that women were poised to "take over the rule of the country, politically and economically" within the next hundred years.

Marston's high opinion of the innate power of women was likely influenced by the women he was closest to. He lived in an unconventional polyamorous relationship with two well-accomplished women, Elizabeth Holloway Marston and Olive Byrne, both of whom embodied the feminism of the day. Elizabeth, his wife, earned a BA in psychology from Mount Holyoke College, a law degree from Boston University, and a master's in psychology from Radcliffe College, an all-female subsidiary of Harvard, paying her own tuition for her law degree when her father refused to support her. She worked alongside Marston on his systolic blood pressure research, coauthoring the findings, and had jobs at universities, magazines, and in insurance, continuing to work even after she had children.*

Olive, Marston's domestic partner, was also well educated, and she had extremely close connections to the birth control movement. Her mother, Ethel Higgins Byrne, opened America's first birth control clinic in 1916 alongside Olive's aunt, Margaret Sanger, birth control's most famous advocate.† That Marston was the de facto son-in-law of such a pioneering feminist likely strengthened his own feminist leanings. He saw the women in his life achieve great things and thought that all women could do the same if given the chance.

In the late 1930s, Marston became the consulting psychologist for *Family Circle* magazine, and his article "Don't Laugh at the Comics" caught the eye of All-American Publications' publisher,

---

*Marston had two children with Elizabeth and two children with Olive. They all lived together as one family, and Marston and Elizabeth worked while Olive stayed home raising the kids and running the household.

†Ethel took the fall when the clinic was quickly shut down by the police, and the conditions of her release from prison demanded that she never be involved in such clinics again. Spared prosecution by her sister, Margaret Sanger was able to continue with the movement and eventually make birth control available to all women.

Max Gaines. The article discussed the growing popularity of comic books, praising Gaines in particular for the success of Superman, and Gaines hired Marston to be on All-American's editorial advisory board. Several parental and educational groups were upset about comics and thought they were harmful to children, arguing that they were too violent and kept children from reading "real" books. In response, many comic book publishers hired panels of experts in education and psychology to review and approve their books. In a 1943 article in *American Scholar*, Marston stated that "it seemed to me, from a psychological angle, that the comics' worst offense was their blood-curdling masculinity." In response, Marston pitched a female superhero to All-American editor Sheldon Mayer to give young readers an alternative to all of this male-dominated violence. Marston called her "Suprema the Wonder Woman," which Mayer wisely shortened.

Marston wrote his comics under the penname Charles Moulton, a combination of his and Gaines's middle names. H. G. Peter drew Wonder Woman's origin, as well as nearly every single Wonder Woman story until 1958, in three different series: *Comic Cavalcade*, *Sensation Comics*, and *Wonder Woman*. Not much is known about Peter, or what he thought about Marston's feminist themes, but his nearly two decades of drawing the character suggest that he wasn't particularly bothered by them.

Peter had a unique style that was notably different from the work of his younger peers at DC Comics. He had drawn cartoons for humor magazines and worked on a number of comic strips, and he had an old-fashioned, cartoonist technique. Many of the young artists on superhero comics drew female characters in a sexualized way, with made-up faces and exaggerated figures. Peter didn't much go for overstated figures or skimpy clothes, and his faces were pleasant instead of provocative. Because of Peter, when Wonder Woman debuted she looked unlike any other comic book woman on the newsstands, and this distinctive style gave consistency to her early adventures.

Wonder Woman's origin story began in *All Star Comics* #8 in December 1941 when an American fighter pilot, Steve Trevor, crash-landed onto Paradise Island, the home of the mythical Amazons. Thousands of years earlier, the Amazons had been imprisoned by Hercules in his quest to accomplish his famous twelve labors. The ninth labor was to capture the girdle of Hippolyte, Queen of the Amazons, which he did through trickery and deceit. After the Amazons escaped from Hercules, they quit the aggressive, violent world of men and were led by Aphrodite to a hidden island where only women would reside.* Once there, Queen Hippolyte sculpted a baby daughter out of clay who was given life by the gods, and she named her Diana.

It was Diana who rescued Steve and took him to the Amazons' hospital. Men weren't allowed on Paradise Island, and Aphrodite and Athena told the queen that Steve had to be returned to America. However, the outside world was at war and Steve carried important military information. The goddesses declared that an Amazon warrior must go back to America with him because "America, the last citadel of democracy, and of equal rights for women, needs your help!"

Queen Hippolyte held a tournament to find an Amazon champion. She didn't let Diana enter because she didn't want to lose her daughter, but the adventurous Diana disguised herself and entered the tournament anyway, winning it easily. She became Wonder Woman, donning a star-spangled outfit so that she would be recognized as a friend of America. She flew Steve home in her invisible plane and established a secret identity as Diana Prince, Steve's nurse and later his secretary, so she could stay close to her charge. When

---

*In order to never forget the cruel treatment of Hercules and the brutal nature of men generally, the Amazons adapted the shackles they wore while imprisoned into bracelets. Wonder Woman's famous bullet-deflecting bracelets weren't just a handy tool but a constant reminder of this injustice, and they turned an object of oppression into an object of strength.

any danger arose, Diana Prince transformed into Wonder Woman and foiled the fiendish plans of whatever villain she encountered.

While *Wonder Woman* was ostensibly just a fun comic for kids, it also tied in closely with Marston's psychological theories. In 1929, Marston released *Emotions of Normal People*, which described his approach to psychology and presented DISC theory, a method of explaining human interactions. DISC (dominance, inducement, submission, and compliance) broke down all human relationships, be they parental, educational, romantic, or otherwise, into two binary relationships: active versus passive and antagonistic versus favorable. In an antagonistic relationship, the active participant was dominant, forcing the passive participant into an unpleasant compliant role. Marston argued that most psychological problems came from these kinds of relationships. In a favorable relationship, the active participant induced the passive participant into pleasant submission. Marston thought this provided "a double dose of pleasantness attached to the process of learning." Harsh dominance led to forced compliance, while kind inducement led to willing submission.

Marston claimed that men were more likely to be dominant, while women were more likely to excel at inducement and submission, though they were by no means submissive. Women were more loving and selfless and thus more willing to happily give of themselves to others, but they were also far better suited to inspire this sort of behavior in others. Because of this, Marston contended that "women, as a sex, are many times better equipped to assume emotional leadership than are males." Women's superior ability to rule was biological, and, Marston wrote, "there isn't love enough in the male organism to run this planet peacefully. Woman's body contains twice as many love generating organs and endocrine mechanisms as the male." The rule of dominant men led society to violence and strife, and Marston stated that "only when the control of self by others is more pleasant than the unbound assertion of self in human relationships can we hope for a stable, peaceful human society." Female rule was humanity's best chance for this peace.

Marston thought that this female rule was fast approaching. In an article in the February 1942 issue of *Tomorrow* magazine, Marston wrote that "the future is woman's—as quickly as she realizes her present frustration, and her tremendously powerful potentialities [. . .] Women will lead the world." In his 1937 *New York Times* interview, he declared that "the next one hundred years will see the beginning of an American matriarchy—a nation of Amazons in the psychological rather than physical sense." Once World War II began, he argued that women's participation in the war effort would give them even more strength and speed up this coming matriarchy. Wonder Woman comics were his way to prepare young readers for this inevitable revolution.

Marston's editor, Sheldon Mayer, said that Marston "was writing a feminist book, but not for women. He was dealing with a male audience." Women were well on their way to taking over the world, and men needed to get out of the way. Marston stated, "these simple, highly imaginative picture stories satisfy longings that ordinary daily life thwarts and denies. Superman and the army of male comics characters who resemble him satisfy the simple desire to be stronger and more powerful than anybody else. Wonder Woman satisfies the subconscious, elaborately disguised desire of males to be mastered by a woman who loves them." The vast popularity of comic books offered a way to reach the malleable minds of America's male youth. Wonder Woman comics were essentially Marston's psychological theories masquerading as superhero adventures.

But his theories weren't without their flaws. A matriarchy maintains an unequal society, just with reversed roles, and Marston optimistically refused to entertain the idea that power would corrupt women as much as it did men. Furthermore, while the idea that women were superior to men was rare and progressive for its time, Marston's concept of gender relied on reductionist generalizations. The female aptitude for love was both maternal and sexual, reducing women to a Madonna/whore stereotype. Marston's theories

idealized women and sexualized their power, basically stating that they were better suited to rule solely based on their ability to fulfill the desires of the men they subjugated. There is a sort of fetishism inherent in Marston's theories that says much more about what Marston was into than about gender relations and feminism.

However, comic books aren't psychology textbooks. The sexual undercurrents in *Wonder Woman* were buried below the surface.* In a genre entirely reliant on idealized heroes, Marston's female idealization as embodied in Wonder Woman becomes much less problematic. Though inspired by DISC theory and the dubious implications therein, the nature of comic books simplified these messages. They were adventure stories for kids that presented simple, surface-level messages about a strong and capable heroine, and children flocked to the book.

Wonder Woman outsold *Superman* at times, with upward of five million kids reading each issue. The character was an instant success. She launched in the back of a team book already filled with established heroes, but starred in three series of her own less than a year later. Given the widespread popularity of comics at the time, both boys and girls would have devoured her adventures. Marston may have had some complicated and problematic theories at play in his comics, but they worked primarily as pure superhero fun for Wonder Woman's legions of fans.

The Women of *Wonder Woman*

Although Marston and Peter were the primary forces behind Wonder Woman, the feminist message of the comics extended behind

---

*Marston's bondage fetishism was a constant subtext in *Wonder Woman* comics that had some dark implications, but to unlock it all requires a fairly intimate knowledge of Marston's other work. It would've been over the heads of the vast majority of comics readers.

the scenes, where several women played important roles in the character's development. Women were very rare in the comic book industry, but the *Wonder Woman* team put Marston's belief in the superiority of women into practice, relying on their advice and putting them in positions with real responsibility.

Marston's partners were key to the creation of Wonder Woman. When Marston wanted a superhero who would be motivated by love and not violence, Elizabeth insisted that the hero had to be a woman, declaring "Come on, let's have a Superwoman! There's too many men out there." Olive is often credited as the inspiration for Wonder Woman's appearance, most notably her bullet-deflecting bracelets. Olive was fond of large, metallic bracelets, and Marston co-opted the look for his new heroine.

When Wonder Woman expanded to a second comics series in the summer of 1942, she did so with a noteworthy associate editor, Alice Marble. Marble was an eighteen-time Grand Slam tennis champion who was named the Associated Press Athlete of the Year in 1939 and 1940. After retiring from tennis, she was excited by the arrival of a female superhero and worked on *Wonder Woman* for several years. Although her title was largely ceremonial, Marble was credited with writing the regular "Wonder Women of History" feature, which spotlighted a famous woman in each issue.

Wonder Woman had another female in editorial, Dorothy Roubicek. Unlike Marble's ceremonial role, Roubicek worked down in the trenches at All-American Comics. Roubicek was the first female assistant editor in the main offices, and along with her usual editorial duties, All-American publisher Max Gaines tasked Roubicek with handling the advisory board's objections to some of the content in *Wonder Woman*, a significant job given that *Wonder Woman* was a bestselling book and the objections were stern. Some sources suggest that Roubicek wrote a few *Wonder Woman* stories in the early 1940s, but there is no evidence to back that up.

Nonetheless, Roubicek was a key player at All-American, alongside Gaines and Mayer.

Although it's unlikely that Roubicek wrote *Wonder Woman*, there was another woman who definitely did. Joye Murchison was Marston's assistant from 1944 until his death in 1947. When Marston became ill with polio and later cancer, Murchison helped him write the comics, scripting several herself. Although she wasn't credited at the time, today her name is listed in reprints of the original stories and she is officially the first woman to ever write Wonder Woman.

On the art side, H. G. Peter was the sole credited artist on most of Wonder Woman's early stories, but he worked with a studio full of artists. Peter took care of the layouts and the main characters, but other artists would help with side characters and backgrounds. There were a few women in the crew who helped Peter with the inking and occasionally some penciling, though the only name we know is Helen Schpens. Several issues were also lettered by Louise Marston, Marston's daughter-in-law.

Utopian Genesis and a New Approach to Crime Fighting

Before Steve Trevor came crashing in, Diana had never met a man or interacted with the outside world, and her entire existence was spent in an all-female utopia. Queen Hippolyte described Paradise Island by saying, "With its fertile soil, its marvelous vegetation—its varied natural resources—here is no want, no illness, no hatreds, no wars. [. . .] That is why we Amazons have been able to far surpass the inventions of the so-called manmade civilization! We are not only stronger and wiser than men—but our weapons are better—our flying machines are further advanced!"

The Amazons had divine benefits on top of their technological and societal superiority, including eternal life, so long as Hippolyte

retained her magic girdle.* The queen made it clear that their utopia would remain so long as "we do not permit ourselves to be again beguiled by men!" Paradise Island was a means for Marston to illustrate, albeit in fanciful form, the benefits of a female-ruled society.

In her early adventures, Wonder Woman was often described as possessing "the beauty of Aphrodite, the wisdom of Athena, the strength of Hercules and the speed of Mercury." But these qualities applied to every Amazon. Hippolyte declared that the Amazons were "a race of Wonder Women!" Princess Diana wasn't especially gifted among her Amazon sisters; in the tournament to decide the Amazon champion, all competed fiercely in the twenty-one grueling challenges, and all of them had the ability to be a Wonder Woman in the world of man. This athletic prowess wasn't limited to Amazons either. In *Wonder Woman* #23, Queen Hippolyte spoke directly to female readers and stated, "You girls can develop strength and courage like our Amazon youngsters if you lead clean, athletic lives and realize the **true power** of **women!**"

Wonder Woman had no past tragedy to resolve, no anger or sorrow burning deep within her. Instead, she grew up in the world's most idyllic environment and became a hero to help others and spread Amazon values. While a lot of superheroes had a sidekick to help them in their crime fighting, Wonder Woman developed an entire network of powerful women.

In America she had the Holliday Girls, the members of the sorority Beeta [sic] Lambda at Holliday College. The Holliday Girls first appeared in *Sensation Comics* #2, when Wonder Woman took their marching band to distract a group of Nazi spies by having a dance.

---

*Mythologically speaking, Hippolyte's girdle was a *zoster*, a belt that represented a warrior's power and heroism. Hercules was tasked with taking Hippolyte's girdle because it was the ultimate symbol of a leader's power. To possess her *zoster* was absolute proof that he had conquered his foe. Marston appears to have had a similar take on Hippolyte's girdle: all of the utopian aspects of the island were rooted in the queen possessing this symbol of power and would disappear if a man possessed this power. Usually only male heroes earned this symbol of power, and through violence, but Marston showed that this power in the hands of a woman equaled peace and utopia.

Once Wonder Woman gave the word, each Holliday Girl subdued her dance partner and handcuffed him. The Holliday Girls were led by Etta Candy, a rotund young woman who loved chocolates. Etta's appearance was a stark contrast to the svelte, wasp-waisted women depicted in most comic books, and Etta was a brave and heroic leader who was always in the thick of the fight beside her friend Wonder Woman. Whatever the adventure, the Holliday Girls were involved. In fact, the Holliday Girls were more useful to Wonder Woman than the American military, often showing up to help her fight the Nazis or Japanese way before any soldiers arrived on the scene.

Wonder Woman's Amazon sisters also helped her battle villains and defend the planet, fighting alongside her and providing her with advanced technology. The brilliant and inventive Amazons had knowledge that far surpassed what was available in the world of men. Wonder Woman regularly used the Amazons' mental radio for contacting the Holliday Girls, Paradise Island, or Steve, and she also had access to their teleportation and time travel devices when the need arose.

When these women worked together, they were unstoppable. Although they regularly used force to stop villains, violence wasn't the only option. Wonder Woman frequently tried to talk to criminals and show them that another path would be a better choice.

Wonder Woman's general approach to women was to encouragingly point out their own strengths and set them free of the dominant men in their lives. When Marva, the wife and assistant of the evil Dr. Psycho, lamented that "Submitting to a cruel husband's domination has ruined my life! But what can a weak girl do?" Wonder Woman told her to "get strong! Earn your own living—join the WAACs or WAVES and fight for your country! Remember the better you can fight, the less you have to."* Employment was always Wonder Woman's first suggestion to help women gain independence.

---

*The WAACs were the Women's Army Auxiliary Corps, the women's branch of the US Army. The WAVES were Women Accepted for Volunteer Emergency Service, a women's branch of the US Navy.

Instead of busting Gloria Bullfinch, a store owner whose employees were being mistreated by her fiancé, Wonder Woman and the Holliday Girls hypnotized Gloria and made her think she was an employee at her own store. Once she saw the appalling conditions, she snapped out of her hypnotic state, left her fiancé, improved conditions, and doubled the workers' wages, declaring "Wonder Woman made me work like you and now I understand!"

Noting the dancing abilities of the villainous Cheetah, Wonder Woman exclaimed, "You're a born dancer—your dancing could attract **millions** of admirers! Oh, Cheetah, why don't you dance and make people **love** you?" Superman and Batman never offered encouraging suggestions for alternate career paths to Lex Luthor or the Joker, but Wonder Woman saw the good in everyone.

Although male villains were left to the police or the military, Wonder Woman usually took female villains to Reform Island, a smaller companion to Paradise Island where criminals were rehabilitated by the Amazons. It first appeared in *Wonder Woman* #3, and its inmates included some of Wonder Woman's most notorious enemies, like the Nazi spy Baroness Paula von Gunther and Priscilla Rich, the Cheetah. Wonder Woman believed that even criminals had the potential to learn the Amazon way of life.

Baroness Paula von Gunther became the poster girl for the transformative effects of Reform Island. Gunther was a Nazi spy with a group of female slaves at her command. She first appeared in *Sensation Comics* #4, where she kidnapped women and brainwashed them to become Nazi agents. Ultimately, she was sent to Reform Island, but she escaped. Rather than merely recapturing Paula, Wonder Woman took the time to talk to her and learned that her daughter, Gerta, was in the hands of the Nazis. Wonder Woman rescued Gerta, and Paula pledged herself to rehabilitation, even saving Wonder Woman from a fire and burning herself terribly in the process. Wonder Woman represented Paula at her trial for her past criminal deeds and had her sent back to Reform Island, where she soon became the Amazon's chief scientist. Her transformation

was so complete that she was able to leave Reform Island and work on Paradise Island, and later moved to a secret laboratory in the United States. A recurring character in Wonder Woman comics, she became a staunch ally who used her scientific genius to help Wonder Woman. Her female slaves were sent to Reform Island as well, where they were taught the benefits of submitting to a loving authority instead of the cruel and dominant rule of their former mistress. Reform Island was a busy place, resulting in an ever-growing network of women who lived the Amazon way of life.

2

Damsels in Distress

Wonder Woman is inarguably the most famous female super-hero in the history of comic books, but she wasn't the first. Comic book historian Trina Robbins found that the earliest cos-tumed heroine was the Woman in Red, a policewoman named Peggy Allen who wore a red robe and mask to fight crime.* The Woman in Red first appeared in Nedor Comics' *Thrilling Comics* in March 1940, well over a year before Wonder Woman debuted. After a few sporadic stories, the Woman in Red last appeared in 1945. Several other female heroes predated Wonder Woman, including Timely Comics' Black Widow, Quality Comics' Phantom Lady and Miss America, and the comic strip heroine Miss Fury.†

---

*Robbins is the foremost expert on women in comics; her book *The Great Women Superheroes* recounts the stories of Golden Age heroines who have been long forgotten.

†Miss Fury is particularly noteworthy because she was written and illustrated by June Tarpé Mills, one of the few women making comics in the Golden Age. She created the strip under the pseudonym Tarpé Mills, dropping her first name to hide her gender. Miss Fury strips were collected in comic book form in several issues from 1942 to 1946.

These Golden Age heroines had short life spans, often just appearing in a backup feature of a series for a few issues before disappearing. Headlining their own comic was rare and always short-lived. With 56 issues of *Wonder Woman*, 106 issues of *Sensation Comics*, and 29 issues of *Comic Cavalcade* released in the 1940s, no other superheroine came close to matching Wonder Woman's presence on the newsstands. The female characters who did regularly appear in superhero comic books broke down into two categories: love interests and villains.

Nearly every male superhero had a love interest who served a variety of purposes. Often captured by nefarious types, she afforded the hero opportunity to demonstrate his prowess when he saved her. Upon her rescue, she would become his cheerleader, fawning over the hero and professing his greatness, and by constantly rejecting her advances, the hero proved his dedication to crime fighting, forsaking all else for his noble mission.

These damsel in distress roles were very common in the 1940s. Superman had Lois Lane, Batman had Julie Madison, Captain Marvel had Beautia Sivana, the Flash had Joan Williams, and the Spirit had Ellen Dolan. These women weren't particularly well-rounded characters. Instead, they were defined only through their male love interests, existing solely to be rescued, and had no real identities of their own.

This phenomenon wasn't limited to comics, either. In their book *America on Film*, Harry M. Benshoff and Sean Griffin discuss movies from this era, writing that "the perseverance of classical Hollywood narrative form [. . .] has always worked to privilege men as the active and powerful heroes of Hollywood film, while relegating women to the role of love interest waiting to be rescued."

Feminism and cultural studies scholar Linda K. Christian-Smith has detailed the rules of conduct that dictated how female characters behaved in 1940s teen romance novels. Tenets like "The Code of Romance" and the "Code of Beautification" present teen romance as a power relationship where the boyfriend was entirely in charge.

The infatuated female lead did everything she could to make herself desirable for her boyfriend, losing herself in the process. Because "her value was acquired through affiliation with males," she allowed herself to be entirely defined by what her boyfriend wanted her to be.

While these passive, adaptive love interests always got their fairy tale ending, the novels also included a cautionary alternative. Christian-Smith describes a good girl/bad girl binary with an assertive and independent bad girl character, usually a friend of the good girl protagonist. Bad girls refused to change for their boyfriends, and thus their relationships were doomed to failure and their lives destined for perpetual sadness.

In her famous essay "The Image of Women in Science Fiction," Joanna Russ presents a similar good girl/bad girl framework. She claims that most female sci-fi characters were weak and ineffectual, essentially prizes won by male protagonists. Active or ambitious women were not only rare but often evil. Russ writes that "this literature was chockfull of cruel dowager empresses, sadistic matriarchs, evil ladies maddened by jealousy, domineering villainesses and so on." Women who weren't love interests, and who were shown to be smart and independent, were always villains.

Superhero comics had a lot in common with these two genres, sharing the younger audience of teen romance novels and the extraordinary characters and settings of science fiction. Comics continued the good girl/bad girl binary and combined the two approaches to bad girl narratives, presenting many female villains who had doomed romantic links with male heroes. Batman regularly faced off against Catwoman, the Flash battled the Star Sapphire and the Thorn, Green Lantern tangled with the Harlequin, and the Spirit came across all manner of femme fatales, such as P'Gell, Sand Saref, and Silken Floss. These women were in no way subservient love interests. Instead, they established their own identities, though this transgressing of the social order rarely ended well for them.

Wonder Woman flipped this paradigm by embodying the strength, assertiveness, and independence usually associated with

bad girls and villains in a positive and heroic light. The Golden Age Wonder Woman was a blatant rejection of the good girl/bad girl binary and even offered a critique of the good girl role. Compared to Lois Lane, a typical damsel in distress, Robin, a sidekick, and Catwoman, a villain, Marston's unique approach to Wonder Woman stands out in stark contrast.

Wonder Woman

For Marston, it wasn't enough to just have a female superhero. The prescribed gender roles had to be subverted even further, so he made Wonder Woman demonstrably more capable and comprehensive a superhero than her male peers.

At DC Comics, the covers of Batman and Superman comics showed daring wartime escapades. Superman rode a missile alongside fighter jets, while Batman and Robin delivered a gun to a soldier on the front lines, but the stories inside the comics had nothing to do with the war at all. While Batman and Superman used their covers to promote war bonds and stamps, they never actually fought the war themselves.

Wonder Woman supported the war effort as well, and the last panel of her comics often ended with "Wonder Woman says do your duty for Uncle Sam by buying US savings stamps and bonds!" She was a superpowered Rosie the Riveter, constantly encouraging women to join the auxiliary forces or get a wartime job. But while Superman and Batman sat out the war, Wonder Woman fought on every possible front. She regularly took on German and Japanese forces on the main lines of the war and defeated all of them with ease and often singlehandedly, with the American military only arriving afterward to cart off her captured foes.

Wonder Woman's war adventures were extensive. She shut down Japanese bases all over the world, from Mexico to South America to China. She, by herself, seized a German U-boat, overturned a

Japanese dreadnought, and captured an entire fleet of Nazi battle-ships. The Nazis attempted to infiltrate America several times and were stopped by Wonder Woman at every turn. Whether it was a plot to poison the water supply or disrupt American industry, or a Nazi spy impersonating an American general to find out their military plans, Wonder Woman thwarted every Axis foe.

She also wrangled with more typical superhero opponents, battling supervillains and fantastical invaders. Wonder Woman always foiled the evil plans of the Cheetah and Dr. Psycho, and saved the world from certain doom at the hands of subterranean molemen or an invading army from Saturn. She pulled off the latter in typical Wonder Woman fashion; she fought the Saturnian forces when necessary, but ended the conflict by negotiating a peace treaty and trade agreement with the king of Saturn.

Regularly saving the world didn't distract Wonder Woman from local justice, and she worked to improve conditions for workers, stopped price-gougers, and fought small-time criminals everywhere she went. Even bullying was important to Wonder Woman, and in *Sensation Comics* #23 she stopped a gang who were picking on a young boy, showed the head bully the error of his ways and learned about his home situation, spoke to his father about his abusive tendencies, and then helped the father get a job in a wartime factory. She always took the time to get to the root of a problem.

Wonder Woman completely eschewed a damsel in distress role by instead being a superhero of unparalleled skill, and the inversion of the typical gender roles didn't stop there. Like her superhero peers, Wonder Woman had her own damsel in distress, a fawning love interest who always got captured and had to be rescued. "Her" name was Steve Trevor. A major in the US Air Force, Steve was a highly decorated pilot who was often called on to perform important secret missions. He appeared to be the quintessential American hero and was drawn that way by H. G. Peter, with a strong jaw, muscular build, and handsome face.

However, the man was entirely inept. No matter the mission, he'd end up ambushed or captured and Wonder Woman would have to save him. When Steve was taken by Nazi gangsters, Wonder Woman raided their boat and knocked out the Nazis with a large anchor, rescuing the bound and helpless Steve. When the not-yet-reformed Baroness Paula von Gunther was about to shoot Steve at point-blank range, Wonder Woman's lasso stopped her in her tracks. Whenever Wonder Woman was in trouble, Steve was no help. He showed up too late, was knocked out and woke up to find Wonder Woman had set herself free, or was captured as well so Wonder Woman had to free herself *and* Steve.

One of the few times Steve did anything helpful, stealing keys and freeing himself from his cage on the planet Eros, Wonder Woman took charge as soon as she was released. The panel showed Wonder Woman at the head of a large group of angry women, and the text read: "Tearing off door after door from the prisoners' cells, **Wonder Woman** leads her army of imprisoned Eros women to freedom!" Steve just ran along behind. Wonder Woman was the undisputed star of the book, and Steve existed solely to show off her strength and skill.

He ably played the role of love-struck admirer as well. Steve often declared that "**Wonder Woman** is the most gorgeous **being** in the world!" Whenever Wonder Woman bounded off to another adventure, he was prone to call out, "**Wonder Woman**—my beautiful angel! Don't leave me. Stay with me always!" Although flattered by Steve's professions of love, Wonder Woman rejected his advances, as her mission was of paramount importance.

Wonder Woman was adamant in her rejection of Steve and wouldn't even let him touch her. A panel description in *Sensation Comics* #13 read: "Steve, overjoyed at having the case solved and finding **Wonder Woman** alive, throws his arms about her and is repulsed violently!" The panel showed Wonder Woman shoving Steve to the floor while he says, "Oh, my beautiful angel, I adore you—oof—unf!" In another issue, Steve tried some smooth talking,

saying, "Look, angel—this plane can fly by itself . . . why don't you let it, and pay me some attention." He was promptly rebuffed. Wonder Woman's identity was, in short, completely independent of Steve. While Steve was madly in love with her, Wonder Woman seemed to treat Steve like she was his babysitter. Diana Prince, on the other hand, saw Steve very differently.

Wonder Woman's secret alter ego, Diana Prince, was everything Wonder Woman was not. While Wonder Woman was strong, Diana was weak. While Wonder Woman was colorful and bold, Diana was a dull wallflower. They even looked completely different; Wonder Woman was flamboyant and agile, with long flowing hair, while Diana was reserved and bespectacled, with her hair tied up neatly in a bun. Diana's relationship with Steve was entirely different too. She acted as Steve's nurse after Wonder Woman returned him to America following his crash on Paradise Island, and when Steve left the hospital she cried, "Oh, Steve is going! I'll never see him again! I can't bear it!" and begged Steve, "Will—(sob) you—(sob)—let me be your secretary?" Diana couldn't handle being apart from Steve and did whatever she had to do to be close to him.

Being in love with Wonder Woman, Steve wanted nothing to do with Diana. When she tried to warn Steve that he was about to be betrayed, he answered, "Ha! Ha! Diana the sleuth! You'd better go back to nursing—I know my own business!" not realizing that the secretary he treated so derisively was in fact the woman he loved.

Diana was ignored not only by Steve but by the rest of the world as well. Unlike her superhero alter ego, Diana was inept and hapless, much like a damsel in distress. During one of the rare times Diana actually tried to take a stand, she ended up bound in chains and about to drown before she transformed into Wonder Woman and escaped. Afterward, she lamented, "I'm almost jealous of myself as Wonder Woman—nothing I do as a normal woman, Diana Prince, ever impresses anybody—I have to become the sensational Wonder

Woman before any body notices me!" Diana was a far cry from her superpowered alter ego, and such a contrast suggests that Diana Prince was more than just a secret identity.

In a soliloquy in Quentin Tarantino's *Kill Bill: Volume 2*, Bill discusses Superman and states:

> Superman didn't become Superman, Superman was born Superman. [. . .] What Kent wears—the glasses, the business suit—that's the costume. That's the costume Superman wears to blend in with us. [. . .] Clark Kent is Superman's critique on the whole human race.

The same can be said of Wonder Woman. Princess Diana of Paradise Island *was* Wonder Woman; it was a title and role she earned before entering man's world. But Wonder Woman was *not* Diana Prince.* Diana Prince was simply a way for Wonder Woman to get inside knowledge on the war and to be close to her protectee, Steve.

Wonder Woman was the embodiment of strength, independence, and assertiveness, while Diana couldn't accomplish anything and was hung up on a man who ignored her. Wonder Woman once stated that "[Diana] will have to go on mooning over Steve Trevor, while he goes on mooning over **Wonder Woman**," essentially declaring that those two hapless characters could engage in typical gender roles but Wonder Woman wouldn't be a part of such an inane system. Wonder Woman even described Steve as "the man Diana loves." As her true self, she was fully detached from these romantic shenanigans. The personality of Diana Prince exemplified what an Amazon princess thought of American

---

*In fact, "Diana Prince" was literally someone else entirely. In *Sensation Comics* #1, soon after Wonder Woman arrived in America she met a nurse who was crying because her husband had found a job in South America and she couldn't afford to go be with him. The two women looked exactly alike, so Wonder Woman gave her money to go join her husband in exchange for taking over her identity.

women. It was a harsh critique, and no character was the target of this analysis more than the Golden Age's archetypical damsel in distress, Lois Lane.

Lois Lane

The modern Lois Lane is the *Daily Planet*'s top reporter, a brash and adventurous journalist who gets the stories no one else can. In the Golden Age, however, things weren't going as well for Lois. Created by Jerry Siegel and Joe Shuster, she appeared alongside Superman in his first comic, *Action Comics* #1, in June 1938. Lois Lane and Clark Kent were both reporters, but at the *Daily Star* instead of the *Daily Planet*. Clark was the top reporter while Lois was a minor writer, frequently out-scooped by Clark. Though unabashedly determined, her big plans rarely got her recognition at the *Daily Star*. Instead, she'd end up captured by a villain, trapped in a burning building, or caught in some kind of jam from which Superman would have to save her. And, of course, she adored Superman for it.

Whether he was rescuing her from kidnappers, catching her as she plummeted to her doom, or proving that he actually was faster than a speeding bullet, saving Lois was a full-time job for Superman, because her ambitious investigating always resulted in trouble. Once endangered, Lois was the perfect damsel in distress, wholly incapable of saving herself.

Lois, in the classic love interest role, was head over heels for Superman. Describing him to Clark, she exclaimed, "He's grand! He's glorious! He's terrific!—He's everything you're not! Brave, bold, handsome—superb!" The love-struck Lois praised Superman at every turn and was the Man of Steel's biggest fan. When Superman zoomed off after saving her, she would cry, "Don't go! Stay with me . . . always." But Superman didn't reciprocate her feelings.

In fact, Superman was downright mean to Lois. When he saved her for the first time he told her, "I'd advise you not to print this little episode."* If she asked Superman about himself, he'd say, "Save the questions!" Even though he knew that news of Superman would be career-changing for her, he refused to help Lois. Superman had all the power and Lois had none.

This dynamic continued with Clark Kent in the workplace. Lois faced considerable sexism at the *Daily Star* that held her back in her career. Striving for big stories, she was often told by the editor that they were "too important!—This is no job for a girl!" She was instead relegated to a job the editor felt was far more suitable for a female reporter: the lovelorn column, where she gave relationship advice to the women of Metropolis.

However, sexism couldn't hold back the ambitious Lois Lane. Her persistence sometimes paid off and she'd finagle her way into a potentially good story, but Clark Kent would steal it out from under her. When danger arose, Clark ducked out, leaving Lois alone and confused, and Superman would show up to save the day in spectacular fashion. If there wasn't a phone booth nearby, Clark often knocked Lois unconscious with a nerve pinch so he could change into Superman. After all of the action, Lois would rush back to the *Daily Star* only to find Clark there already, story in hand. In *Superman #3*, after this had happened several times, Lois realized something was amiss and stated, "Oh, how I hate Clark Kent!—I tell you, he deliberately set out to take my job from me!" Later in that same issue, Clark took Lois out to console her, only to steal her big revelation about jewel smugglers and take the front-page story.

While a normal man wouldn't have been able to keep the ambitious Lois so thoroughly restrained, Lois was dealing with a superpowered Kryptonian with the patriarchal values of 1930s America,

---

*Lois ignored this demand and was at her editor's desk the next morning trying to get the story published, but her editor didn't believe her. Every man in Lois's life actively kept her down.

furthering his career and holding back hers. Trying anything outside of her damsel in distress role only led to failure for Lois.*

Comparing Lois Lane and Wonder Woman isn't really an accurate reflection of their roles in their respective comic books. Wonder Woman had far more in common with Superman, while Lois, Diana Prince, and Steve Trevor were very alike. Wonder Woman and Superman saved their particular damsels in distress, with one significant difference: Superman was an antagonistic rescuer, while Wonder Woman was benevolent. Lois's interactions with Superman weren't pleasant, even though she was in love with him. Superman was curt with Lois and refused to let her write about their encounters, and the only reason Lois needed rescue was because she got into dangerous situations trying to out-scoop Clark.

Steve, on the other hand, was saved from bad situations, but he wasn't demoted or antagonized. In fact, he was regularly praised for helping to incarcerate the spies and criminals Wonder Woman captured. She singlehandedly stopped the Japanese invasion of South America, yet Steve was recommended for the Distinguished Service Cross even though he showed up after the fact. With her inherent moral superiority and loving nature, Wonder Woman was created as a response to the dominant traits of male superheroes, and her dealings with Steve demonstrate the contrast Marston was trying to make.

While Wonder Woman was a criticism of superheroes like Superman, Steve and Diana were a commentary on the typical female gender role demonstrated by Lois Lane. But where Diana was all an

---

*This slowly changed over time, and Lois got a cover story here and there, though it was often only because Superman felt bad and let her have one. Years into the series, Clark was still out-scooping Lois at almost every turn. Lois is fascinating in that she so well embodies the progress and limitations of working American women in the late 1930s. That Lois even had a job was impressive considering that only a quarter of American women worked outside the home at the time, but being relegated to a position with very little room for advancement in a hostile work environment was the unfortunate plight of many working women.

act, Lois was no act at all and wasn't in her situation by choice. She didn't have a superhero alter ego to turn into. Lois tried to escape her circumstances, but in doing so she only became more firmly entrenched in them.

Lois and Steve fulfilled similar roles and the way they each saw their rescuer was virtually identical. "Don't leave me. Stay with me always!" and "Don't go! Stay with me . . . always," are pretty much interchangeable. But Steve benefited from his connection with Wonder Woman, while Lois Lane was only suppressed in her relationship with Superman. Marston's approach to gender roles was not only flipped but also more beneficial for everyone involved.

Robin, the Boy Wonder

In *Detective Comics* #38, published in April 1940, Bruce Wayne attended a circus that featured the Flying Graysons, a family of trapeze artists. During the performance, the ropes mysteriously snapped and John and Mary Grayson plummeted to their deaths, leaving their son, Dick, an orphan. After the show, Dick overheard some men taking credit for their deaths, but as he was about to call the police he was stopped by Batman. Batman told Dick that his parents' deaths were orchestrated by Boss Zucco, a local mobster who was trying to extort money from the circus. Dick wanted to help Batman avenge the crime; seeing something of himself in the young boy, Batman agreed and trained him to be his assistant, Robin. Bruce Wayne took on the boy as his ward, and together they became the Dynamic Duo. Created by Bob Kane, Bill Finger, and Jerry Robinson, Robin was an instant hit with young readers and has remained a staple of the Bat-canon for decades.

Although Robin was male, he often fulfilled a helpless damsel in distress role, frequently being captured and subsequently rescued. A subordinate role was common among the damsels, and Robin's character was both a child and a sidekick to Batman. Robin also replaced an actual damsel in distress. Before Robin came along, Bruce Wayne

had a fiancée named Julie Madison. She appeared in a few issues of *Detective Comics*, and Batman saved her from the clutches of an evil vampire known as the Monk. After Robin showed up, Julie was mentioned a few times and appeared in one issue, but then less than a year after Robin's debut she called off the engagement with nary a protest from Bruce. Instead of Julie, it was Robin who fulfilled the companion role in Batman comic books by serving as someone Batman could care about and save from perilous situations.

In the first twelve issues of *Batman*, Robin was knocked out, detained, or in some other way debilitated no less than fifteen times. Most of these situations required Batman's help; the Caped Crusader had to stop chasing a villain to tend to an unconscious Robin, independently dispatch a group of thugs while Robin sat tied in a corner, or give up and allow himself to be captured because the bad guy threatened Robin's life.

Despite his general inability to stay conscious or untied, Robin's relationship with Batman wasn't a subordinate one for long. The Dynamic Duo operated more as a partnership than an unbalanced power relationship. Initially, Batman tried to take charge, and was annoyed when Robin challenged him. In Robin's first issue, he attacked Boss Zucco and his men by himself, prompting Bruce to later say to him, "You reckless young squirt. I ought to whale you for jumping those men alone. Why didn't you wait for me?" But by the end of the story, Boss Zucco was captured and both Bruce and Dick smiled in celebration of their success.

In the following issue, Batman told Robin to stay behind while he went out, but his young ward disobeyed. Batman's only response when he saw that Robin hadn't listened and was instead fighting a group of thugs was "Well doggone! All I can say is, he certainly is an apt pupil!" Batman's attempts to corral Robin lasted all of two issues. Although not quite as skilled as Batman, Robin was certainly a capable crime fighter and was eventually treated almost as an equal by Batman.

As a male embodying several aspects of a typically female role, it would seem that Robin might have had a lot in common with Steve

Trevor. Beyond their uncanny knack for getting captured, however, the two shared very few traits. Despite his military rank, Steve was useless and couldn't do anything on his own. Essentially, Steve existed to be captured. In contrast, Robin could actually do things. He had to be rescued often, but he could also be a good rescuer himself. Batman trusted Robin with solo missions and regularly gave him opportunities to demonstrate his combat abilities.

Robin more resembled Etta Candy and Paula von Gunther, Wonder Woman's female companions. They were taught the Amazon way of life and Wonder Woman led them, but she treated them as if they were her sisters and her peers. They constantly helped Wonder Woman; a well-placed distraction by Etta's Holliday Girls or some invention of Paula's often played a key role in Wonder Woman's plans, and when Wonder Woman was incapacitated it was usually Etta or Paula who came to her aid.

In conventional comic books, the gender roles were very rigid. As much as Robin appeared to have the qualities associated with a typically female role, he actually ended up as a sort of junior Batman. Marston was equally committed to his inverted approach, and Steve was never anything more than a damsel in distress while Wonder Woman mentored several junior Wonder Women.

Catwoman

Catwoman is one of the most varied and continually changing characters in comic book history. In a literal sense, her appearance changes all the time; Catwoman has had more costumes than she has lives. The character herself changes too. In current DC Comics continuity, Catwoman is a wealthy socialite named Selina Kyle, rather ambiguous in her aims. Sometimes she works with criminals and breaks the law and other times she allies with Batman or the Justice League and enforces it. Her domain is Gotham City's East End, and she protects its residents through whatever means she sees fit.

The 1960s live-action Batman TV show demonstrated Catwoman's proclivity for change by having three different women portray Catwoman: Julie Newmar and Eartha Kitt played Catwoman on the show, and Lee Meriwether played her in the 1966 film. Change was also the hallmark of the Golden Age Catwoman. Created by Bill Finger and Bob Kane, Catwoman first appeared as the Cat, a notorious cat burglar, in the first three issues of *Batman*, but she wasn't given a proper name. In *Batman* #10 she was called Cat-woman or Cat Woman and was identified as a wealthy socialite named Marguerite Tone. Eventually, as a beautician named Elva Barr in *Batman* #15, she arrived at Catwoman. After numerous other secret identities, she became Selina Kyle in 1952 and it stuck. Despite these variations, throughout the Golden Age Catwoman was a classic femme fatale, a woman who used her sexual wiles for personal gain, and who was punished for violating the social order. Catwoman represented the bad girl, a woman who refused to be defined by a man and who worked for her own goals. In the world of superheroes, that made her a villain.

Batman had a fondness for Catwoman, and she gladly used that attraction to her advantage. Although Catwoman occasionally seemed to take on the role of the damsel in distress, she did so only to manipulate Batman and achieve her own ends. She knew Batman would rescue her if she were truly in a dangerous situation, and she knew she could easily escape him afterward.

During their first encounter, the Dynamic Duo escorted Catwoman back to shore after foiling her attempted robbery of a cruise ship, and she suddenly jumped overboard. As Robin prepared to jump after her, Batman bumped into him, impeding his pursuit and allowing Catwoman to escape. Robin proclaimed, "I'll bet you bumped into me on purpose! That's why you took her along with us . . . so she might try a break!" Batman flatly denied this before spending the next panel rhapsodizing about Catwoman's lovely eyes.

Two issues later, Batman was about to arrest Catwoman, but she kissed him and, taking advantage of his distracted state, pushed

him away so she could escape. Robin was about to give chase, but Batman called him off and then said, "What a night! A night for romance, eh, Robin?" Similarly, in *Batman* #10 Catwoman's kiss left Batman in such a state that Robin had to yell at him to snap out of his preoccupied bliss long after Catwoman had left the premises. In most of these stories, Catwoman not only escaped, she also got away with jewels she'd stolen. Batman, the consummate crime fighter, was completely powerless in her presence.

Catwoman was similar to the femme fatales of crime novels or film noir. The complete opposite of the typical good girl, she was assertive instead of passive, ambitious instead of subordinate, and entirely self-defined. Her sexuality wasn't something to be chastely protected, but rather was a tool to be used for her own enjoyment or advancement. However, femme fatales regularly ended up dead by the end of the novel or film. Because of this, many scholars view the femme fatale as a tragic figure and see her inevitable demise as a punishment for betraying the sexual codes of patriarchal society.

However, the serialized nature of comic books made death rare for major characters. New stories had to be written every month, and repopulating them would've been a laborious task. Any well-received heroes or villains were kept alive and became recurring characters. Catwoman may have stayed alive, but like the femme fatale had to die as condemnation for her independence, so too was Catwoman presented in a negative, villainous light. While Batman was attracted to Catwoman, he ultimately lamented, "It's too bad she has to be a crook!"

In the end it was Catwoman who most resembled the Golden Age Wonder Woman. They both used men and eschewed romantic entanglement, working to accomplish their own goals regardless of societal expectations. But while they shared similar traits, they had completely different roles. Catwoman embodied these traits in a framework meant to reinforce typical gender roles, and so she had to be shown in a bad light. Wonder Woman was focused on inverting typical gender roles, and so she took those traits that

were so often negatively portrayed and embodied them in a positive and heroic light. Catwoman had transgressed the patriarchal social order, and because of it had to be a crook, but Wonder Woman was establishing a new matriarchal social order and she was its heroic model.

The Inverted World of Wonder Woman

Discussing the creation of Wonder Woman in a 1943 article in the *American Scholar*, William Moulton Marston wrote that "not even girls want to be girls so long as our feminine archetype lacks force, strength, power." Marston suggested that most comic book readers had disdain for female characters because they showed only the "weak" qualities of women, and he argued that "the obvious remedy [was] to create a feminine character with all the strength of a Superman plus all the allure of a good and beautiful woman."

In Wonder Woman, Marston presented a brand-new kind of character. While his ideas about female superiority never really caught on, the long-term impact of the first powerful, independent female superhero cannot be understated. In a genre that so rigidly enforced typical gender roles and relied on a very narrow view of femininity, Wonder Woman shattered these expectations for millions of young readers each month. It's sometimes hard to see the ingrained societal structures that dictate daily life, but by inverting these structures Wonder Woman comics shed a light on the tenets of these systems, along with a sharp critique.

Marston intended to prepare boys for matriarchy, but it seems that girls got the most out of the comics. It can't just be a coincidence that the first generation of girls raised on empowering female characters like Wonder Woman and Rosie the Riveter became the generation of the women's liberation movement. Marston's Wonder Woman was a wholly unique character in the Golden Age of comics, and while his theories may have been problematic, the legacy of his creation lives on still.

3

Amazon Princess, Bondage Queen

While the Golden Age Wonder Woman was impressive, there was more to her than just fighting crime. Her adventures, from helping a bullied child to saving the world from alien invaders, gave her a range Superman and Batman didn't have. Wonder Woman was a superior superhero, and intentionally so. William Moulton Marston believed that every woman could be a metaphorical Wonder Woman and that women would soon take over the world. His worldview was unique, remarkably progressive, and all of his theories were channeled into his creation. Many of Wonder Woman's early stories still stand up as strikingly feminist seventy years later, even compared to modern comic books and female characters in today's books, TV shows, and movies.*

---

*The Golden Age Wonder Woman would certainly have a thing or two to say to Bella Swan about that vampire fellow and her complete and total inability to do anything for herself.

All of Marston's work preached a strong message about female power, and while his vision of a female-ruled society hasn't panned out yet, it was nonetheless a rather forward-thinking idea. However, the more we dig into the subtext and metaphors of his work, the more another side of Marston emerges. His comics were rife with bondage imagery, adding a sexual component to the books that reflected his own fetishism and the troubling places it could lead.

The rampant fetishism in Wonder Woman comics complicates their feminist message, but it doesn't undermine it. In fact, the feminism and fetishism were inextricably linked, both of them deriving from Marston's psychological work. You can't have one without the other.

A Staggering Amount of Bondage

The idea of Wonder Woman as a bondage queen may seem far-fetched. Getting captured and tied up by bad guys is an occupational hazard when you're a superhero, so some argue that while Wonder Woman got tied up sometimes, so too did everyone else. In *The Great Women Superheroes*, Trina Robbins makes an interesting Golden Age–specific argument about Captain Marvel. Robbins points out that because Billy Batson had to say "Shazam!" to turn into Captain Marvel, he often ended up bound and gagged by fiendish villains so he couldn't transform into a superhero and thwart their plans. Similarly, Wonder Woman's main weapon was a lasso, which she used to tie up a lot of people in her comics. Both characters had reasons to have an abnormal amount of bondage in their stories.

A comparative analysis of the first ten issues of *Captain Marvel Adventures* with the first ten issues of *Batman* confirms Robbins's initial point. Be it ropes or chains or gags, anytime someone was bound and restrained in a way that encumbered or incapacitated him or her, that panel was noted. *Batman* was chosen for two reasons: the book was never really associated with bondage, and Robin

was always tagging along so there were two heroes to be captured and tied up.

The overall percentage of bondage in both series was the same with each coming in at about 3 percent, but in terms of personal bondage there was a clear winner. On average, Batman and Robin combined were tied up in only 1 percent of the panels in *Batman*, while Captain Marvel was bound in *Captain Marvel Adventures'* panels twice as often. This is a sizeable difference, particularly since it was one hero's total against two.

Captain Marvel was definitely tied up more than the average superhero, but his numbers get dwarfed by Wonder Woman.

The chart below shows how often Captain Marvel and Wonder Woman were bound in the first ten issues of their own series, debunking the "all superheroes get tied up" argument. Wonder Woman's lowest percentage of personal bondage in *Wonder Woman* was the same as Captain Marvel's highest percentage of personal bondage in *Captain Marvel Adventures*. When your worst is the same as the other guy's best, that's a substantial amount. The averages show the same divide: Captain Marvel was tied up about 2 percent of the time in his books, and Wonder Woman was tied up 11 percent of the time in hers. Captain Marvel doubling Batman and

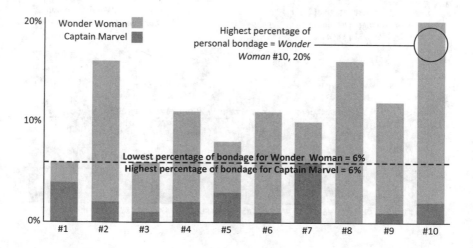

Robin's personal total was fairly impressive, but Wonder Woman trumps Captain Marvel more than five times over.

In *Wonder Woman* #10, one out of every five panels in the issue showed Wonder Woman tied up in some fashion. The series was drawn on a six-panel-per-page grid, so on average Wonder Woman was tied up at least once a page in that issue. That's excessive on its own, but other people were tied up in *Wonder Woman* as well.

The following chart shows the total amount of bondage in *Wonder Woman* and *Captain Marvel Adventures*, including the heroes plus everybody else who happened to be tied up. If *Captain Marvel Adventures* #1, the issue with the highest amount of bondage, doubled its total, it still wouldn't reach *Wonder Woman*'s lowest total. On average, *Captain Marvel Adventures* contained 3 percent total bondage, while *Wonder Woman* had 27 percent. That's more than a quarter of the book and amounts to nine times as much bondage as *Captain Marvel Adventures*, our paradigm of an above-average bondage comic book.

These numbers are colossal, and they get even more curious when comparing personal and overall bondage. Captain Marvel accounted for most of his book's bondage. His personal total was

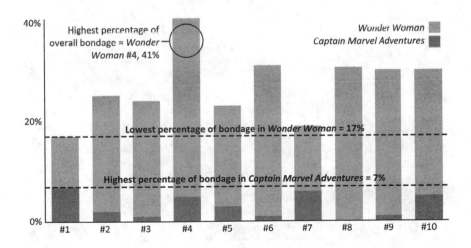

2 percent and the overall total was 3 percent, so Captain Marvel comprised two-thirds of the book's bondage, a clear majority at nearly 70 percent. Wonder Woman was tied up 11 percent of the time, while her book's overall total was a massive 27 percent; at 40 percent of the total bondage, this is a minority. Sixty percent of the bondage imagery in *Wonder Woman* didn't actually feature Wonder Woman at all. Marston spread the bondage around to other characters.

The bondage panels in *Wonder Woman* were both numerous and widespread. Going far beyond the occupational hazards of being a superhero, bondage in Wonder Woman comic books was a vast and all-encompassing phenomenon, and it was there for a reason.

Bondage and the Coming Matriarchy

Contemporary thought on bondage is much different than Marston's approach. When we think of bondage these days, it's usually in terms of the bondage/discipline, dominance/submission, and sadism/masochism subculture, conveniently amalgamated into the far easier to remember acronym of BDSM. This type of bondage has very specific associations with things like leather and whips and is usually tied to role-playing and escapism. For example, the businessman who runs a company all day and gets to boss people around goes home, puts on a leather unitard, gets chained to the wall, and lets someone with a riding crop be in charge for a while. It's escapist and focuses on one party dominating the other.

For Marston, bondage was about submission, not just sexually but in every aspect of life. It was a lifestyle, not an activity, and he used bondage imagery as a metaphor for this style of submission. In 1942, Marston conducted a fake interview with his domestic partner, Olive Byrne, for *Family Circle* magazine. Byrne used the pseudonym "Olive Richard" and pretended to be a casual friend of Marston interested in Wonder Woman and his ideas behind

her.* The article was called "Our Women Are Our Future" and it allowed Marston to spell out his theories on the coming matriarchy. Byrne, still upset over Pearl Harbor, asked Marston, "Will war ever end in this world; will men ever stop fighting?" He replied, "Oh, yes. But not until women control men."

Patriarchy amounted to a lot of war, greed, and general strife and was motivated by aggression. It was a forced system where those in power weren't looking out for everyone's best interests. Marston told Byrne that he saw women taking over society "as the greatest— no, even more—as the only hope for permanent peace." Men had to choose to surrender to the "loving authority" of women if things were going to get better.

Men choosing to give up power to women en masse seems as unlikely today as it did in 1942, and Byrne pretended to be incredulous about the idea. Marston replied that men actually wanted to submit to women, because women were "nature-endowed soldiers of Aphrodite, goddess of love and beauty, and theirs is the only conquering army to which men will permanently submit—not only without resentment or resistance or secret desires for revenge, but also with positive willingness and joy!" To Marston, this is what every man wanted deep down, and once women realized their power and took over, men would quickly fall in line.

Marston always described patriarchy in active terms; it was aggressive and forceful and selfish, a whirlwind of men taking what they wanted and leaving destruction in their wake. Marston told Byrne that the success of *Wonder Woman* was a sign that this process of submission, of taming the whirlwind, had already started. He said that "boys, young and old, satisfy their wish thoughts by reading comics. If they go crazy over Wonder Woman, it means

---

*For an article about how women should take over the world, Byrne went out of her way to make Marston sound big and powerful. She referred to him as "the mammoth," "the big man," "the psychological giant," and a wise "oracle" who responded with "rumbling whoops of laughter."

they're longing for a beautiful, exciting girl who's stronger than they are." Wonder Woman tapped into "the subconscious, elaborately disguised desire of males to be mastered by a woman who loves them," and intentionally so.

In a letter to his publisher, Max Gaines, Marston echoed his comments in *Family Circle* and wrote, "The only hope for peace is to teach people who are full of pep and unbound force to enjoy being bound." This bondage meant giving up selfish, dominant aims in favor of deference. If boys were taught the values of submission instead of the forceful, patriarchal values of other superhero comics, then matriarchy would come about more quickly and smoothly.

The bondage imagery that made up more than a quarter of *Wonder Woman* was actually an elaborate series of metaphors about submission. Different forms of bondage had different meanings, but they all revolved around this theme. Nearly every Amazon activity on Paradise Island involved some form of bondage, even their holiday festivities. At Christmastime, the Amazons celebrated Diana's Day, a moon goddess festival. Part of the celebration involved chasing down Amazons dressed as deer, hog-tying the ones who were caught, and then pretending to bake the bound Amazons in a massive pie. Once an Amazon was "sliced" out of the pie, Wonder Woman called out a zany task for her to perform and earn her freedom.

Bondage was especially important for women who were new to the island and learning the Amazon lifestyle. In one issue, Wonder Woman brought a group of female athletes to Paradise Island for a competition, and the athletes were surprised to see so many women walking around with their hands and feet chained together. One athlete asked an Amazon initiate if all Amazons had to wear chains, and she enthusiastically replied, "Oh yes, we love it!" Whenever Wonder Woman returned home, the backgrounds of panels regularly featured characters walking around with chains of some sort, usually without comment. It was just an everyday part of life for all Amazons, even Wonder Woman.

Wonder Woman not only directed bondage activity, she accepted it as well. In *Wonder Woman* #13, seven Amazons wrapped all manner of chains and ropes around her, lashing her to a wooden post. Wonder Woman was having a great time and called out, "Bind me as tight as you can, girls, with the biggest ropes and chains you can find!" One of the laughing Amazons replied, "We are, Princess—even **you** can't escape **these** bonds!" Wonder Woman did escape, of course, snapping her bonds with ease.

Bondage was a game to the Amazons, a sport they all played and enjoyed. When Wonder Woman was subduing female guards in Atlantis in *Sensation Comics* #35, she mentioned a few of the Amazon bondage moves by name, like "the kitten hold." As she quickly bound a guard in her lasso, Wonder Woman said, "On Paradise Island where we play many binding games this is considered the safest method of tying a girl's arms!" The intent of bondage was never to hurt, ridicule, or shame someone, and there were rules of safety and care.

The Amazons incorporated bondage into their society as an expression of trust to emphasize that their utopia was based on kinship with a hierarchy of submission. All of the Amazons were committed to their patron goddess, Aphrodite; love was their very foundation. Queen Hippolyte would consult Aphrodite directly and ruled the island with the help of her love-based wisdom. They also submitted to Diana, their princess, but through bondage she regularly surrendered to them in return, promoting mutual respect and love.

While Paradise Island was the end result of submission, the goal of Reform Island was to teach villains to give up their own egocentric desires and learn submission. Most of them were rather committed to their criminal lifestyles and incredulous that they would be in any way changed by Reform Island. Tigra Tropica, a felonious tiger trainer, was nabbed by Wonder Woman and told that on Reform Island she'd learn to "obey loving authority." The infuriated Tigra replied with her exotic accent, "You weel regret zis! I weel get

revenge!" But even a simpleton like Steve Trevor knew how effective Amazon rehabilitation was, and exclaimed, "Horsefeathers! You'll end up loving **Wonder Woman** like all the rest of us!" And most of the inmates did. When Wonder Woman visited Reform Island in *Sensation Comics* #22, a reformed criminal ran up to her and proclaimed, "These bonds feel wonderful! Keep me here in Amazon prison and train me to control my evil self!"

On the all-female Amazon islands, bondage was practiced in its purest forms. It was pleasant and instructive, and the result was a utopian society where even the most evil villain learned to love peace. Things were a lot more difficult out in the world of men, but Wonder Woman carried the power of submission with her in her golden lasso. The lasso was crafted from the girdle of Hippolyte, the symbol of the queen's power and the Amazon matriarchy.

While interrogating a suspected Nazi spy, Wonder Woman bound the woman in the lasso, saying, "I shall **make** you tell the truth—while bound with the golden rope you **must** obey me!" The lasso gave Wonder Woman complete control over whomever she tied up. A lot has been written about the links between the lasso and Marston's work developing the lie detector test, but while there's certainly some connection, the lasso was much more than just a magical polygraph. Marston told Byrne that he created Wonder Woman as a "dramatized symbol of her sex. She's true to life—true to the universal characteristics of women everywhere. Her magic lasso is merely a symbol of feminine charm, allure, oomph, attraction every woman uses." Every woman could be a Wonder Woman and every woman had her own lasso. It wasn't a lie detector test; it was her sexuality.

When Byrne again feigned doubt about the power of women, Marston replied that "woman's charm is the one bond that can be made strong enough to hold a man against all logic, common sense, or counterattack." Just like getting ensnared in an actual lasso, a woman could capture a man with her feminine wiles and get him to submit to her. And, because they were women and women were inherently loving, they used these powers for good.

Wonder Woman could do anything she wanted with her lasso, and she chose to use it to fight crime and help others. While villains occasionally stole the lasso and used it for nefarious purposes, in the hands of Wonder Woman it was only used for good. Even in the world of men, with one lone lasso against all of the forces of patriarchy, the power of submission was extremely effective and beneficial.

Although Marston depicted his theories in an unusual way, the underlying message of his bondage imagery was consistent and progressive. There weren't many other people, much less men, advocating that women should be in charge in the 1940s. Paradise Island, Reform Island, and the golden lasso illustrated the strength and power of women.

However, in the world of men Marston showed a different type of bondage, where women were kept down.

While bondage among the Amazons was empowering, in the world of men, bondage had the opposite effect. Because men were cruel and dominant, being bound took what made women most powerful—the benefits of submission—and twisted it, leaving women literally, physically powerless.

The first time Wonder Woman had her bracelets chained together by a man, her mother appeared to her and said, "Daughter, if any man welds chains on your bracelets, you will become weak as we Amazons were when we surrendered to Hercules." All of Wonder Woman's superpowers that came from her Amazon upbringing disappeared once a man had power over her. Wonder Woman was even reduced to tears in one instance as her captor taunted her, saying, "Aye weep, captive girl! Behold yourself helpless!" She sobbed as she gazed forlornly at her bonds.

Marston took the metaphor even further in *Wonder Woman #5*. Not only did the fiendish Dr. Psycho capture Wonder Woman and lock her in a cage, he then used a special device to rip her spirit from her body. As Wonder Woman's body slumped lifelessly in its cage, Dr. Psycho chained her spirit to the wall. Wonder Woman tried desperately to send out a mental distress call to the Holliday Girls, but it was no use;

she couldn't do anything without her body. It wasn't a subtle message, but it was certainly evocative: don't let men have control or they will steal your spirit and render you a powerless shell of your true self.

The brutality of the bondage of women by men was meant to critique patriarchal society and illustrate the political and social oppression of women. When Byrne expressed concerns that patriarchy was too powerful for women to overcome, Marston offered a ray of hope, stating, "My Wonder Woman often lets herself be tied into a bundle with chains as big as your arm. But in the end she easily snaps the chains. Women can do lots of things by letting men think they're fettered when they're not." Even with Dr. Psycho, eventually Wonder Woman's spirit escaped its bonds, jumped back into her body, and defeated him. The dominant patriarchal society was strict, but in the end it could never keep a strong woman down.

The Bondage Battle

Soon after All-American Publications began publishing *Wonder Woman*, *Sensation Comics*, and *Comic Cavalcade*, Max Gaines received several concerned letters from the company's editorial advisory board. Josette Frank, the staff advisor of the Children's Book Committee at the Child Study Association of America, wrote to Gaines that "this feature does lay you open to considerable criticism from any such group as ours, partly on the basis of the woman's costume (or lack of it), and partly on the basis of sadistic bits showing women chained, tortured, etc." Frank advised Gaines to take her criticisms "very seriously" because she'd heard a lot of concerns about the bondage imagery.

W. W. D. Sones, a professor of education and director of curriculum study at the University of Pittsburgh, agreed and wrote, "My impressions confirmed those of Miss Frank that there was a considerable amount of chains and bonds, so much so that the bondage idea seemed to dominate the story." Responding to Marston's claims about submission and metaphors, Sones was unconvinced

and stated, "I could not help but feel that such subtle and almost mystic purposes were a business and social risk."

Assistant editor Dorothy Roubicek was given the job of sorting out these complaints. She sent Marston some sketches of less revealing costumes Wonder Woman could wear, and suggested that Wonder Woman avoid Paradise Island, which was obviously a hub for bondage imagery. Marston refused to make any changes; he replied to Gaines with lengthy letters arguing against Frank and Sones's comments. After months of acting as a go-between for Marston and the advisory board's letters, Gaines was weary of all the psychological mumbo jumbo and was about to drop the issue when he received another letter that he found very unsettling.

It was a fan letter addressed to Marston that had arrived at the All-American offices, from an US Army sergeant who wrote, "I am one of those odd, perhaps unfortunate men who derive an extreme erotic pleasure from the mere thought of a beautiful girl, chained or bound, or masked, or wearing extreme high-heels or high-laced boots—in fact, any sort of constriction or strain whatsoever. [. . .] Have you the same interest in bonds and fetters that I have?" The sergeant also said that he was a big fan of William Seabrook, the traveler and occultist, who wrote a lot about "chained women."*

This didn't go over well with Gaines at all. Psychological squabbling was one thing, but a reader aroused by the bondage imagery was far more troubling. Gaines was the man behind *Picture Stories from the Bible*, after all. He wrote to Marston right away, stating that "this is one of the things I've been afraid of (without quite being able to put my finger on it)."

Gaines was so concerned that he got Roubicek to quickly come up with some alternatives to bondage, and included them in his

---

*Seabrook was an author who was particularly interested in Satanism and voodoo, sadistic bondage, and cannibalism, and participated in all of these activities. He was also an alcoholic and a drug addict. The sergeant called Seabrook his "idol."

letter to Marston. Gaines wrote, "Miss Roubicek hastily dashed off this morning the enclosed list of methods which can be used to keep women confined or enclosed without the use of chains. Each one of these can be varied in many ways—enabling us, as I told you in our conference last week, to cut down the use of chains by at least 50 to 75% without at all interfering with the excitement of the story or the sales of the books."

Marston, on the other hand, couldn't have cared less.

His reply to Gaines's letter about the sergeant was astounding. He was completely indifferent to Gaines's worries. Marston wrote back, "I have the good Sergeant's letter in which he expresses his enthusiasm over chains for women—so what?" He then entirely embraced the sergeant's reaction, writing that "you can't have a real woman character in any form of fiction without touching off many readers' erotic fantasies. Which is swell, I say—harmless erotic fantasies are now generally recognized as good for people." He refused to change his series in any way.

Gaines remained concerned, but ultimately he did nothing about the book. *Wonder Woman* editor Sheldon Mayer later said, "The fact is, it was a runaway best-seller." In early 1944, Josette Frank resigned from the advisory board for all three Wonder Woman titles, writing that "the strip is full of significant sex antagonisms and perversions" and "personally, I would consider an out-and-out strip tease less unwholesome than this kind of symbolism."

Marston's critics thought that he used bondage imagery in an intentionally erotic manner to lure in readers, and they weren't entirely wrong. To Marston, there was a definite erotic component to submitting to women. In his fake interview with Olive Byrne, Marston argued that men's desire to submit to women came from a combination of two feminine qualities. First, "normal men retain their childish longing for a woman to mother them," so they want a caring, maternal figure. Second, "at adolescence a new desire is added. They want a girl to allure them."

Mayer later said that Marston "was writing a feminist book, but not for women. He was dealing with a male audience." It was a bait and switch, playing on male desires with the bondage to bring them in and then hitting them with his metaphors and messages about female superiority. In an article about movies he wrote in 1929, Marston argued that "the unique appeal of the erotic actress" was the key to the success of the film industry, and it seems that he was trying to do the same for comic books with the unique appeal of the erotic superheroine. According to Marston, any powerful female character could get a boy riled up, and *Wonder Woman* just happened to be full of those.

Sex with Marston

Not surprisingly, Marston wrote a lot about sex in his psychological work, and he had a different, more positive approach to women and sex than his contemporaries. In the 1920s, when Marston was developing DISC theory and all the ideas that would lead to Wonder Woman, the study of sexology had recently emerged as a new field in psychology. Researchers like Edward Carpenter, Richard von Krafft-Ebing, and Sigmund Freud all broke with the prudish and repressive Victorian approach to sexuality, but Havelock Ellis was probably the most famous early sexologist. He argued for the sexual rights of women and took men to task for their poor lovemaking skills, famously writing that "the husband is sometimes like an orang-outang with a violin."

There was a sort of sexual renaissance in the 1930s when marriage manuals became popular. Based on the research of sexologists, these manuals espoused sexual harmony for married couples and the importance of sexual satisfaction for the husband *and* the wife.*

---

*At the time, in many countries it was illegal for nonmedical professionals to purchase or sometimes even read medical texts about sex, so translating these scientific ideas into more practical marriage manuals was how this new approach to sex was disseminated.

Although the theories of sexologists were certainly better for women than anything that had come before, there were still a lot of repressive ideas about women and sex. Sexology was rooted in evolutionary theory, so researchers looked to the animal kingdom, where males often put on a display or some show of strength to capture the female. This propagated a framework where men were defined as active, aggressive captors while women were passive and wanted to be captured. Because women were meant to be captured, any resistance was deemed part of the mating ritual. If a woman refused a man, it was considered a feigned act. Some Freudians went so far as to argue that if a woman were forced to have sex against her will, her unconscious self had actually consented to the act, basically justifying the rape.

Similarly, since men were made to be aggressive captors, these theories resulted in a rationalization, and in some ways an endorsement, of brutality. Ellis wrote that sexual sadism was "in its origin an innocent and instinctive impulse" and "compatible with a high degree of general tender-heartedness." If all sexual behavior was natural and instinctive, sexual sadism was therefore natural too.

For sexologists, the binary of active, aggressive men and passive women was like a law of nature, hardwired into the brains of humans. Marston disagreed entirely. To Marston, men's aggressiveness and women's passivity were things that could be changed with ease, because they were the product of society. Patriarchy encouraged men to be dominant and ruled by their egocentrism, forcing women into a subordinate role.

The only law of nature Marston ascribed to was the superiority of women. When Marston said that women should be in charge, he meant they should be in charge everywhere, especially in the bedroom. In *Emotions of Normal People*, he claimed that "however much dominant resistance the majority of males may feel, [. . .] women's bodies are designed for the capture of males and not for submission to them."

Marston turned the sexologists' framework around entirely, and described every step of a romantic relationship in his own terms.

Women were never passive at any stage. In dating, for instance, "the male becomes a constant attendant upon his captivatress, obeying her spoken commands and seeking to submit to her inarticulate emotional nature in every way possible." The woman was actually slyly capturing him.

Marston argued that during sex the woman's body literally captured the man's.* Once captured, the woman should initiate all of the movements and the man should respond to her actions, and only with her permission. This would be best for both parties, because women would get what they wanted and "normal males get the maximum of love happiness from being controlled, captured, or captivated by women." This may be more about Marston and what he liked than an accurate theory of human behavior. Nonetheless, Marston's ideas were a significant break from those of his contemporaries.

By denying that male sexual aggression was a law of nature, Marston also undercut the justification of sexual sadism. In fact, Marston spoke out quite strongly against sadism, calling it an "abnormal extreme" and arguing that sadism "imposes various tortures upon the body of the person subjected, revealing the fact that the subjected person is regarded, for the time, as an inanimate antagonistic object."

Given his stance against sadism, it's no surprise that Marston reacted strongly to his critics suggesting that the bondage in *Wonder Woman* was sadistic. He wrote massive letters defending the series against its advisory board critics, arguing that the bondage wasn't sadistic because Wonder Woman always escaped. Marston stated

---

*Usually when people talk about sex, it is about the man penetrating the woman. Marston totally flipped that around, seeing sex as a woman literally capturing a man's penis with her vagina. To Marston, that's why men have erections. Women use their feminine wiles on men to get them erect, making their penises easier to capture.

that sadism was "the enjoyment of other people's actual suffering" and claimed this could never happen in his comics because Wonder Woman wasn't actually suffering; she was bound so she could demonstrate her strength and power when she broke free.

The Limits of Metaphor

Marston certainly had some eccentric ideas, but when he defended them he always said the right things. He was firmly against sadism, strongly advocated the strength of women, and while his bondage metaphors were elaborate, they in theory hold up. However, his intent didn't match up with his execution, and there was a disconnect between his defense of the comic and the comic itself. If you were trying to teach boys the benefits of submitting to women, you'd expect that the comics would feature a lot of men bound by women. You'd expect them to be having fun, too, happily bound so as to demonstrate the positive qualities of letting a woman be in control. Instead, the vast majority of bondage imagery in *Wonder Woman* featured unhappily bound women. This raises some serious questions about the effectiveness of Marston's metaphors.

Returning to the comparison series from the start of the chapter, *Wonder Woman* had far more bondage, but how often were men bound in *Batman* and *Captain Marvel Adventures*? All of the time. In *Batman*, panels featuring tied-up male characters made up 96 percent of the book's total bondage imagery. *Captain Marvel Adventures* was a bit higher at 97 percent. That's nearly all of the bondage; women only accounted for 8 percent and 6 percent of the series' bondage imagery, respectively.* Of the twenty issues of both

---

*These numbers don't add up to 100 percent because there were a few panels that featured both men and women in some sort of bondage scene, so there's a slight overlap.

series that were tabulated, only five featured any bound women at all, so three-quarters of the issues featured only bound men.

Men accounted for only 20 percent of the bondage imagery in *Wonder Woman*, far less than the other two series. Women made up 84 percent of the book's bondage, over four times as much as the men. We're used to *Wonder Woman* being a different sort of book, but this is puzzling. It seems that Marston used his bondage metaphor rather sparingly on his male characters and focused all of his attention on having females tied up. There are several possible explanations for this, but none of them hold up.

Wonder Woman had a female lead character, and lead characters always got into tight spots. Thus, there was higher male bondage in *Batman* and *Captain Marvel Adventures* with their male stars, and higher female bondage in *Wonder Woman* with its female star. However, Wonder Woman accounted for only 40 percent of her book's total bondage. Women were tied up 84 percent of the time in *Wonder Woman*, which leaves 44 percent of female bondage unaccounted for. This 44 percent is still more than double the percentage of male bondage. Wonder Woman was tied up a lot, but didn't even make up a majority of the female bondage. If a woman was tied up in *Wonder Woman*, more often than not it wasn't even Wonder Woman.

It's interesting to note that when the golden lasso was used in the examined issues, it involved Wonder Woman tying up someone else only 52 percent of the time. The other 48 percent of the time, Wonder Woman was tied up in her own lasso. So really, the golden lasso that symbolized women's power was almost as much a hassle as it was a help.

Amazons played lots of bondage games on Paradise Island, which could explain all of this female bondage, but the numbers don't back it up. Bound Amazons accounted for less than 10 percent of *Wonder Woman*'s total bondage. Paradise Island was an important metaphor for female rule, but it wasn't in the book all that much.

While most of the bondage took place in the world of men, Wonder Woman always escaped and, according to Marston, was never actually suffering. One would assume that getting tied up in the world of men must have been a joke for Wonder Woman, since she could just snap her bonds and defeat the bad guys with ease. She wasn't smiling much, though. Of the 341 panels where Wonder Woman was bound, she was smiling, laughing, or shown to be happy/amused through the art or text in only fourteen panels. Bondage was only demonstrably fun for Wonder Woman 4 percent of the time.

For the other 96 percent of her bondage panels, Wonder Woman was not at all pleased. She was frustrated because she couldn't help her friends, crying because she was helpless, trying very hard not to die, or having her spirit ripped from her body. These unpleasant panels outnumbered the pleasant ones 24 to 1. Wonder Woman was Marston's champion of female power and superiority, but in her bondage panels the pleasant, loving aspects of submission were completely overshadowed by cruel dominance.

If you look at the bondage imagery as elaborate metaphors for Marston's theories, the metaphors do hold up. Paradise Island is a utopia, criminals get rehabilitated on Reform Island, and the world of men is a terrible, terrible place for everyone. Clearly, *Wonder Woman* shows that things are better with women in charge.

However, when we look closer we can see that there were fixations. Marston's metaphors weren't evenly presented. Instead, a lot of the book focused on one specific component: women bound in an unpleasant manner. These panels represented Marston's critique of patriarchal society, but in the comics they were shown ridiculously disproportionately to the rest of his theories. All of the pleasant, positive aspects of submitting to women were shorted. Instead, readers were presented with a lot of very unhappy, very tied-up women.

Marston acknowledged that the book would inspire erotic fantasies, that it was "swell" readers got turned on by the bondage in *Wonder Woman*. But what was ultimately presented was a children's

comic book, full of images of unhappily bound women, meant to excite male readers. That suggests that there may have been some sadistic fetishism at play, where female characters were dominated for the reader's erotic pleasure.

Taking a look at the series as a whole, though, while Marston illustrated his theories by having Wonder Woman tied up in all manner of painful, unpleasant, and arguably sadistic scenarios, the series was never overtly sexual. Marston acknowledged the erotic nature of bondage, but there was nothing in the comics themselves that directly tied bondage to sex or sadistic fetishism. *Wonder Woman* was fiction for children, and because of its G-rated content we can only take our sadistic fetishism concerns so far.

But Marston also wrote fiction for adults.

Venus with Us, Marston's Ancient Roman Sex Romp

While Marston couldn't delve into the sexual aspects of bondage and submission with *Wonder Woman*, he definitely did with *Venus with Us*. By taking a look at his novel, we can see how his metaphors played out in a more adult setting and then apply this knowledge to *Wonder Woman*.

Venus with Us told the life story of Julius Caesar, the first emperor of Rome, with a very Marston twist. The description on its first edition in 1932 read, "The title is from the Latin 'Venus nobiscum,' which was Julius Caesar's battle cry and motto. He maintained all his life that women controlled the world; that men lived, fought and ruled, that nations grew; changed and disappeared under the stimulus of women. Each step in his own career, in his judgment, decided by a woman."

The novel detailed all of the events of Caesar's life that one would expect, adding that each of his achievements was motivated by women. For example, according to Marston, Caesar went to Egypt not to defeat Pompey and become the sole ruler of Rome but to rescue his kidnapped granddaughter, Gaia, and his lover, a British

slave named Ursula. That he defeated Pompey and found another lover in Cleopatra were bonuses, it seemed.

The cover of the 1932 edition was simple with an orange color scheme, and it showed Julius Caesar battling a gladiator in an arena, about to deliver the decisive blow with his cape billowing behind him like an ancient superhero. As heroic as Caesar looked on the cover, the real stars of the book were the women who influenced his life. Clearly, Marston provided another example of the benefits of submitting to the loving authority of women, this time through the guise of a serious novel for adults.

There is, however, a second edition. In 1953, after Marston's death, the book was reprinted as *The Private Life of Julius Caesar*, with a new description and cover. The back cover of this edition read: "Here is the whole bold panorama of Roman times—the debauchery, the wars, the barbaric revels and cruelties, the old pagan rites on the altar of Venus." The description went on to exclaim that "from Egypt to England, from Greece to Gaul, he came, he saw, he conquered. But slave girl and vestal virgin, courtesan and queen, each in turn conquered Caesar!" So it had quite a different vibe; the original didn't mention anything about debauchery or conquering.

On the new front cover, Caesar reached for a woman who lay back on a bed and gazed at him suggestively, while a nude female slave knelt at his feet. In the background, several nude women were being whipped. The back cover had a series of images that included a naked woman being crucified, and even more nudity with another unclothed woman pouring water over Caesar as he reached up the dress of, you guessed it, yet another woman.

This edition also kept some sketchy company. There were several other pulp novels advertised in the back, like *Paprika*, a tale of "the lurid life of an uninhibited Gypsy lass"; *His Majesty O'Keefe*, the "epic saga of the white man who became master of a South Seas island and its golden women"; and two books in one, *Dope Doll* and *The Bigamy Kiss*. Marston had no control over this edition of

the book, but it's clear what the publishers thought of it. Comparing the two, the 1953 edition's cover and description more accurately reflected the novel. It was a lurid, suggestive sex romp.

There was no sex whatsoever in Wonder Woman comics, just a lot of reading between the lines, but in *Venus with Us*, blatant sexual content was regularly discussed in terms of Marston's theories. Marston rephrased his ideas in Roman terms; instead of talking about "submission" and "dominance" there were "servants of Venus" and "servants of Eros." This described submission/dominance in sexual terms where Venus, the female goddess, represented submissive love while Eros, the male god, represented dominant lust.

When a former Vestal virgin named Metala tried to seduce Caesar, he rebuffed her and said, "Is it possible that you do not understand the difference between worshiping Eros and submitting to Venus? The pleasure of Eros may rightly be enjoyed only when Venus commands." He added that "love without pleasure is a dreary occupation; but pleasure without love is death to body and soul." For Marston's Caesar, sex was about submission.

Marston did slip into his psychological vocabulary occasionally. Speaking to Alda, a Gallic slave who was his lover throughout the novel, Caesar commented, "I have a notion it's really rather good for people to be compelled to submit to others." Just like Paradise Island demonstrated the ideal form of submission in *Wonder Woman*, Caesar and his circle of women did the same in *Venus with Us*. And did so with bondage, of course.

Caesar's female associates willingly became each other's slaves throughout the novel, regularly donning chains and clothing that reflected their slave status. In one scene, Gaia and Ursula made a wager over a fencing competition in which the loser of the bet had to be the other's slave for a month. Ursula lost, and much tickling and spanking ensued as she served Gaia. Bondage and submission were fun games for Marston's Roman women, just as they were for his Amazons. There was mutual love and trust all around, and it was pleasant for everyone involved, though *Venus with Us* added a

sexual dimension to this pleasure. While a slave, Ursula stated, "I *love* to call you Mistress . . . it gives me a thrill every time I say it."

It was Caesar who got the most thrills. He had several sexual relationships, and submitted to all of the women gladly, most notably the vestal virgin Florentia, his first love. The novel stated that for them "it was the girl who ruled, and it was the man who submitted." Caesar's total submission was described in this somewhat risqué paragraph:

> She made him boast himself her slave—weeping, pleading, imploring. She made him hers so utterly that even she could never grant him freedom. She enveloped him in bonds of herself whose softness was unbreakable.*

Florentia ruled Caesar entirely, and all of the women in his life had a similar role. Just like Wonder Woman had incomparable strength and power in the world of men, Caesar was unrivaled by his peers and accomplished great things, all because of submission to the loving authority of women.

As a counter to the benefits of submitting to women, there had to be a dark side that critiqued patriarchal society. Outside of Caesar's circle, bondage wasn't fun at all. In fact, it became sinister. The most notable instance involved poor Florentia. Metala was jealous and had her pirate lover, Alcibiades, kidnap Florentia. Metala kept her as a slave, humiliating the proud servant of Venus. But slavery wasn't enough, and Metala demanded that Florentia be crucified in the most painful way possible. Caesar quickly tried to buy back Florentia from Alcibiades, but he didn't have enough money with him. The pirate, who had cut down Florentia from the cross to sell her to Caesar, "drove his sword savagely into Florentia's side and kicked her body over the cliff." She landed on the deck of Caesar's ship "with a soft, hollow thud," and died. Metala and Alcibiades

---

*This all sounds a lot like the penis capturing discussed earlier.

were like an ancient Roman version of Cheetah and Dr. Psycho, the villains who so often captured Wonder Woman and showed the evils of dominance.

Venus with Us and *Wonder Woman* both included a select group that demonstrated the benefits of submitting to the loving authority of superior women, and in both this submission was perverted outside of the core group by dominance and cruelty. Where the comics had Wonder Woman, *Venus with Us* had Caesar. Both characters espoused Marston's theories and lived them out to their benefit, but there was something more with Caesar.

Early in the novel, Caesar was confronted by Roman troops trying to arrest him, "but Caesar, with a natural gift for psychology, detected an undercurrent of query, of calculation," and used his psychological knowledge to escape. Caesar espoused Marston's theories, was interested in psychology, and lived a polyamorous lifestyle with several women. In many ways, Caesar was an analogue of Marston, so it stands to reason that when we read Caesar's thoughts on bondage and submission, these words reflect what Marston thought were acceptable, enlightened practices.

Early in the novel, Caesar stormed the palace of Mides, a rich island ruler, to rescue Alda, one of his many lovers. There he found a room with several small, gilded cages. Inside each was a nude slave girl with a golden chain tied around her ankle; the girls were described as "human pets," and the chain was called "a golden leash." After entering, "Julius glanced about the room and laughed appreciatively. His beauty-loving soul approved Mides' idea. It did not disturb his enjoyment to think that several of these girls had been stolen from his own villa. On the contrary, he felt relieved to discover that their new master was a true esthete, capable of enjoying the girls' beauty in such an ingenious fashion." This wasn't fun bondage games in the style of Paradise Island. This was a man who stripped woman, put them in small cages, and thought of them as pets for his own enjoyment. That Caesar approved of this is problematic for Marston's arguments.

Later, when Caesar was in Egypt, Cleopatra built him a barge with a quartz floor so he could see the rowers below. These rowers were all nude slave women, masked and chained together at the wrists and ankles, forced to row the barge. When he saw this, Caesar called it "the prettiest sight I have ever seen," "the most marvelous spectacle ever prepared for a love-starved Roman," and "poetry of motion." During his time touring the Nile on the barge, the novel states that "Caesar had not felt so well for twenty years. [. . .] He felt relaxed, satisfied, rejuvenated." Caesar enjoyed the arduous forced labor of women that was prepared specifically for his erotic pleasure. These women didn't willingly submit to this onerous and degrading task; they were made to do it against their will.

While Caesar wasn't the dominant force behind these scenarios created by Mides and Cleopatra, he did enjoy them. He loved them, even, and they turned him on sexually. Marston described sadism as a dominant action that reduced people to objects. Forced labor and imprisonment were obviously dominant actions, and the captured and bound women enjoyed by Caesar weren't viewed as people with their own wills but rather as objects meant for male pleasure. By his own definition, Marston's hero enjoyed dominant, sadistic bondage.

Reading Caesar as Marston's representative, these scenes are essentially an endorsement of finding sexual pleasure in dominance. *Venus with Us* doesn't disapprove of Caesar's enjoyment. Instead, it celebrates it, describing the scenarios and Caesar's pleasure in detailed, glowing terms. Bondage imagery was supposed to make men want to submit to women, but here the message was that it was pleasant for men to dominate women. Dominant bondage was supposed to be a critique, but here it was a celebration.

If it was acceptable for Caesar to be aroused by Mides's caged women or Cleopatra's chained rowers, then it would translate that it was OK for a reader to be turned on by a bound and powerless Wonder Woman, subjected to the sadistic whims of her villainous captors. Because Wonder Woman was tied up in such a fashion for the vast majority of her bondage panels, her comic books have a new

dimension. There were messages of female empowerment, but there was also imagery that would rile up dominant men and their sadistic fetishes. According to Marston, that was totally fine.

William Moulton Marston, Bondage Connoisseur

With *Venus with Us*, we see that bondage took a dark turn. It's difficult to talk about how Marston felt about bondage outside of his psychological theories, because that's the only way he discussed it. We know he used bondage as a metaphor, and we know this metaphor becomes strained when examined closely. But was the bondage a limited metaphor that crumbles when dug into, or was it a fetish that Marston shoehorned into his fiction with a psychological cover?

In *Wonder Woman* #6, dated Fall 1943, Wonder Woman appeared at a charity function to benefit the women and children of Europe affected by the war. The main event was a Houdini-like escape, where Wonder Woman was chained up and submerged in a tank of water. It was one of the rare instances outside of Paradise Island where Wonder Woman was willingly bound. Of course, everything went wrong; the Cheetah added the golden lasso to Wonder Woman's bonds and she barely got out of the tank alive. Nonetheless, escaping from a tank of water was a fairly pedestrian use of bondage.

Except that Marston gave the scene an extra twist. Before Wonder Woman entered the tank, two panels described the various types of restraint that were used. The emcee said, "This is the famous 'brank'—a leather mask worn by women prisoners in St. Lazare prison, France. It covers the entire face and muffles a prisoner's voice! The wide iron collar on **Wonder Woman's** neck comes from Tibet—it prevents the prisoner from bending his head. This ancient Greek manacle clamps the ankles firmly together." Also added was a pile of chains and, secretly, the golden lasso. Now this is ridiculously elaborate. It wasn't enough to have chains and masks and manacles, they had to be fancy too. They were foreign or ancient or

infamous, and Marston took up a lot of space to describe them. The items were specific, and Marston knew what he was talking about.*

A brank, also known as a scold's bridle, was an iron mask that resembled a Hannibal Lecter–style muzzle. The goal was to cover the mouth, not the whole head. Inside the mask was a long bridle bit that went in the mouth so that the wearer's voice was muffled. Sometimes this bit had spikes on the bottom, to discourage any attempt at talking. Basically, it was a torture device, and it was used mainly on women to silence them.

In certain areas of Europe from the sixteenth to the early nineteenth century, if a woman was suspected of being a witch, wearing the brank was one of the punishments she might receive. It was also used on wives who were gossips or nagged or talked back to their husbands. If a wife was considered impertinent, her husband could drag her to the local judge where she'd be sentenced to wear the brank. Usually a chain and a bell were attached and she would be

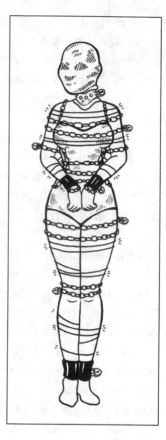

An interpretation of the brank, neck collar, leg manacles, chains, and interwoven lasso on a female form. KATE LETH

paraded through the streets where people could throw things at her and beat her. It was a degrading and humiliating punishment.

---

*This was the favorite issue of the army sergeant who had written the fan letter to Marston.

However, the brank in *Wonder Woman* was slightly different. It was a leather mask that covered the entire head and was unique to St. Lazare's prison, an actual place. Formerly a hospital, St. Lazare's became a prison during the French Revolution, then exclusively a women's prison in 1896 that housed mainly murderers and prostitutes before it was closed down in 1935. The leather brank was used on dangerous female prisoners when they had visitors. The mask prevented the guest from transferring notes, poisons, or small metal files to the prisoner via a kiss. The brank was used at St. Lazare's as late as the 1920s. Interestingly, one of the prison's most famous inmates during the French Revolution was the Marquis de Sade, the libertine torture enthusiast from whom we get the term "sadism."

Marston made a very specific, and very accurate, reference with his use of the brank. The specificity alone is peculiar enough, suggesting he might have been more into bondage then he let on publicly. How did Marston know about St. Lazare's prison and its unique use of the brank? There's an interesting lead.

In the early twentieth century, newspapers regularly bought ready-made articles from large syndicates to fill up their page counts. The International Feature Service included a Europe-based writer named Carl De Vidal Hunt, who wrote a six-part series entitled "As the Fabulous French Women's Prison Falls After 14 Years, Comes the First Look-in on Its Million Secrets," a thorough history of St. Lazare's prison published in American newspapers in 1932. One of the article's most shocking revelations was the prison's use of the leather brank. We can't know if Marston ever read this series, but there aren't many other references to St. Lazare's and the brank elsewhere. Also, two of the six parts of the article were dedicated to white slavery, in which naïve girls were duped and forced to do all sorts of unpleasant work for cruel men, much like every Marston Wonder Woman story written.

If Marston didn't read the article, he still knew a lot about the prison and the brank. But if he did, it affected him so strongly that he remembered it for a decade. Either way, he ultimately referenced a

bleak prison known for holding the father of sadism and put his heroine in a ridiculously degrading device in a comic book for children.

This doesn't sound like a man who was just using bondage as a metaphor. This sounds like a man who knew his bondage very well, a connoisseur who sporadically slipped in meticulous details about his fetish. There were curiously precise things like the brank, but there were creative things as well, like embedding Wonder Woman in a three-inch-thick statue of herself or freezing her in a block of ice or turning her into a being of pure color and shackling her inside a tube of boiling water meant to melt her like a crayon. The bondage was elaborate and detailed, and knowing that Marston thought it was acceptable to be sexually aroused by sadistically bound women casts his comics in a new light.

Yet Wonder Woman escaped. Every single time. As much as we can call Marston a bondage fetishist, that Wonder Woman freed herself from every predicament redeems him on some level. Consider the brank: historically it was meant to silence women, to render them helpless. Both the scold's bridle and the St. Lazare's leather mask rendered a woman's mouth ineffective. So what was the first thing Wonder Woman did when she was thrown in the tank and realized she was trapped in her lasso? She bit through the mouth of the brank, ripping it apart. She then used her teeth to undo the lasso, smashed her other bonds, and escaped. Wonder Woman literally tore apart the source of the brank's power, straight away.

Marston's bondage fixation was fetishistic, even sometimes sadistic. Wonder Woman escaping these bondage scenarios was undoubtedly feminist, empowering, and redemptive. It seems that Marston created, and was himself, quite a paradox.

The Interconnectedness of All Things

When scholars and writers talk about the bondage in *Wonder Woman*, they usually do one of two things. They either call Marston a quack or a pervert and dismiss everything he wrote entirely,

or they pretend that the bondage is inconsequential and focus on his progressive, feminist theories.

Both the feminist and fetishist aspects of Wonder Woman came from the same place: Marston's focus on submission, which surfaced in everything he wrote. On the one hand, he believed that women were the superior sex and would soon rule the world, leading him to create a strong female character who could defeat any foe and escape any predicament. On the other hand, the way Marston depicted submission led down a crooked road that resulted in the sadistic, sexual objectification of his heroine. Complicated and contradictory, the two sides cannot be separated.

Dismissing the bondage imagery to focus on the positive, feminist aspects of Wonder Woman means that one would have to dismiss the theory of submission that's at the root of bondage. By cutting away those roots, you lose the foundation of Wonder Woman's feminism as well. To state that this fetishism invalidated Wonder Woman's feminism, one would have to ignore the undeniably unique and progressive elements of the character. Both approaches are wrong; Wonder Woman was feminist *and* fetishist.

INTERLUDE 1

Wonder Woman's Extra Features

These days, the contents of most comic books are very basic, consisting of the story and some ads. However, from the 1940s through the 1960s, comics were filled with a variety of extra features. They usually included an essay or a prose story, some funny or informative short comic strips, and sometimes games or puzzles. *Wonder Woman* had many of these supplementary materials until the 1968 revamp, although most of them are now long forgotten because they rarely get reprinted in modern collections. This is unfortunate, because the changes to these features perfectly mirrored the changes to Wonder Woman herself as she moved from the Golden to the Silver Age. The progressive, feminist features during Marston's tenure gave way to strips about marriage and romance in the 1950s as our quirky, feminist heroine became much more interested in settling down as a housewife.

The Golden Age

Reviewing the contents of *Wonder Woman* #1, we get a sense of what was included in a Golden Age issue of *Wonder Woman*:

- It started with a "Wonder Women of History" strip about Florence Nightingale that covered all of Nightingale's life; it showed how her caring for injured animals when she was a child led to her serving in war hospitals when she grew up, and how this then led to her founding schools for nursing. It's her entire biography jam-packed into four pages.
- There was a two-page prose story by Jay Marr titled "A Message from Phil." In the story, a girl named Phillys saved a submarine by communicating telepathically with her injured engineer twin brother, Phil.
- After the story came a two-page comic strip called "Sweet Adeline: Songs Without Music" by Art Helfant. A hapless family frustrated with running a hotel decided to dig for oil instead, and were overjoyed to find a geyser of black gold until a maintenance man told them they'd just hit the building's oil tank.
- On the back inside cover was "Good Books Worth Reading," a book recommendation from editorial advisory board member Josette Frank. She suggested *Little Oscar's First Air Raid* by Lydia Mead, with art by Oscar Fabres, a timely choice.
- Below the book recommendation was "Superman's Secret Message (Code Pluto No. 8)," an encoded message that could be deciphered by readers who had the key. Take a crack at this impenetrable cipher: GWCZ NQZAB TQVM WN LMN-MVAM QA BPM TQVM IB BPM EQVLWE AMTTQVO ABIUXA IVL JWVLA!*

---

*"Code Pluto No. 8" simply means to go back eight letters, so A is S, B is T, C is U, etc. This message translates to: "Your first line of defense is the line at the window selling stamps and bonds!"

There was quite a range of features in the Golden Age, along with over fifty pages of Wonder Woman stories. It was a lot of material for ten cents!

The comic strips changed nearly every issue but were a regular component of the series, though Phillys and Phil were never heard from again. Soon *Wonder Woman* was host to the adventure stories of Jon L. Blummer's heroic aviator Hop Harrigan, which tied into the popular Hop Harrigan radio show. While there were various extra features in *Wonder Woman*, they were dwarfed by "Wonder Women of History"; its four pages often equaled or topped the page count of every other feature combined.

"Wonder Women of History" was the pet project of *Wonder Woman*'s celebrity associate editor, Alice Marble, the tennis star who became involved in comics after she retired from her stellar sports career. The first issue of *Wonder Woman* included an announcement of Marble as the book's associate editor and a message from Marble herself. She wrote that in her travels around the country she had realized "what a large part comics and comic books play in the life of the average American boy and girl!" and added, "Wonder Woman being my favorite comic character, I am very happy, indeed, to become associated with it!" Marble's editorial role was fairly ceremonial, but she wrote "Wonder Women of History" every issue, and she eagerly looked for ideas for which women to profile.

After the first issue premiered, Marble sent packages to several notable American women asking for their help. The package contained items like *Wonder Woman* #1 and a copy of Marston's article "Women: Servants of Civilization" from *Tomorrow* magazine, as well as a letter. Marble wrote that "women still have many problems and have not yet reached their fullest growth and development" and that "*Wonder Woman* marks the first time that daring, strength and ingenuity have been featured as womanly qualities." She asked each of the recipients to use an included form to list the famous women they'd like to see profiled and to send it back to her. The whole campaign was a very thorough operation.

However, it looks like Marble left her editorial position after sixteen issues, or roughly four years, because the byline "as told by Alice Marble" no longer appeared on "Wonder Women of History" after *Wonder Woman* #16. While the exact details of her departure are unknown, it was likely for personal reasons. In 1944, the newly married Marble suffered a miscarriage after a car accident, then days later learned that her husband had been killed in the war. She attempted suicide soon after, though she survived and recovered,* but it's reasonable to assume that comic books weren't much of a priority for her during this time. Despite the loss of Marble, "Wonder Women of History" continued after her departure, profiling over fifty women before it was canceled.

Each edition of "Wonder Women of History" followed the same pattern: the subject overcame some kind of adversity, usually related to her gender, and ultimately accomplished something of great importance. They were heroic stories, and showed how one woman could have a big impact and influence the world. As fantastic as Wonder Woman was, presenting real-life role models alongside her adventures showed that being a strong and successful woman wasn't just for people with superpowers.

Due to their short length, the writing on "Wonder Women of History" had to be to the point, but that didn't stop Alice Marble and, after she left, famed editor Julius Schwartz from crafting thorough and engaging stories. The art was intriguing as well. It used a realistic style to present an authentic depiction of each woman's historical setting. The first six strips were drawn by legendary comics artist Sheldon Moldoff, one of the main artists for Batman during the Golden and Silver Ages. He was followed by notable artists like

---

*According to her posthumously published autobiography, she became a spy. Her former lover was a Swiss banker, and she used him to track down Nazi financial data until she was eventually shot by a Nazi agent. She survived and recovered from that too.

Paul Reinman, Bob Oksner, and Alfonso Greene.* The strips were always engaging as well as informative.

"Wonder Women of History" covered an impressive array of professions. No matter what career a young reader was interested in, the feature likely had an ideal role model. Medicine was the best-represented field, and the strips included five nurses, three doctors, and various medical researchers and health reform advocates. There were obvious choices like Florence Nightingale and Clara Barton, but also many lesser-known women like Florence Rena Sabin, the first woman to graduate from the Johns Hopkins University School of Medicine, and Dorothea Lynde Dix, an advocate for the mentally ill whose work led to the creation of America's first mental asylums.

Women's rights was a popular topic as well. The women profiled spanned the history of women's fight for the right to vote, from Lucretia Mott and Emma Willard in the early 1800s to Susan B. Anthony in the latter half of the century to Carrie Chapman Catt and the passing of the Nineteenth Amendment in 1920.

Abolitionists and civil rights advocates had several representatives too, including Sojourner Truth, a former slave turned abolitionist; Julia Ward Howe, the writer of "The Battle Hymn of the Republic"; and Lillian D. Wald, one of the founders of the NAACP. The rest of the biographies depicted a myriad of professions; there were three astronomers, three authors, two aviators, two First Ladies, two lawyers, two Nobel laureates, a journalist, a missionary, an opera singer, a saint, a sculptor, a sharpshooter, and many others.†

---

*Greene was one of the few African American artists working in comics during the Golden Age. He drew nine strips for "Wonder Women of History."
†QUIZ INTERLUDE: Try to guess all twenty women based on the professions listed here, and the full list will be in a footnote later on in the chapter. Some are more obvious (the sharpshooter, the saint, and the aviator) while others are tough (the missionary, any of the astronomers).

As if showcasing strong women wasn't enough, the feature was also diverse in terms of race and nationality. While Americans dominated "Wonder Women of History," with Great Britain and France close behind, there were women like Madame Chiang Kai-Shek, the famed wife of the Chinese general; Mumtaz Mahal, the Indian empress for whom the Taj Mahal was built; Emilja Plater, a Polish/Lithuanian revolutionary; and Queen Margrete, a medieval queen of Scandinavia, just to name a few. The Native American population was represented too, with Sacajawea, Lewis and Clark's Shoshone guide.

Between "Wonder Women of History" and the adventures of the amazing Amazon, the early years of *Wonder Woman* presented women as heroes in both a literal and a fanciful manner. Young girls could play as Wonder Woman in the backyard every afternoon after they studied hard at school each day to be the next Marie Curie or Clara Barton. This progressive double feature was incredibly rare in the 1940s; women had just earned the right to vote two decades before, and many people still weren't pleased about that. While the war may have given women some new opportunities in the workforce, that quickly ended once the fighting was done and the men came home. Encouraging young girls to grow up to be anything other than housewives and mothers wasn't a huge priority, but *Wonder Woman* told them they could be anything they wanted to be. However, by the late 1940s, the supplementary contents of *Wonder Woman* began to change.

The Interregnum

After Marston's death in 1947 and before *Wonder Woman*'s shift to the Silver Age in 1958, the additional contents of the series were completely revamped. This started soon after Marston passed away, thus the timing seems more than coincidental. Marston died in May 1947, and 1948 saw two big changes to the book's

supplementary materials. First, "Wonder Women of History" lowered its page count, and second, the prose section shifted from stories to essays.

Before 1948, almost every edition of "Wonder Women of History" had been four pages long, but the profile of Sacajawea in *Wonder Woman* #27, published in January 1948, was only two pages. As was the profile of Elizabeth Barrett Browning in the following issue. The next two subjects, Dorothea Lynde Dix and Nellie Bly, each had three-page strips, but Jenny Lind and Mary Slessor were the only women to have a four-page profile after 1948. From January 1948 until the feature's final appearance in May 1954, the twenty-nine women profiled got an average of 2.4 pages each.

Furthermore, "Wonder Women of History" became increasingly intermittent over these six years. It sporadically skipped months, and then the feature disappeared for seven issues after *Wonder Woman* #57 in January 1953, finally returning more than a year later. But this return was short-lived; the next two women profiled, medical scientist Florence Rena Sabin and lawyer Gail Laughlin, were the last two new profiles, receiving only one page each. Laughlin's profile was buried with the advertisements at the very end of the comic book, and after *Wonder Woman* #66 the feature was over for good. "Wonder Women of History" faded away without any fanfare, a rather inauspicious end for a strip that had been in *Wonder Woman* since its very first issue.

The shift from prose stories to essays was, in its initial years, insignificant. The adventure stories were replaced by mildly interesting essays on seemingly random topics: the first essay was entitled "Race to the Top of the World" and discussed attempts to reach the North Pole; the second, "You Name It," explained the origins of several common last names; topics for the next several essays included the calendar, the Colossus of Rhodes, pineapples, and unique headdresses from around the world. The essays were gender neutral, aimed only at those curious about fruit, headwear, or the ancient

wonders of the world. This informative new endeavor lasted for a few years, but by 1952 the essays had a different aim. The topics were geared toward girls, as the following list of essays shows:

- *Wonder Woman #51*—"Let's Dance!"
- *Wonder Woman #52*—"What the Well-Dressed Women Wore 300 Years Ago"
- *Wonder Woman #53*—"Fashions of the Far East"
- *Wonder Woman #54*—"Swing Your Partner!"
- *Wonder Woman #55*—"Those Rings on Your Finger"
- *Wonder Woman #56*—"Women in War"
- *Wonder Woman #57*—"Her Crowning Glory"
- *Wonder Woman #58*—"Those Lovely Liberty Belles"
- *Wonder Woman #59*—"Background to Stardom"
- *Wonder Woman #60*—"With This Ring . . ."

These ten essays included two about fashion, two about dancing, two about jewelry, one about hairstyles ("Her Crowning Glory" is about hair, not crowns), and one about becoming a movie star. Now, while many boys enjoy dancing and fashion and the like, these were topics aimed squarely at young girls.

Two of these essays didn't quite fit this format: "Women in War" was about warrior queens, and "Those Lovely Liberty Belles" discussed the need for women in the armed forces. However, "Those Lovely Liberty Belles" made sure to point out that a woman in the armed services "can wear her hair in bangs or a chignon, and she can wear nail polish," adding hairstyles and fashion to the mix.*

By and large, the essays continued in this manner from then on. There was the occasional essay on the Leaning Tower of Pisa or

---

*The bizarre ending of the article reads: "Those of us who love a parade will love it just a little bit more to view column after column of those lovely Liberty Belles smartly marching down the street." Apparently, the author was looking forward to ogling female military officers.

umbrellas, but dancing and perfume and jewelry and dolls were the types of topics that dominated the feature. This isn't to say that those topics were bad; there's nothing inherently wrong with learning about different hairstyles throughout history. There's just a stark juxtaposition between "Wonder Women of History" telling the reader about the first female doctor or Nobel Prize–winning scientist and "Your Favorite Color" offering readers some tips on what colors of clothing best matched their hair and complexion. The subtext couldn't be more different.

A close look at May 1954's *Wonder Woman* #66, the last issue where "Wonder Women of History" appeared, gives us a sense of the extra features in this era:

- The inside cover featured a strip from the National Social Welfare Assembly called "Binky Says: Welcome Amigo!" that taught children to be kind and welcoming to Mexican immigrants.
- There was a half-page strip titled "Broken Engagements!" that showed superstitions about what could break off an engagement, like a woman putting cream in her coffee before the sugar or sitting on a table while talking to her fiancé.
- A full-page strip called "Clothing of Fortune!" was also about superstitions. The reader learned how doing up your buttons wrong would lead to bad luck all day, and that it's important for a girl to take off a garment when a tear needs to be mended "lest she lead a threadbare existence the rest of her life."
- Another full-page strip, "Wedding Forecast," provided some "sooth-saying" suggestions for how to tell when and who you'll marry, such as pulling out enough strands of your hair to match your age, and then burning them one by one until you see a vision of your future husband.
- The next strip was "Romantic Notions . . . ," and it provided even more marriage-related superstitions. For example, you shouldn't marry someone whose last name starts with the

same letter as yours because "If you change the name and not the letter, you change for the worse and not the better."

- There was a two-page essay on "The Dazzling Dolls," a history of doll collecting from ancient Rome to Belgium and China. It said that "psychologists tell us that little girls love dolls because of an innate mother instinct" and suggested that this desire to play with dolls and pretend to be a mother "is nature's way of preparing them for their future roles in life."

- Buried at the very back of the book was the one-page "Wonder Women of History" strip on Gail Laughlin. We very succinctly learn how Laughlin earned a law degree, met President Coolidge to argue for equal rights, fought for women's suffrage, and argued a case before the Supreme Court. There were no tips on how to get a man, though.*

If you take out "Wonder Women of History," which they did the very next issue, you can see that marriage and children were the main focus of the extra features by the mid-1950s. The informative essays became pro-domesticity propaganda, and the humor strips disappeared entirely. Interestingly, these new romance-centric strips had the same style as "Wonder Women of History," with realistic art and more narration than speech balloons, giving the superstition-laden strips the appearance of the same weight and factual value as the tales of women's historical achievements. As the Silver Age began, these random strips evolved into regular features that dominated the extra materials in *Wonder Woman*.

---

*The feature was near an advertisement for a FREE set of ten stamps featuring portraits of Adolf Hitler, which promised that if you ordered them, "your friends will envy you for it and want to buy the set from you." Why they were having trouble selling Hitler stamps is hard to say . . . you'd think they would fly off the shelves. *Wonder Woman* #66 was a weird issue.

The Silver Age

The Silver Age of superhero comic books began around 1956, and by that time the essay feature of *Wonder Woman* was nearly out the door. It lasted for a few more years, discussing stereotypically "girly" topics, but its page count dropped from two to one, and it made a final appearance in *Wonder Woman* #115 in July 1960. The title was "Maids of the Manor," and the essay discussed the amusements available to ladies in eleventh-century France and the hard working conditions for the wives and daughters of serfs. From the timing, it seems that the essay section was cut in favor of the series' new letter column, which had just premiered in the issue previous. Once the essays were gone, superstitious strips ruled the extra features in *Wonder Woman*.

They premiered in *Wonder Woman* #52 in March 1952, with the half-page strips "Leap Year Proposals" and "Ancient Beauty Secrets." In their early appearances they seemed like filler, short pieces to take up half a page while an advertisement filled the rest. There weren't any regular strips initially, though thematically they were all similar, dealing with traditions and superstitions surrounding marriage and romance, fashion, jewelry, or beauty. After they began, every issue of *Wonder Woman* for over a decade contained at least one of these strips.

Soon each strip was an entire page, and some became semi-regular features. One of the first regular strips began with "Strange Beliefs About Wedding Gowns" and continued with this motif. "Strange Beliefs About Gloves," "Strange Romantic Beliefs," and "Strange Romantic Customs" followed. The first feature with a regular title was "Gems of Destiny," which was about various precious stones and historical pieces of jewelry. It first appeared in *Wonder Woman* #68 in August 1954, with information about moonstones, diamonds, pearls, and opals. While both the "Strange" strips and "Gems of Destiny" appeared sporadically, at most once a year, soon there was another strip that became a constant presence in the book: "Marriage a la Mode."

"Marriage a la Mode" was published consistently after its first appearance in October 1954's *Wonder Woman #69*. The first strip was a full page and described several marriage traditions and superstitions, including the fact that "one of the important duties of the best man at a wedding in Wales was to give the bride a daintily cut piece of bread and butter, with the expectation that it would induce her children to have pretty and small mouths." The feature appeared in fifty-four of the next seventy-two issues of *Wonder Woman*, sharing wedding folklore from all over the world.

For all intents and purposes, "Marriage a la Mode" was the new "Wonder Women of History." It premiered three issues after "Wonder Women of History" ended, had a similar art style and format, and was the only regular feature in *Wonder Woman* after the essays ended. The layout for "Marriage a la Mode" was very consistent: each strip contained four panels that showed four different wedding traditions. Ultimately, that added up to well over two hundred different bits of wedding folklore. They covered a wide range of marriage-related topics, from traditions about proposals, ceremonies, and attire to superstitions concerning the success of the marriage, wealth, and children. "Marriage a la Mode," along with "Marriage Charms," "Lucky Brides," "Hope Chest," "Wedding Notions," "Future Mates," "Dream Sweetheart," "Romantic Rings," and scads of other strips placed a strong focus on love, marriage, and starting a family.

An issue that well captured this era is *Wonder Woman #116*, the first issue without an essay and thus the first issue where strips accounted for all of the book's extra features:

- First up was "Marriage a la Mode." We learned about the silver compote of sweets that "Moslem" couples enjoy on their wedding night, how on Borneo a Dyak boy initiates courtship by carrying a load of wood for a girl, that in ancient Japan the bride shaved off her eyebrows "to symbolize her subservience to her husband," and finally that two suitors wrestle for the right to marry a woman on "Mombasa Island, Somaliland."

- The next strip was "New Moon Superstitions," with a tip for women who have just moved into a new house: when she first sees a new moon, she needs to rush to the bedroom and make up the bed with fresh sheets. This keeps misfortune from her home.
- The only thing that stopped the dominance of these marriage-centric strips was the National Social Welfare Assembly's public service strips. In "Superman Says: Lend a Friendly Hand," we learn that it's important to be a good neighbor to refugees, even if they don't speak English and don't know how to play ball.

Though there were fewer extra features by the 1960s due to lowered page counts and increased advertisements, there was nothing to counterbalance the marriage and domesticity messages that dominated the strips. Not even Wonder Woman offered much of a different perspective.

By 1963, "Marriage a la Mode" and the other strips appeared less frequently. When *Wonder Woman* was revamped in 1968, these strips had become sporadic at best, down to just three or four appearing every year, and the revamp ended them for good. "Marriage a la Mode" appeared twice after the mod revamp and made its last appearance in *Wonder Woman* #191 in November 1970, discussing how in Madagascar the bride's father performed the marriage ceremony by cracking a coconut on the groom's head. The Bronze Age marked the end of extra features in DC Comics' series as a whole, and the main story and advertisements became the sole content of their books.*

---

*The "Wonder Women of History" quiz answers: **Astronomers (3):** Annie Jump Cannon, Caroline Herschel, Maria Mitchell. **Authors (3):** Elizabeth Barrett Browning, Fanny Burney, Hannah Adams (though if you guessed Hannah More, give yourself a point). **Aviators (2):** Amelia Earhart, Harriet Quimby. **First Ladies (2):** Abigail Adams, Dolley Madison. **Lawyers (2):** Gail Laughlin, Myra Colby Bradwell. **Nobel Laureates (2):** Jane Addams, Marie Curie. **Journalist:** Nelly Bly. **Missionary:** Mary Slessor. **Opera Singer:** Jenny Lind. **Saint:** Joan of Arc. **Sculptor:** Vinnie Ream Hoxie. **Sharpshooter:** Annie Oakley.

★ PART 2 ★

The Silver Age

4

A Herculean Task

*T*he Golden Age Wonder Woman was ahead of her time, much like Rosie the Riveter in presenting a symbol of what women could become but weren't allowed to be. The masses of women who entered the workforce during World War II got a taste of a different life, but it was only temporary. While surveys showed that 80 percent of female wartime workers wanted to continue working in their new field once the war was over, nearly all of them were let go when the men returned. The world returned to the status quo, with a renewed focus on domestic roles for women. Wonder Woman, Rosie the Riveter, and women workers ultimately became important touchstones for women's rights, but in the immediate postwar era their strength and independence had little lasting effect. The young girls who grew up with these role models eventually launched the women's liberation movement, but they had to get through the 1950s first.

After Marston's death in 1947, the writing duties of *Wonder Woman* and *Sensation Comics* went to Robert Kanigher. Before he worked in comics, Kanigher had written for various media, even publishing a book entitled *How to Make Money Writing* in 1943. He joined DC Comics in 1945 as both an editor and a writer and

created new characters like Black Canary, Rose and Thorn, and the Harlequin while writing for *Hawkman*, *Green Lantern*, and other books. Kanigher also filled in for Marston a few times when he was ill, writing a handful of Wonder Woman stories.

Once he took over the book, Kanigher edited and wrote *Wonder Woman* for over twenty years, but until 1958, Kanigher's work on *Wonder Woman* was basically a poor Marston impression.* He didn't continue Marston's feminist or fetishist themes with any detail, but his stories were clear attempts to ape Marston's style. H. G. Peter stayed on the book for several years as well, continuing his distinctive look. It wasn't until *Wonder Woman* #98 that Kanigher made the book his own, along with the series' new penciller, Ross Andru, and inker, Mike Esposito.

Andru and Esposito's modern style was a big change from Peter's old-fashioned art. Peter's work was compact and uniform, and it felt very flat, especially toward the end of his run when Peter was getting old and the art was churned out by committee. Andru and Esposito used different perspectives and angles to communicate the action of a scene, and their work more resembled contemporary comic book art than Peter's unique but dated style.

Wonder Woman #98 marked a clear break from the Marston-influenced run on the book. It was followed seven issues later by Kanigher's brand-new origin story for Wonder Woman. Aspects of Kanigher's new Wonder Woman were very much a product of DC Comics' Silver Age approach to superheroes, and this approach was born out of the ashes of this chaotic decade.

---

*In fact, the stories were still credited "By Charles Moulton," and continued as such until the mid-1960s. During his twenty years writing Wonder Woman, Kanigher was never credited as a writer, only as an editor. This was the fate of many Superman and Batman writers as well, whose stories still bore the taglines "By Jerry Siegel and Joe Shuster" and "By Bob Kane" long after those men had stopped working on the books.

Prelude to the Silver Age

When World War II ended, so too did the superhero boom. After Superman premiered in 1938, superhero comics had dominated the comic book industry, but the end of the war also meant an end to the desire for costumed heroes. Many books were canceled, and superheroes began to disappear. At DC Comics, *Flash Comics* and *Green Lantern* both ended in 1949, and the last adventure of their superhero team, the Justice Society of America, was published in 1951. Timely Comics' Human Torch and Namor the Sub-Mariner both ended in the late 1940s, and attempts to revive the characters throughout the 1950s routinely failed. Even Captain Marvel, who regularly had the top-selling comic book during the war, faced a staggering drop in sales. The decreasing profitability of the character was a major factor in Fawcett's decision to settle DC Comics' copyright infringement lawsuit and shut down its comic book division in 1953.

By 1954, only three superheroes still had comic books. Superman and Batman both survived the superhero collapse and starred in two books each, as well as costarring in a third, *World's Finest*. Wonder Woman also survived, but only with her self-titled series. *Comic Cavalcade* changed its format in 1948 and ended a few years later, and *Sensation Comics* was canceled in 1952.

Nothing better exemplifies the shift in the comic book market than the fate of Captain America. He had been hugely popular during the war but ran into the same sales decrease that rocked the genre in the late 1940s. Just before his series, *Captain America Comics*, was canceled, Timely Comics changed the name to *Captain America's Weird Tales* and tried to salvage the book as a horror series. The revamp failed and the series was canceled in 1950; Captain America didn't even appear in its final issue. Throughout the industry, horror, crime, and suspense comic books became the new hot genres.

Coincidentally, the most infamous publisher of horror and crime comics had direct ties to Wonder Woman. In 1944, National Comics

officially merged with All-American Publications to form DC Comics, and Harry Donenfeld bought out All-American's publisher, Max Gaines. Gaines left the publisher, taking only *Picture Stories from the Bible* with him, and formed a new company he called Educational Comics. When Gaines died in a boating accident in 1947, his son, William, took over.

Bill Gaines, as he was better known, had a very different vision for the company. He changed the name to Entertaining Comics and found a slew of writers and artists with distinctive styles and a taste for the macabre. EC Comics began to publish several horror comic books, most famously *Haunt of Fear*, *Tales from the Crypt*, and *Vault of Horror*, all of which featured gruesome and frightening artwork.* EC also had a strong stable of crime and suspense series, including *Crime SuspenStories*, *Shock SuspenStories*, *Two-Fisted Tales*, and *Weird Stories*. They were all luridly illustrated and presented shocking tales of horrific crimes, revenge, and violence.

EC Comics wasn't the only publisher of such series; nearly every company still in the business in the early 1950s had some horror or suspense comic books on the newsstands, but no one did it quite like EC. Despite its numerous imitators, EC remains the gold standard for horror and suspense comic books to this day. In fact, the art of EC Comics is often heralded as some of the most innovative and influential art to ever appear in comic books. However, in the 1950s these sensationalistic comic books faced a slew of very powerful critics.

Dr. Fredric Wertham was a noted psychologist who did some remarkable work in the 1950s. In 1953, he argued against Ethel Rosenberg's solitary confinement during the trial of the famous American communist spies. In 1954, he gave testimony during the landmark *Brown v. Board of Education* case in which he described

---

Tales from the Crypt was later adapted as an HBO television series of the same name, which ran in the early 1990s and was hosted by the congenial Crypt Keeper.

the adverse psychological effects of segregation on African American children. Throughout the entire decade, he ran a mental health clinic in Harlem in order to serve the often-ignored minority community. Despite these impressive actions, though, Wertham is today best remembered as the man who nearly destroyed the comic book industry.

In the late 1940s and early 1950s, Wertham wrote several articles about the dangers of comic books, calling them out as a contributing factor to juvenile delinquency. His comic book research culminated in his 1954 book *Seduction of the Innocent*, which received several favorable reviews in national magazines and was even excerpted in an issue of *Reader's Digest*. In the book, Wertham outlined his major objections to comic books, which were:

1) The comic-book format is an invitation to illiteracy.
2) Crime comic books create an atmosphere of cruelty and deceit.
3) They create a readiness for temptation.
4) They stimulate unwholesome fantasies.
5) They suggest criminal or sexually abnormal ideas.
6) They furnish the rationalization for them, which may be ethically even more harmful than the impulse.
7) They suggest the forms a delinquent impulse may take and supply details of technique.
8) They may tip the scales toward maladjustment or delinquency.

Wertham's major concern was that the horror and suspense stories that dominated the genre spent most of their time depicting crimes, violence, and offensive/racist rhetoric, and very little time showing that those things were wrong. He argued that while the perpetrator was regularly caught and punished at the end of a story, for a young mind that last page of justice didn't balance out the twenty pages of injustice that preceded it.

As such, Wertham believed that comic books placed a strong focus on negative activities, and that this focus was a contributing

factor to the alarming rise in juvenile delinquency in the mid-1950s.*
The popularity of *Seduction of the Innocent* was noticed by the
Senate Subcommittee on Juvenile Delinquency, which was led by
Senator Estes Kefauver, famous for his hearings on organized crime.
Soon Wertham was invited to speak before the committee.

The Senate hearings were a disaster for the comic book industry.
Wertham stepped up his rhetoric; while his book focused primarily on crime and horror series, he painted all comic books with the
same brush before the Senate, decrying the output of the industry
as a whole. Ultimately, Wertham stated that "Hitler was a beginner compared to the comic-book industry. They get the children
much younger. They teach them race hatred at the age of four before
they can read." Wertham's alarmist testimony shocked many, and
Bill Gaines had to follow his blistering attack later that afternoon.
Unfortunately, Gaines was even more damaging than Wertham.†

Gaines started off well enough, but when he was asked what
were the limits of what he would print in a comic book, Gaines
stated, "My only limits are the bounds of good taste, what I consider
good taste." Senator Kefauver then showed the cover of *Crime SuspenStories* #22, which depicted a woman's body lying on the floor
and a man holding a bloodied ax and the woman's severed head. The
senator asked Gaines if the cover was in good taste and Gaines, having painted himself into a corner, had to say that it was. He added
that "a cover in bad taste, for example, might be defined as holding
the head a little higher so that the neck could be seen dripping blood
from it and moving the body over a little further so that the neck of
the body could be seen to be bloody." Gaines made the front page of

---

*Wertham further alleged that Batman, Robin, and Wonder Woman were
homosexuals and that Superman was a Nazi.
†Gaines was set up to be a scapegoat, but he didn't do himself any favors
by appearing before the Senate after taking diet pills earlier in the day that
were wearing off. In the 1950s, diet pills usually meant dexedrine, a powerful
stimulant with quite a comedown.

the *New York Times* the very next day with the headline No HARM
IN HORROR, COMICS ISSUER SAYS; COMICS PUBLISHER SEES NO
HARM IN HORROR, DISCOUNTS "GOOD TASTE." The Senate hearings received national press coverage, and the comic book industry
came out of them in terrible shape.

Back in the 1930s, educational and parental groups had some
problems with comic books, but their ire was more of the angry
letter variety and was calmed by advisory panels. After the Senate hearings, several municipal governments across America banned
comic books outright, and there were even comic book burnings.
With a full-blown crisis on its hands, the comic book industry had
no choice but to band together.

Rather than having the government impose regulations upon
them from the outside, comics publishers came up with their
own rules and created the Comics Code Authority. The CCA was
extremely strict and specific; the goal was to make comics as unobjectionable as possible so that the *Seduction of the Innocent*/Senate
hearings outrage would fade away as quickly as possible. The CCA
prohibited vulgar language and poor grammar, salacious or exaggerated depictions of women, and the ridiculing of religious groups,
racial groups, or the police and other authority figures. According
to the Code, comic books were supposed to show that "in every
instance good shall triumph over evil and the criminal punished for
his misdeeds." Basically, the publishers took every criticism leveled
against them and made it mandatory that comic books do the exact
opposite.

Most important for the industry, the CCA forbade the use of
the words "terror" and "horror" from comics titles, as well as the
depiction of gruesome imagery and "scenes dealing with, or instru-
ments associated with walking dead, torture, vampires and vampir-
ism, ghouls, cannibalism and werewolfism." These rules destroyed
horror comics, and intentionally so. All of the publishers without
a solid horror line saw an opportunity to kill the genre that was
slaughtering them on the sales charts, and they went for it. Retailers

wouldn't sell comic books without the CCA's "seal of approval" on the cover, and publishers who refused to participate, like Gaines's EC Comics, very quickly went out of business.

For the publishers who survived, there was still a lot of work to do. Without the genres that had dominated the newsstands for years, publishers began to look for new, more wholesome and unobjectionable types of comic books to replace them. The editors at DC Comics decided to return to their superhero properties, and thus the Silver Age of comics began.

The Dawn of the Silver Age

In the early 1940s, DC Comics had been the biggest publisher of superhero comic books, and after the catastrophic events of 1954 it decided to revitalize some of its old characters. The first hero to come back was the Flash, who was revamped by John Broome, Carmine Infantino, and, coincidentally, Robert Kanigher. This new Flash was Barry Allen, a police scientist who developed superspeed when lightning struck his laboratory and spilled electrified chemicals over him. His first appearance in *Showcase* #4 in October 1956 is generally agreed upon as the official start of the Silver Age.

Many other reimagined heroes soon followed. Alan Scott, the original Green Lantern, had a magical power ring, but Hal Jordan, who appeared as the new Green Lantern in October 1959, was a member of an intergalactic police force with a power ring given to him by an alien. The new Hawkman, Katar Hol, was a policeman as well; he first appeared in February 1961 as a police officer from the planet Thanagar, unlike the original Hawkman, who was a reincarnated Egyptian god. The original Atom, Al Pratt, was just a short guy with a superpunch, but the new Atom, Ray Palmer, was a physicist who could shrink down to subatomic size. Other heroes were brought back without significant changes, like Aquaman, who kept his original costume and powers and was given a slightly different backstory.

There were entirely new characters too, like the Martian Man-hunter, a shape-shifting Martian accidentally transported to Earth who became a police detective, and Supergirl, Superman's younger Kryptonian cousin. All of these new and revitalized characters led to an explosion of new series, and superheroes became a dominant force in the comic book industry again.

The origin stories of these new characters marked a significant change in tone from those of their Golden Age counterparts. Their abilities tended to be rooted in science and technology instead of magic and mysticism. The Guardians of the Universe who ran the Green Lantern intergalactic police force used power rings built with super advanced alien technology to give their members superpowers. Hawk-man had the ability to fly because of Thanagarian technology and the antigravity Nth metal. The Atom could shrink down as small as the tiniest particle because he built a belt powered by a white dwarf star.

When Marvel Comics debuted its own superheroes in the early 1960s, it took this scientific focus even further and used fantastical versions of real-life science to explain its heroes' powers. For example, the Fantastic Four gained superpowers after being exposed to cosmic rays while in space, Peter Parker became Spider-Man after being bitten by a radioactive spider, and gamma rays turned mild-mannered Bruce Banner into the raging Hulk. In this age of atomic science and the beginnings of space exploration, it was no wonder that the creators of Silver Age heroes looked to the stars and modern science for their origins.

More significantly, the origin stories of Silver Age superheroes often lacked the tragic genesis that was so common in the Golden Age. These new heroes were well-adjusted men who saw crime fighting as an adventure, not a sacred duty or quest for vengeance. The orphan motif disappeared, and most of the new heroes had a very stable home life, including a girlfriend or a wife. The Flash, Green Lantern, and the Atom all had girlfriends, while Hawkman arrived on Earth with his wife, Shayera, and Aquaman quickly found an undersea queen, Mera.

The tragic elements of their origin stories were minor at best. Hal Jordan inherited his ring from Abin Sur, who died when his spaceship crashed onto Earth, and the Martian Manhunter was separated from his family back on Mars, but these examples pale in comparison to being the last of an extinct race or witnessing the murder of your parents.* The superheroes of the Silver Age were an upbeat, happy-go-lucky group, and the positivity of their origins seemed to reverberate throughout the entire DC Comics universe.

Before the Silver Age, Superman and Batman had some dark elements in their lives in terms of the tragedies at the root of their motivation. Both of them had lost their family in a deeply unpleasant way, and while they had pals like Jimmy Olsen and Robin, one buddy hardly made up for their loss. The Silver Age, however, brought with it a new lease on life for the Man of Steel and the Caped Crusader.

Under editor Mort Weisinger, Superman's supporting cast started to resemble a family. Superman was the father, Lois Lane the mother, Jimmy and Supergirl were the children, and *Daily Planet* editor Perry White was like a curmudgeonly grandfather. Along with this faux family, the addition of Supergirl in 1959 gave Superman a real, Kryptonian family member in his cousin, Kara Zor-El. Furthermore, in 1958 Superman rescued Krypton's capital city of Kandor, which had been miniaturized and bottled by the villain Brainiac before Krypton was destroyed. Superman couldn't restore Kandor, but he kept it in his Fortress of Solitude and developed technology so he could shrink down and visit his fellow Kryptonians. His parents, real and adopted, were still dead, but he had a new family-like group

---

*In modern DC Comics continuity, both Hal Jordan and the Martian Manhunter have more tragic origin stories. Hal's father was a test pilot, and Hal witnessed his father's death in a terrible plane accident when he was a child, while the Martian Manhunter is the last living Martian and his entire family and race were wiped out. Both of these stories are *retcons*, or retroactive continuity, a story that is written later on and retroactively added to the canon of a character. In their original Silver Age incarnations, neither story was present.

of friends, his cousin, and the residents of his home world's capital city for company.

Similarly, Batman's supporting cast also grew; inspired by Batman's war on crime, Kathy Kane became Batwoman, and her niece Betty Kane joined her as Bat-Girl. These women provided love interests for the Dynamic Duo while also creating a Superman-style faux family. In fact, in 1961 *Batman Annual* #2 featured a pinup picture of the entire Bat-family. Batman and Batwoman were the parents; Robin and Bat-Girl were the two children; Batman's butler, Alfred, and Gotham City's police commissioner, James Gordon, appeared as grandfathers or kindly uncles; on the floor lay their pet, Ace the Bat-Hound; and perched on Batman's shoulder was Bat-Mite, an imp from another dimension, who looked like a young toddler.* The pinup read "Greetings from the Batman Family," and the Caped Crusader, that dark denizen of the night, beamed broadly. The world was a happier place for heroes in the Silver Age, and that had a lot to do with the Comics Code Authority.

The Silver Age Batman faced all manner of unusual scenarios, including being turned into an alien, sent back to ancient Babylon, and battling gods, dragons, and interdimensional imps. The Silver Age was, frankly, rather silly. Under the strict guidelines of the CCA, regular crime stories and dangerous villains were strongly discouraged. The result was campy adventures with innocuous story lines and fantastical creatures, more juvenile science fiction than crime fighting. Aliens and bizarre creatures were nothing new for superhero comic books, but they became much more common after 1954.

Robert Kanigher Revises Wonder Woman

Kanigher's Wonder Woman followed these dominant trends in terms of campy adventures and a familial focus, but he went the

---

*Bat-Mite was a mischievous creature who idolized Batman and popped into Gotham City sporadically to set up strange adventures for his hero.

opposite direction with her origin. The Golden Age Wonder Woman had powers rooted in her utopian upbringing, unlike the tragedies of her peers. While Silver Age superheroes moved on to upbeat origins rooted in the hopefulness of science and space travel, Kanigher's origin for the Silver Age Wonder Woman went backward into a tragic genesis. He removed the utopian aspects of her creation and changed the nature of her powers and mission.

The cover of *Wonder Woman* #105 declared that Wonder Woman would face "The **Amazon's** Most Startling Opponent—**The EAGLE of SPACE!**" and the book certainly did deliver that riveting tale, but a small banner at the top promised the never-before-revealed secret origin of Wonder Woman. The story began centuries in the past, when baby Diana was visited by four impressive guests. The first was Aphrodite, who bequeathed to her the gift of beauty; second came Athena, who gave her wisdom; third was Mercury, who gave Diana speed; and finally came Hercules, who bestowed her with strength.

The story then jumped ahead several years to when Diana was a teenager, and horrible news reached Queen Hippolyta's throne room.* The Amazons had husbands, brothers, and sons who had all gone off to war, and they'd been wiped out by their enemies. The news prompted one distraught Amazon to cry, "Woe is us . . . we are alone . . . now—!" A tearful Hippolyta told Diana, "You must be . . . brave . . . Diana . . . as befitting . . . a . . . princess—!" The crying young princess responded, "Y-y-yes . . . mother . . . !" Everyone in the throne room wept and wailed in a very un-Amazon fashion.

Overcome with grief, Hippolyta decided to leave their home to escape the wars. The superpowered Diana built a boat by herself,

---

*The spelling of the queen's name has changed several times over the decades. Marston favored "Hippolyte," but Kanigher switched to "Hippolyta" when he took over the book. That spelling remained until the relaunch of Wonder Woman in 1987, when George Pérez went back to "Hippolyte," but "Hippolyta" became the norm again after Pérez left the title, and has been so ever since.

and on their journey to a new home she saved her fellow Amazons from a whirlpool, a sea of fire, and a sea of dangerous gas fumes. Finally they reached Paradise Island, where Athena was waiting and granted them immortal life so long as they remained on the island. Diana singlehandedly built the Amazons a city to live in and became their guardian, battling any beast that came near their new home.

When the Silver Age Diana became Wonder Woman, it had nothing to do with World War II or America as a citadel of freedom and democracy. Instead, Athena appeared to Hippolyta in a dream one day and instructed her to choose an Amazon who would go to "man's world to battle crime and injustice—and help people in distress!" Hippolyta held a competition to choose a champion and, to prevent favoritism, all of the Amazons dressed like Diana and wore Diana masks so Hippolyta couldn't tell them apart. Kanigher's tasks were less dangerous than Marston's original tournament and included a tug of war, log rolling, and a wrestling match on a high wire. Of course, Diana won and was given a final task of going to man's world and turning a penny into a million dollars.*

In a remarkable coincidence, just as Diana was about to leave, an airplane exploded overhead and Steve Trevor came plummeting toward Paradise Island. Wonder Woman caught him in midair and flew him back to America while he hailed her as an angel. Once in America, she learned that the city was looking to pay a million dollars for a new bridge. Using her Amazon strength and violating the laws of physics, she stretched the single, three-gram penny out into a long cord and wove an entire suspension bridge. Along the way she also disarmed a nuclear bomb, destroyed an enemy submarine, and saved a children's camp.

---

*The story was entitled "The Million Dollar Penny," and Wonder Woman enthusiasts might know that Kanigher had written another Wonder Woman story entitled "The Million Dollar Penny" five years before in *Wonder Woman* #59. Kanigher and repetition go hand in hand.

Wonder Woman's new origin story made some notable additions to the Wonder Woman mythos, including the ability to fly. While she could always jump extremely high with her superstrength, she needed her invisible jet for any sustained flight. However, when she saved Steve Trevor from falling to his doom, Wonder Woman realized that she could manipulate updrafts in order to propel herself toward Steve, and gained the power of flight.

Wonder Woman #105 made further changes to the character, marking the beginning of Wonder Woman's teenage adventures as Wonder Girl. The younger Amazon princess wore a modified Wonder Woman costume and had the same abilities as her adult self.* The adventures of a teenaged Clark Kent as Superboy were very popular in Superman comics at the time, so it seems that Kanigher borrowed the idea to expand on the types of stories he could tell with Wonder Woman. Over the next decade, Wonder Girl appeared in the series almost as often as Wonder Woman.

Kanigher's origin story also offered a new approach to the mythology of the Amazons. Marston was a mythology buff, and his stories were rooted in the Greek legends of the Amazons, but Kanigher appeared unconcerned with mythological consistency. Adding men to the Amazon homeland was an odd choice, made even more confusing by having them off fighting wars while Queen Hippolyta and the Amazon women stayed at home. There were men in a few Amazon myths, but they were the stay-at-home type, often because their Amazon mothers hobbled them as infants so they could never overthrow their female rule. The defining characteristic of the Amazons throughout history was that they were a race of warrior women, so having men fight for them, not to mention fleeing the wars after the men all died, was an unusual approach.

---

*Including flight, even though she only learned that skill when she was an adult and left Paradise Island to become Wonder Woman. Kanigher wasn't much for continuity.

Looking at Kanigher in light of Marston, these changes drastically altered the message of the book. Marston's Amazons were an extension of his psychological theories, however problematically, and Kanigher removed or altered all of the key components. For Marston, the Amazons willingly rejected involvement with men and were better because of it. For Kanigher, it appeared that the Amazons would gladly welcome their men back at any time, and only established Paradise Island so that the world wouldn't bring them any more grief. This eliminated the Amazons' original feminist message of female superiority, but Kanigher wasn't done.

In this new origin story, Wonder Woman's superpowers were gifts from the gods that made her unique among her Amazon sisters. She was given beauty, wisdom, speed, and strength when she was an infant, and as Wonder Girl she demonstrated these abilities at a young age. Her fellow Amazons all marveled at her prowess; Wonder Girl could accomplish in minutes what would have taken days or weeks for everyone else. This Wonder Woman was clearly stronger and more skilled than the rest of the Amazons.

In the Golden Age, Wonder Woman gained her abilities from being raised in the advanced, utopian society of Paradise Island, and her fellow Amazons had the same skills. The original Wonder Woman wasn't special or different, and she didn't have any sort of divine giftings; she was simply the most capable warrior in a race of advanced, powerful women. By making Wonder Woman unique and changing the source of her powers, Kanigher further unraveled the messages Marston had instilled in the character. The benefits of female rule went by the wayside when everyone else became normal. It's also significant that two of Wonder Woman's benefactors were men. Half of her abilities, and the ones that were actual superpowers, came from males, obliterating Marston's focus on female superiority.

One of these men was Hercules, the greatest enemy of the Amazons in Greek myth. In Apollodorus's ancient account of Hercules's ninth labor, Hercules took Hippolyta's girdle and then, when the

Amazons rose up to stop him, he killed the queen. Other accounts have him imprisoning the queen and killing her later, or letting Theseus take her to be his tamed Amazon bride. Hercules was never a friend of the Amazons, and this continued with Marston. Hercules was the ultimate symbol of male dominance, the archetype for the aggressive, violent male that Marston believed led to the world's wars and strife. To Kanigher, Hercules was the source of Wonder Woman's strength, and even the subject of a few screwball romance stories with Hippolyta later in the series. Kanigher's Wonder Woman fought crime and wore the same outfit as Marston's Wonder Woman, but the similarities end there.

Now, it looks like Kanigher performed a terrible hatchet job on Wonder Woman and blatantly undid everything that Marston instilled in his creation. We should be appalled at Kanigher's campaign to reverse the very nature of the character. Regardless of which version we prefer, this degree of disrespect for what came before is hardly becoming. However, such outrage would be based on the notion that Kanigher consciously undid Marston's underlying messages and intentionally replaced them with his own view of the world. Marston was a creator who wrote with a message and plan, and submission and female superiority was at the core of every single thing he did. He put a great deal of thought and effort into Wonder Woman.

Robert Kanigher didn't. By all accounts, Kanigher was winging it; the man just sat down and typed.

Although he was quite prolific, Kanigher wasn't very well regarded as a writer. Throughout the 1960s, the Academy of Comic Arts and Sciences gave out the Alley Awards, annual prizes to comic books based on fan votes. The awards were closely associated with *Alter Ego*, a comic book fan magazine, and were the first ever fan-based awards for comic books. The categories were generally positive, celebrating "Best Writer" or "Best Series," and even their negative categories were politely named, like "Comic Most Needing Improvement." Robert Kanigher's work on *Wonder Woman* holds

the dubious distinction of winning the only two Alley Awards ever given for "worst" comic book. In 1961, *Wonder Woman* won the award for "Worst Comic Book Currently Published," and in 1964 it was awarded "Worst Regularly Published Comic." They were also the only two Alley Awards the series ever garnered.

Kanigher's work was repetitive and his grasp on continuity was practically nonexistent. In *The Comic Book Heroes*, Will Jacobs and Gerard Jones write that "Kanigher's plots hurtled from event to event with an illogic that even the most lax editor couldn't have approved (had he not also been the writer)." His writing style was haphazard, and it didn't bring him a great deal of praise. In an interview with the *Comics Journal* in 1983, Kanigher described his methods by stating, "I'm an instinctual writer. I am not a writer who sits down, knowing what he is going to do in advance." Throughout the course of the interview, it became very clear that Kanigher wasn't interested in underlying messages or planning ahead. His sole focus was the story, which he began not knowing where it was going.

The interviewer even asked Kanigher a question about giving Wonder Woman a father in his origin story, and Kanigher replied, "Impossible! She never had a father." He then added, "According to Marston's origin, she COULDN'T possibly have had a father. Wonder Woman was fashioned out of clay." Kanigher remembered Marston's origin very well and had no recollection of ever writing his own, contrary version. In fact, Kanigher felt that he had been very faithful to Marston's vision, saying that after Marston died his family still had a "strong influence" on how Wonder Woman was written, and that they had selected him to take over the character.* Kanigher believed that he'd carried on Marston's legacy, and the very notion that he would write anything contrary to what Marston had established struck him as impossible.

---

*In reality, the widows Marston didn't much care for Kanigher's work, but Kanigher's memory was not the best. Simultaneously, he also maintained a very high opinion of himself, which may have colored his recollections.

This doesn't change the fact that he did write a completely contrary origin story for Wonder Woman, but it illustrates how insignificant the story was to him. It was likely a story he came up with on the spur of the moment; it wasn't intended to radically revise the character. Nonetheless, the new origin story exists, and it became a staple of the Silver Age Wonder Woman. When DC Comics released a series entitled *Secret Origins* in 1961 to reprint the origin stories of all of its superheroes, Kanigher's new story appeared for Wonder Woman.

5

Focus on the Family, or Superman Is a Jackass

*L*ove, marriage, and family were constant themes for the women in superhero comic books in the 1950s, even the ones with superpowers. Normal women longed for husbands and children, superpowered women longed to be able to give up their life of fighting crime and settle down, and teenage girls longed to learn the skills that would soon land them a husband and domestic bliss. At DC Comics, it seemed that every woman in the Silver Age had marriage on the brain.

Along with this focus on marriage came another peculiar phenomenon: the men were complete jerks. They either callously rejected advances or were irate when their own advances were brushed aside. There was a constant attitude of "How dare you?" no matter the circumstances, stemming from the notion that men knew better. Indignant outrage was common, leading to a lopsided gender dynamic whereby women had to constantly jump through hoops to appease men. Whether they were attempting to sooth their damaged egos or being taught a valuable lesson after upsetting them, women

acquiesced to men's every demand and the men always had full control of the relationship. Several archetypical female characters in the Golden Age had markedly different experiences, but in the Silver Age they were all in the same boat.

In the late 1950s, the championing of marriage and the nuclear family was ubiquitous in American popular culture. In *Homeward Bound: American Families in the Cold War Era*, historian Elaine Tyler May calls this "domestic containment." In a world of uncertainty, May writes, the nuclear family "would create a feeling of warmth and security against the cold forces of disruption and alienation." The outside world seemed rife with godless communist spies, atomic bombs, and numerous other threats, so Americans looked inward to their families for stability. This resulted in a celebration of traditional roles: the father as the stalwart head of the home, the mother as the loving caregiver and domestic wizard, and the children as precocious but obedient.

Coupled with the rise of suburbia and strong economic growth, a family with a working father and a stay-at-home mother became the norm. Such a setup was common in the TV shows of the day: *Leave It to Beaver, Ozzie and Harriet,* and *The Donna Reed Show* are but a few examples. The wife cooked and cleaned and took care of the children. When the husband came home, dinner was on the table and his wife was at the door in a lovely dress, his favorite drink in hand, waiting to take his coat. And, of course, she loved it.

The Comics Code Authority had a rule that stated that "the treatment of love-romance stories shall emphasize the value of the home and the sanctity of marriage." But there was one caveat for romance stories in superhero comic books: no one could really settle down, leading to frustration all around.

The serialized, almost timeless nature of storytelling in comic books made marriage impossible. Lois Lane could never land Superman as a boyfriend, much less as a husband with kids and a house in the suburbs. Doing so would kill the suspense and eliminate a whole slew of possible love triangle story lines. Plus, the neighbors would

probably notice Superman shooting off from the Kents' backyard. This constant limbo aggravated every character involved. Ozzie and Harriet were already married, and the show revolved on their escapades as a family; superhero comics were about adventures and thwarting villains, and marriage was a secondary story that could never be fulfilled.

This limbo took several forms for female characters in the Silver Age, but they all centered on not being able to have the life they desired. Everyone wanted to settle down and be part of a family, and the dictates of the medium just didn't allow it. This exacerbated tensions for everyone involved so each woman, from the superpowered Wonder Woman to the everywoman Lois Lane, was in the same position, trying to please the increasingly frustrated man in her life.

Wonder Woman

Despite the oppressive Cold War culture, Wonder Woman was still a superhero, as powerful and capable as ever. Her origins had changed and she became mired in ridiculous romantic situations, but when a villain needed defeating or someone needed saving, she was there. Steve remained as inept as ever, and Wonder Woman saved him from various exploding aircraft, spaceships, volcanoes, and other deadly scenarios. She may have lacked the female superiority underpinnings of the Marston area, but she was still a superhero.

When DC Comics decided to assemble its best superheroes into the Justice League of America in 1960, Wonder Woman was the only female member. During the Golden Age, Wonder Woman was a part of the Justice Society of America but was relegated to the role of the team's secretary. In the Justice League, Wonder Woman was a full-fledged member. For almost the entire duration of the Silver Age, she was the sole woman alongside Superman, Batman, the Flash, Green Lantern, the Atom, Martian Manhunter, Green Arrow, and Hawkman. Finally Black Canary joined nearly a decade later, and Zatanna became an official member in the mid-1970s.

Wonder Woman's teenage adventures as Wonder Girl were equally heroic. Wonder Girl saved Paradise Island from countless sea monsters and mythical beasts, and she also protected a nearby underwater city of mer-people from various aquatic threats. In terms of her superpowers and heroic prowess, the Silver Age Wonder Woman was as strong and capable as ever. However, the campy nature of the era brought her a slew of new, fantastical creatures to defeat.

Kanigher wasn't creative in his choice of villainous beasts. He had a few favorites and they appeared frequently with just slight variations. One of these was his regular use of clams in underwater tales. For example, in one issue, a clam was a gateway to travel through time, and in another Wonder Girl battled a cannibal clam.* Enormous creatures were a common foe in *Wonder Woman* generally, particularly giants and massive birds. As both an adult and a teenager, she fought giants from different dimensions, planets, and time periods as well as pterodactyls, rocs, dimorphodons, and even a space eagle. Her adventures were larger than life, her enemies fantastical and mythological as opposed to rooted in any semblance of reality. With such a proliferation of absurd and extraordinary enemies, it was the romantic aspects of her stories that brought Wonder Woman back into something reminiscent of the real world, though not in a good way.

Steve had always been in love with Wonder Woman, though it never got him far in the Golden Age. Whenever he tried to make a move on Wonder Woman, he was rebuffed, often violently, and when he asked for her hand in marriage Wonder Woman would say that Amazon law forbade it and end the discussion.

By the Silver Age, Steve and Wonder Woman were an item. They were referred to as "sweethearts" and often went on dates together.

---

*Technically, the cannibal clam should have eaten other clams, but in actuality it seemed to only like to eat humans. This doesn't make it a cannibal but instead an anthropophagus.

Moreover, Wonder Woman was far more affectionate with Steve, like in *Wonder Woman* #102 when Steve gave Wonder Woman perfume for her birthday and got a kiss in return. When asked on a date, she'd eagerly reply, "I'd love to, Steve! You know I like to be with you!" She still rejected his marriage proposals, but for a different reason. Whenever Steve professed his love for her, she'd heartily pledge her love in return but would add, "I **can't** marry you—until my services are no longer needed to battle crime and injustice! Only **then** can I think about myself!" Wonder Woman would have loved to marry Steve but for that pesky superhero job.

She was also very concerned about being a good wife, and asked Steve, "How can I become your wife 100% of the time—and also fulfill my mission as an Amazon and help anyone in distress?" If Wonder Woman married Steve and continued her superheroic mission, she wouldn't be able to be a proper wife and give him all of her attention. She cemented this point in another issue, stating, "It would be unfair to marry you unless I could be a full-time wife!" She pled with Steve to be patient and wait for her and the day when her abilities would no longer be needed.

Along with this newfound romantic inclination came jealousy; it was rather unwise to trifle with the affection of an Amazon. As a teen, Wonder Girl dated Ronno the Mer-Boy, a half-boy, half-fish from the mer-people city near Paradise Island. She wore his seashell fraternity pin and they went to his sea dances, but Wonder Girl was very covetous of his attention. When Ronno danced with a mermaid, Wonder Girl left in a huff, thinking, "I've had enough! And to think of all the time I spent making myself pretty for that ungrateful wretch!"

Steve often faced a jealous Wonder Woman, but with a twist. When he had to pick the real Wonder Woman out of a group of Wonder Woman robots and kissed them all to do so, Wonder Woman was furious. When Wonder Woman disguised herself as a movie star and Steve was attracted to her, she was again irate. Wonder Woman's biggest rival was herself.

These identity issues continued with Diana. In the Golden Age, Wonder Woman and Diana had always been separate personalities, one the real woman and the other merely a disguise. In the Silver Age, the two sides conflated and Wonder Woman wanted Steve to appreciate both sides of her personality. When he ditched Diana to spend time with Wonder Woman, she called him two-faced. When he rhapsodized about Wonder Woman in front of Diana, she later thought, "The nerve of Steve! Always praising **Wonder Woman** in my presence as if I were just a wooden post! He never says a single nice thing about my eyes—or my hair—or my figure!" While she was livid when Steve was interested in an exact copy of herself, at the same time she wanted him to be in love with her *secret* identity.

Wonder Woman always got over her jealous feelings, but the men were much more difficult. If Steve was in a Silver Age issue of *Wonder Woman*, chances were that marriage was going to come up; the man was nothing if not persistent at proposing to Wonder Woman. She always politely declined, not with an outright refusal but by saying she couldn't yet marry him and asking him to be patient. That rarely soothed Steve's hurt feelings, and he was prone to outraged comments like:

- "Angel—if you really cared for me, I should be able to convince you within the next thirty seconds to marry me!"
- "I don't care whether you think it's fair or not—I want you to marry me!"
- "I'm getting sick and tired of hearing that excuse, Wonder Woman!"
- "I'm tired of waiting around for you to make up your mind! I've had enough! **Goodby!**"
- "If you really loved me—you'd let nothing interfere! I've had enough of waiting! I'm through! I'll marry the next girl I meet! I don't care **who**—or **what** she is!"

To calm his outrage, Wonder Woman submitted to ridiculous contests to prove her love. In one, if Steve picked Wonder Woman

out of a crowd three times in twenty-four hours, she'd have to marry him. In another, marriage was again the "prize" if Wonder Woman had to save Steve three times in twenty-four hours. Not only did Wonder Woman agree to these silly contests, but Steve cheated; he marked Wonder Woman with a tracking device so he could find her with ease to win the first contest, and then planned the second contest on a day when he was testing dangerous aircraft, failing to mention that fact when he made the bet. Steve always just failed to win, but not before making Wonder Woman submit to inane activities to prove she still cared for him.

In *Wonder Woman* #118, Steve came to the conclusion that Wonder Woman refused to marry him because she was interested in someone else, and he used government spy equipment to stalk her to see if he had a rival. Upon finding her with Mer-Man, the grown-up Mer-Boy, Steve tried to show her that he was braver and stronger, insisting that she pick one of them, but Wonder Woman refused. This love triangle became a common feature, with both Steve and Mer-Man trying to prove themselves more worthy of her affections by coming up with ridiculous competitions.

The rarely tactful Steve handled the situation with constant irritation, reading into everything Wonder Woman said and did. In *Wonder Woman* #132, Wonder Woman was distracted while out bowling with Steve, upset that he'd brushed off Diana to go out with her. For no discernible reason, Steve thought that she was actually thinking about Mer-Man, and he went on a tirade laden with aquatic-based insults. When Wonder Woman got a strike without even looking, Steve exploded, "Now you're trying to make a fool out of me! [. . .] You'd never act that way with your boyfriend, the half-man, half-fish!"

Both Wonder Woman and Steve had issues with anger and jealousy, but the core of their feelings was completely different. Wonder Woman's problem was one of identity. With Diana Prince no longer just a mask to fit in but now part of who she was, Wonder Woman felt that Steve, by rejecting Diana in favor of Wonder Woman,

was rejecting half of herself. Thus she was furious when Steve was interested in robot doppelgangers and herself in disguise. Steve was attracted to other forms of herself, just not the one she most wanted him to love. She wasn't really angry with Steve but with her own dual nature.

Steve, on the other hand, was angry with Wonder Woman. Paranoia was the hallmark of Steve's fury, and he manufactured things to be upset about and read her dedication to her mission as a lack of affection for him. No matter how many times Wonder Woman proved she loved him, it was never enough. Steve felt he was entitled to the life he wanted with the woman he wanted, and anything less was unacceptable. This unbalanced gender dynamic was a hallmark of the Silver Age, and Cold War culture generally.

Lois Lane

At first glance, life had improved for Lois Lane at the dawn of the Silver Age. Her days writing the lovelorn column were far behind her; now she was a top reporter at the *Daily Planet*. Lois got her own comic book series in 1958, a rare occurrence for a female character. The only problem was that the series wasn't called *Fearless Journalist Lois Lane* or *Lois Lane: Intrepid Reporter*; it was called *Superman's Girl Friend Lois Lane*. Even in her own series, Superman still got top billing and Lois was defined by her relationship to him.

In *Superman's Girl Friend Lois Lane* #17, the staff of the *Daily Planet* threw Lois a surprise party celebrating the anniversary of her joining the newspaper. While discussing her many scoops, Jimmy Olsen pointed out, "It seems you owe your career to **Superman! All** your big scoops are about him!" Lois disagreed, citing three stories she had written without the aid of Superman years before when she was first hired as a reporter. However, as she recounted each scoop, Superman recalled that he had been involved in all of them without Lois knowing. He decided, "I . . . er . . . won't hurt Lois' feelings!

Let her think she got her first scoop all by herself!" She was a top reporter now, but it was all because of Superman.

An advertisement for the launch of *Superman's Girl Friend Lois Lane* included a fact sheet on Lois. It gave her occupation (reporter), hair color (brunette), age (twenty-two), weight (121), and the last line listed her goals. It read, "**AMBITION:** To become **Mrs. Superman**." Lois's quest to marry Superman was the main plot of her series from the get-go.

Nearly every issue of the series featured a scheme to make Superman fall for her. Lois heard the adage that "the way to a man's heart is through his stomach," so she took a leave of absence from the *Daily Planet* to become a chef. She wore a new, exotic outfit every day to entice Superman with the many varieties of woman she could be for him. She used an experimental youth ray to rid her twenty-two-year-old self of any wrinkles.

Lois also hid herself from Superman anytime she thought she wasn't desirable enough. She went out of her way to avoid Superman when a growth ray turned her into "the fattest girl in Metropolis." Lois took more drastic action when she was hypnotized into thinking she had the face of a cat, encasing her entire head in a lead box so Superman couldn't see her, even with his X-ray vision. Marrying Superman was her primary concern, and she'd do anything to make it happen or to prevent any setbacks.

However, Lois didn't love Superman because of his winning personality or their shared interests. She was only interested in his strength and heroism, a point hammered home by the ease with which Lois was prepared to ditch Superman for any other strong and heroic man who came along. Time travel was common in the Silver Age, and Lois instantly fell in love with a local hero named Samson in ancient Rome, then with Robin Hood in medieval England. In the present day, when an alien named Astounding Man arrived on Earth in a spaceship and immediately proposed to her, Lois agreed to marry him and leave Earth right away. She even fell for Clark Kent when she mistakenly thought he was roughing up a rude pedestrian,

thinking, "Whatever got into Clark? I've always **liked** him, but now, he's so manly, I could **love** him!" None of these relationships worked out, but they showed that Lois was keen for any man who met the masculine ideal of the time.

Unfortunately for Lois, the fellow she was most interested in treated her like an impetuous child. The Man of Steel regularly took it upon himself to manipulate Lois in order to "help" her see the error of her ways. In the first story of the first issue of *Superman's Girl Friend Lois Lane*, Lois was in disguise doing research for an article, and Superman decided, "I'll have to teach her a lesson for using such tactics to get a story!" He then faked the death of Lois's story subject, causing a distraught and weeping Lois to exclaim, "Oh dear me—how stupid I was to try a hoax like that! I'll never, never do it again!"

Superman's aim was to get Lois to stop being so curious and impetuous, but in teaching her lessons all he did was cause her extreme grief. During her disguise-wearing lesson, Lois believed that someone had been killed because of her and was beside herself with grief. In another story, Superman told Lois not to touch a box of objects from another planet, and when she did he pretended that Lois had developed Kryptonite vision that caused him terrible pain whenever she looked at him. Lois felt so terrible about hurting the man she loved that she decided to move to Alaska, where she was unlikely to ever see him again.

Superman's sense of superiority to Lois often manifested itself in angry and hurtful outbursts. When teaching Lois a lesson, this anger was staged, but Lois's tears were real. After she touched Superman's space artifacts, Superman yelled, "You little idiot! I warned you to keep **hands off**! Now you're a menace to my life! Go far away! Get lost!!" His outburst resulted in Lois crying for most of the remainder of the story, until Clark came to Alaska with a fake antidote to cure her "condition." Superman's response to Lois's extreme grief was chuckling about how "the biggest laugh of all is that Lois never did

have Kryptonite vision!" He never told her the whole episode had been a ruse.

At times, Superman's anger was genuine. In *Superman's Girl Friend Lois Lane* #16, Superman gave Lois a signal watch so she could alert him if she was ever in trouble. After Lois used it for several nonemergency situations, Superman responded to her last alarm thinking, "Now she's stuck in a revolving door! This is **it**! Here goes my temper!" As Lois thanked him for saving her, Superman exclaimed, "PEST!!" and told her that he'd take the watch back if she didn't stop wasting his time, while a crowd of people watched and laughed. Lois was so upset that she later refused to use her watch after she was captured by a gang of villains and was nearly killed by a bomb in the process.

Superman treated Lois terribly. Their relationship resembled that of an irate, unfit parent frustrated with his child. Superman didn't see Lois as a capable adult, but as a nuisance that he needed to straighten out, and he had Lois in tears with his condescending, patronizing attitude in nearly every issue. Even in her own series, Lois wasn't treated with any respect.

In the Golden Age, Wonder Woman and Lois Lane had very little in common, but they found themselves in a very similar situation in the Silver Age. Their superpower disparity made no difference at all. They were subject to the same oppressive gender dynamics in their unconsummatable relationships. Their angry beaux made them jump through hoops, be it an inane contest to prove their love or an elaborate ruse to teach them a lesson. Steve and Superman both lashed out angrily when they were frustrated, and Wonder Woman and Lois had to appease them.

Both women cared only about having a strong, heroic man and not at all about how he treated them. Much like Lois fell for any tough man who crossed her path, Steve would do something brave and heroic to remind Wonder Woman what a strong man he was and all would be forgiven. Love wasn't about affection, but rather

about a stereotypical ideal of manliness. It didn't matter how domineering the men behaved; their passive girlfriends only wanted to swoon at their strength. The main message of both *Wonder Woman* and *Superman's Girl Friend Lois Lane* was that men controlled the relationship and women shouldn't question their actions, however cruel, demeaning, or unnecessary.

Supergirl

First appearing in *Action Comics* #252 in May 1959, Supergirl was Superman's long-lost Kryptonian cousin. When Krypton exploded, a small portion of the planet survived, and two of its inhabitants were Zor-El, the brother of Superman's father, Jor-El, and his wife. They later had a daughter, Kara, and when their village began to be affected by Kryptonite radiation, they searched the galaxy for a new home where they could send her. Using a superpowered telescope, they learned that Superman was from Krypton, so Zor-El sent Kara to Earth where she too could have superpowers and be spared the deadly effects of Kryptonite radiation.

Superman discovered her rocket, and he decided to put his teenage cousin in an orphanage where she could interact with other children and learn the customs of Earth. He gave the blonde Supergirl a brunette, pigtailed wig, and she chose the alias Linda Lee.

After her first appearance, Supergirl was regularly featured in *Action Comics*, but she also appeared occasionally in *Superman*, *Adventure Comics*, *Superman's Pal Jimmy Olsen*, and *Superman's Girl Friend Lois Lane*. Because of their age difference, Superman assumed a sort of parental, caregiver role for her. For all intents and purposes, Superman was her surrogate father and, as a good child, she obeyed him as such. However, much like with Lois Lane, having Superman in charge wasn't a pleasant experience.

Ostensibly, Superman put Supergirl in an orphanage so she could learn how to fit in on Earth, but an ulterior motive quickly became

clear: Superman wanted to keep Supergirl as a secret weapon. When Supergirl asked if she could reveal herself to the world, Superman responded, "No, **Supergirl!** I have many cunning enemies! If I'm ever in a bad trap, you're the only one who could rescue me!" So Supergirl stayed in the orphanage, and was initially fine with her secret weapon role. When Superman was in trouble or needed assistance, she would jet off and help, all the while making sure that no one noticed her so that her existence remained a secret.

In an early appearance, Supergirl saw a newspaper story about one of Superman's exploits and stated, "I won't get any headlines for my feats like my cousin **Superman** does! But it's still super-fun to work secretly as **Supergirl** and help others!" Supergirl even sabotaged her interviews with couples looking to adopt her so she could remain at the orphanage; in one issue, she used her heat vision to burn a roast she was making in hopes that a couple would think she was careless and a poor cook. She dutifully remained Superman's secret weapon, giving up the establishment of her own identity and the love of a family so that Superman could have a safety net, but her happiness with this arrangement soon wore thin.

Although Supergirl had to stay at the orphanage, she worked hard to get the other children into loving homes. These instances included:

- Helping Timmy Tate with a magic show that impressed his potential parents, resulting in his adoption
- Proving that Paul was not lying about seeing Streaky the Super Cat perform fantastical feats so that potential parents wouldn't be told he was a liar
- Using her superbreath to help Frank Cullen shoot several holes in one, impressing his potential new father, a golfer, so much that he adopted him
- Warming an iron with her heat vision so Nancy could iron her dress and look nice for her interview, after which she was adopted

- Flying underwater to help Eddie Moran rescue a drowning man, who then adopted Eddie

Her commitment to family and adoption extended beyond the orphanage as well: in an adventure in the future, she helped a boy named Tommy Tomorrow find parents, and she found a home for a Bizarro baby with Bizarro parents.* Just as the desire for marriage was a common theme in other DC comic books, so too was the desire for family well illustrated in Supergirl stories. The nuclear family was again paramount, and Supergirl soon wanted a family of her own.

In a guest appearance in *Superman's Girl Friend Lois Lane*, Supergirl thought, "Jeepers! If . . . if cousin **Superman** and Lois got married, they could adopt me! . . . 'Mother Lois'!! . . . 'Father **Superman**'!! . . . Gee! I'd be the happiest girl alive!!!" Note the rare usage of three exclamation points. Supergirl ached to be adopted and have the happiness and security that came with being part of a family, but Superman wasn't interested and punished her when she tried to meddle in his love life. A year and a half after her first appearance, Supergirl was still housed in the orphanage. After seeing another girl get adopted, she thought, "H-how long will I have to wait for a mother and father to adopt me? . . . >**Sob!**<"

Supergirl was finally adopted in August 1961, but only because she had lost her superpowers in the previous issue. Without her powers, she wasn't able to pull her usual tricks to sway couples from adopting her and, with a career as a superhero no longer a possibility, Supergirl became Linda Lee Danvers, the dutiful daughter of Fred and Edna Danvers. Her superpowers did eventually return, and she remained with her adopted parents, but it's striking that the only

---

*Bizarro was a craggy, backward version of Superman created by a malfunctioning duplicator ray, who then created a whole race of Bizarros who lived on the planet Htrae (Earth spelled backward).

way Supergirl could have a family was for her to no longer be of any use to Superman.*

Superman, despite being raised by caring parents who taught him everything he needed to know, actively deprived Supergirl of a loving home. To Superman, Supergirl was little more than a tool. Furthermore, even though he was her only family member in the entire universe, he came by infrequently, popping in only when he needed her help or, even worse, when he wanted to teach her a lesson or submit her to a test.

When Supergirl saw Krypto, the super dog, and flew over to meet him, she was chastised by Superman because Krypto could follow her to the orphanage and expose her secret identity. Superman declared, "You must be taught a **lesson** for breaking my rule!" and he exiled her to an asteroid for one year. After a week, she received a message from Superman to return to the orphanage for a day. It turned out that the exile was a test to see if Supergirl could protect her identity and cover for Linda's weeklong absence, which she did. Again we see Superman forcing a female character to endure an elaborate ruse so he could make an insignificant point. To Superman, the ends always justified the means, even if the means involved making a teenage girl feel ashamed, sad, and alone.

While Supergirl and Lois Lane were both maltreated by Superman in similar ways, Wonder Woman is a more apt comparison to the Maid of Might. With their superpowers, both had the capacity to rebel against the controlling man in her life; Lois, for all her

---

*When Supergirl's powers returned, she wasn't vulnerable to Kryptonite anymore and was thus stronger than Superman; a mischievous troublemaker from the fifth dimension, Mr. Mxyzptlk, had purposely granted her better powers. Noting this, Superman thought, "Now that she's **superior** to me, maybe our relationship ought to be reversed! Perhaps I should become her assistant!" But he never did. After two issues, Supergirl's superior powers disappeared and the original power dynamic was restored, and in those two issues Superman made no further mention of taking on a subordinate role.

gumption, was just a human up against a superpowered Kryptonian. Wonder Woman and Supergirl didn't have to put up with these
domineering males, yet they willingly did. Although their relationships were different, romantic for Wonder Woman and parental for
Supergirl, their superpowers kept them from having a normal life,
and these men offered them the hope that someday they could be
part of a nuclear family. They were kept in a sort of limbo, unhappy
with their lot but unable to change it, looking forward to some idyllic future where they would feel complete.

Star Sapphire

Carol Ferris first appeared in *Showcase Comics* #22 in September
1959 as the daughter of the boss of Green Lantern's alter ego, the
test pilot Hal Jordan. Early in the issue, Hal asked Carol out on a
date, but later that day her father announced that he was going to
travel around the world for two years and that Carol would be in
charge of the company. When Hal later asked Carol if they were still
going out that evening, she replied, "Mr. Jordan, *puh-lease*! From
now on the relations between us will be **strictly business!**" Hal tried
to change her mind, but she stated, "During the next two years I'll
have absolutely no time for romance! I'm your boss. Mr. Jordan—
and that's **orders!**"

In her first appearance, Carol appeared to break out of the Silver
Age mold. She purposefully set aside romance in favor of a career,
and a very high-powered one at that, and committed herself wholly
to her job. While other female characters were wrapped up in relationships with domineering boyfriends and wishing they could trade
their careers for marriage, Carol did the opposite and swore off men
so she could best run her company. It was a remarkably progressive
stance, and it lasted for two-thirds of an issue.

By the end of *Showcase Comics* #22, Carol was out on a terrace
kissing Green Lantern, and two issues later she was sure that he was
going to propose to her and was terribly excited to accept. Naturally,

he didn't propose, and instead a classic love triangle was born. Carol loved Green Lantern, and he loved her too but wanted Carol to love his alter ego, Hal, not his superpowered self.

Carol immediately became fixated on the notion of marrying Green Lantern, and in *Green Lantern* #1* thought to herself while sitting in her office, "Night and day . . . day and night . . . all I think about is **Green Lantern!** I wonder if my dream will ever come true . . . and that someday he and I will marry?" Her commitment to her job had faded; instead of working, she was daydreaming. Soon she even rescinded her dating embargo on Hal and the two sporadically went out on the town. Carol the high-powered businesswoman very quickly turned into Carol the love interest.

The narration of the series unsubtly reinforced this role; in *Green Lantern* #7, Carol was on another date with Hal, and an editor's note stated, "Carol Ferris, in the absence of her father, is in sole charge of the **Ferris Aircraft Company** where Hal works! Nominally, therefore, she is Hal's boss . . . but actually, and mainly, she is his **romantic interest!**" Several issues later, Carol was described as "the young and pretty 'boss' of the **Ferris Aircraft Company**," with boss in quotation marks.

However, the narrow scope of her character was given the opportunity to grow when she became the villainous Star Sapphire. In *Green Lantern* #16, Carol was kidnapped by a race of alien women called the Zamarons, who told her that she would be their new queen. The Zamarons were described as coming "from a world tremendously in advance of ours scientifically! A place inhabited solely by **women!** And if what they say is true, they are all **immortal.**"† There was only one caveat to their immortality: their queen was

---

*After three issues in *Showcase Comics*, Green Lantern moved to his own eponymous series in August 1960.

†With their advanced technology and female superiority, these space warriors were an alien analogue of the Amazons. "Zamaron" is even the letters of "Amazon" rearranged, plus an *r*.

mortal. Whenever their queen died, the Zamarons scoured the universe to find a woman who was the exact physical duplicate of their queen, and that woman happened to be Carol. They wanted to take Carol back to their planet, where she would be crowned Queen Star Sapphire and rule their advanced world. To a business-minded woman involved in the high-tech aerospace industry, becoming queen of the Zamarons would be the biggest promotion possible. On Earth, she was already in charge of her company and had essentially reached the top of the ladder. Leading the technologically advanced Zamarons was a significant step up and a great honor, which Carol promptly refused.

She just couldn't bear to leave the man she loved and wanted to stay on Earth with Green Lantern. But the Zamarons were persistent, declaring, "As our future queen you must be made to realize, highness, how far superior even the **lowest Zamaron** is to **any man**— no matter who he be!" The Zamarons thought that if Carol could see that the powers of the Star Sapphire were greater than those of the Green Lantern, she wouldn't be in love with him anymore, and so they gave Carol superpowers and manufactured a confrontation.

The powers gave Carol a split personality, where her Star Sapphire side wanted to defeat Green Lantern but her Carol side wanted him to win. Ultimately, she beat Green Lantern and returned to the Zamaron ship, but instead of agreeing to go with them Carol begged them to give Green Lantern another chance. The Zamarons could barely believe it; one cried out, "She doesn't seem to realize that **men** are a distinctly inferior species!" and another chimed in, "She acts as if a **man** could be **something important!**" The head Zamaron warrior agreed to give Green Lantern a second chance, and this time he defeated Carol by surrounding her with an impenetrable barrier that cut her off from the source of her powers. Inside this box, she thought, "I feel so weak . . . so helpless . . ." but then realizing she was beaten, "I'm defeated! How terrible . . . **no! How wonderful!**" The Zamarons, disgusted with Carol, wiped her memory and left her in the middle of the desert while they resumed their quest for a queen.

When the Zamarons departed, they left Carol with the Star Sapphire gem that gave her superpowers. Green Lantern took the gem away from Carol, but in future issues she'd occasionally stumble upon it and again be transformed into Star Sapphire. In one of these adventures, she decided to show up Green Lantern and prove that she was the superior hero to weaken his will so she could convince him to marry her. Her Star Sapphire side only wanted to be queen but her Carol side only wanted to marry Green Lantern, so the two sides reached a compromise whereby Green Lantern could become her consort while she ruled the Zamarons.

Using her impressive powers, Star Sapphire captured a criminal gang before Green Lantern could. She then thwarted an alien attack after Green Lantern's initial tactic failed. Star Sapphire took advantage of the demoralized Green Lantern's weak will and convinced him to marry her, but before they were married he wanted to see who Star Sapphire really was. As she took off her mask, he exclaimed "Carol Ferris!"—the magic words for breaking the hold of the Star Sapphire gem—and she reverted to her normal self. Like her previous stint as Star Sapphire, Carol had no recollection of what happened. The story actually ended sweetly, with Green Lantern thinking that it really didn't matter who married who, Green Lantern and Star Sapphire or Hal and Carol, because it was all the same and he loved her.

Unlike Wonder Woman, Lois, and Supergirl, Carol wasn't dealing with a selfish, frustrated man. Hal / Green Lantern could be a little brash and arrogant, but he certainly was no Superman or Steve. This change cast Star Sapphire in a slightly different light than the other three females, but at her core she still wanted the same things they did. She just went about it in a more blatant, extreme manner, ratcheting up her efforts to get married. Star Sapphire's man was far and away the most important thing to her, just like Wonder Woman, Lois, and, albeit in a slightly different way, Supergirl. Star Sapphire actively resisted the superpowers that could defeat the man she loved, only embracing them when she realized she could

use them to get Green Lantern to marry her. Even though she was a villain, she remained focused on marriage and the inevitable happy nuclear family it would bring about.

Four of a Kind

Uniformity was the hallmark of female characters in the Silver Age, and the differences between all four of our women were very slight. Their circumstances were varied, but their end goals and their relationships with men followed the same pattern. Rather than presenting readers with an array of the many things women could do or be, every female character was pigeonholed into the same male-dependent role. This uniformity not only narrowly redefined womanhood, it also sucked in Wonder Woman.

The Golden Age Wonder Woman was unique among the diverse female archetypes of the time, combining elements of each into an entirely new sort of character. She wasn't an exemplar of a larger category of characters, but rather something completely new and different. This distinctiveness was lost for the Silver Age Wonder Woman. She faced the same predicaments as her fellow female characters, and handled them in the same ways. Wonder Woman wasn't a critique of male-dominated women any longer, but instead was an embodiment thereof.

6

Conforming to the Code

*I*narguably, the most significant event for comic books in the 1950s was the publication of *Seduction of the Innocent*. The appearances of comic book publishers at the Senate juvenile delinquency hearings and the subsequent adoption of the Comics Code Authority were both the result of the anti-comics fervor created by Dr. Fredric Wertham's book. While most of the book dealt with crime and horror comics, Wonder Woman, Batman, and Superman were among the very few characters Wertham mentioned by name, and these mentions were in no way complimentary.

The crime and horror comics soon disappeared, wiped out by opportunistic publishers in a mad fervor to appease the public, but the superheroes remained. The genre was again an instant hit, and the new and revised superheroes of the Silver Age embodied the values of the post-Wertham, Comics Code Authority era from their first day. However, Wonder Woman, Batman, and Superman had some strong criticisms to deal with. Wertham's hatchet job on Wonder Woman was particularly brutal, and for the most part the response to his allegations sunk Wonder Woman further into the

mire of Silver Age conformity. Nearly everything from the Marston era was lost, but a new subversive element remained.

Fredric Wertham and the Seduction of the Innocent

In the modern comic book community, Fredric Wertham is generally reviled and seen as an alarmist crackpot. This hatred stems from a misunderstanding of Wertham and *Seduction of the Innocent*; most of those who vilify Wertham think that he believed that comic books directly caused juvenile delinquency and that he wanted to eliminate comic books entirely. While Wertham was prone to hyperbole and overstatement, like in his testimony before the Senate committee, most of his claims weren't that extreme. Wertham believed that comic books were one of many contributing factors to juvenile delinquency, and the one that could be most easily remedied. The remedy he prescribed wasn't to eliminate comic books, but rather to put age restrictions on the sale of comic books where the content was of a violent, frightening, or sexual nature. It was a valid idea; crime and horror comics from the early 1950s routinely featured gruesome plot lines and imagery that weren't suitable for young children, even by today's standards.

Wertham wasn't a bad guy. His controversial support for Ethel Rosenberg, his stance against segregated schools, and his mental health work in Harlem all showed a tolerance and liberalism that was ahead of the time. Although he's most often viewed as a simplistic crusader today, many of Wertham's arguments were fairly nuanced and his more provocative claims were tempered with reasonable qualifiers. There are many problems with *Seduction of the Innocent* in terms of Wertham's research methodology, his focus on sketchy anecdotal evidence, and his blatant sexism and homophobia, but there are interesting points as well, especially about superheroes. People scoff at them today, but he presented some thought-provoking theories.

Superman was one of the heroes singled out by Wertham. "Superman (with the big S on his uniform—we should, I suppose,

be thankful that it is not an S.S.) needs an endless stream of ever new submen, criminals and 'foreign-looking' people not only to justify his existence but even to make it possible." It's easy to contend that Wertham was just calling Superman a Nazi and a racist, but there was more to his critique than that simple interpretation. Wertham was saying that Superman solved problems with violence, and that this approach taught young readers to acquiesce toward strong, violent people or to become strong, violent people themselves. To Wertham, Superman comics equated violence with power and presented a message that "might makes right."

Furthermore, Wertham argued that the bad guys Superman defeated, and thus showed to be inferior, were foreign-looking criminals, which is a fair point. Heroes in the Golden Age were handsome men with chiseled, typically Aryan features, while the criminals tended to be unattractive, with exaggerated features that could be read as stereotypical of various ethnicities. One can disagree with Wertham about Superman, but his points weren't inherently unreasonable. There was more to Wertham than just strong rhetoric.

Nowhere was this truer than with Wertham's discussion of Batman. Many people think that Wertham claimed that Batman and Robin were gay. It wasn't that simple: Wertham's argument was that young readers read homoerotic undertones in Batman and Robin comic books. Wertham described how Batman and Robin were always together and took care of each other, writing that "they live in sumptuous quarters, with beautiful flowers in large vases, and have a butler, Alfred," which he called "a wish dream of two homosexuals living together."

But Wertham wasn't leafing through Batman comics looking for homoerotic subtext and warning the world that it could be dangerous for young readers; his comments on Batman and Robin were rooted in his psychiatric work with gay teenagers who identified Batman and Robin as an example of the lifestyle they desired. Many of these young men wanted a handsome, older man to take care of them and to have fun adventures with before retiring to the mansion

for the evening, and Wertham listed several quotes from his patients that said just that.

Of course, being the 1950s, this gay subtext was presented as dangerous for young readers. America was in the midst of a gay panic, worried that if their boys weren't raised to be strong, manly men then they'd turn into gay psychopaths who molested and murdered children. Homosexuality was seen as unnatural, a psychiatric disorder to be cured rather than something to be in any way accepted or encouraged. Wertham pointed out this subtext as a warning to parents and authorities to prevent these desires from being awakened in other boys.

Apart from his homophobia, though, the research in the Batman and Robin section of *Seduction of the Innocent* was generally sound, rooted in interviews instead of his own interpretations.* His claim wasn't that Batman and Robin were gay, but that they were often *read* as gay, and he had evidence to back it up.

While there were actually well argued, reasonable points in *Seduction of the Innocent*, when it came to Wonder Woman, Wertham engaged in the sort of poor research and unsubstantiated claims for which he is generally reviled today. Gone were the rational arguments and well-evidenced interpretations of characters.

Wertham wrote that "the lesbian counterpart of Batman may be found in the stories of Wonder Woman" and argued that "the homosexual connotation of the Wonder Woman type of story is psychologically unmistakable." He quoted an editorial from *Psychiatric*

---

*Recent research by Carol Tilley shows that Wertham's treatment of these teen testimonials was often sloppy. In one instance, he combined two separate anecdotes into one testimonial. Twice he overemphasized how the reader felt about Batman, omitting that one teen thought other comics characters better fulfilled his erotic fantasies and rewording another testimonial to put the focus more on Batman. This is problematic in terms of research methodology, but the fact remains that several gay teens read homoerotic undertones in Batman comics. The issue is one of degree, not whether or not teens read these undertones in the first place.

Quarterly that decried *Wonder Woman* for its "extremely sadistic hatred of all males in a framework which is plainly lesbian."* However, his evidence for his claims was nonexistent.

While his work on Batman was based on extensive interviews, his Wonder Woman work was pure supposition. He claimed that "for boys, Wonder Woman is a frightening image," and "for girls, she is a morbid ideal," but presented no evidence of young readers who saw Wonder Woman comics in that way. Wertham's only proof of Wonder Woman's supposed lesbianism was that she was always hanging around the Holliday Girls. He then launched into a nonsensical extrapolation:

> Her followers are the "Holliday girls," i.e. the holiday girls, the gay party girls, the gay girls. Wonder Woman refers to them as "my girls."

That, plus their mutual rescuing, was Wertham's only "evidence" for Wonder Woman's lesbianism.

This supposed lesbianism came up again in *Seduction of the Innocent*, entirely without any proof. Wertham stated that "even when Wonder Woman adopts a girl there are Lesbian overtones," referencing "Little Miss Wonder Woman," a story from *Wonder Woman* #49 in September 1951. In the story, Wonder Woman rescued Jan, a young girl lost at sea whose parents had gone missing, and adopted her instead of leaving her in an orphanage. Wertham offered no explanation about what the lesbian overtones of this story were. The relationship between the two was clearly parental: Wonder Woman instructed Jan on the importance of a good night's sleep, a healthy breakfast, and dental hygiene, and helped her fit in at school. Ultimately, they found Jan's parents and the family was reunited.

---

*As far as I can tell, this editorial doesn't exist in any issue of *Psychiatric Quarterly* between 1941 and 1954, the years covering Wonder Woman's first appearance to the publication of *Seduction of the Innocent*. Wertham was terrible at citations, and it's possible the editorial comes from somewhere else, but I've searched every issue of *Psychiatric Quarterly* to no avail.

Nothing in the story matched the homosexual model Wertham outlined in his discussion of Batman and Robin. Jan wasn't Wonder Woman's protégé in some pederastic relationship, nor were they overly affectionate. Also unlike in his Batman section, Wertham didn't mention any of his patients seeing lesbian overtones in this story. This interpretation was purely Wertham's, and frankly, if he was looking for a Wonder Woman story with a lesbian subtext, there were far better ones to choose from. What this adoption story did offer was a female superhero in a maternal role and that, for Wertham, was an inherently impossible situation.

Discussing female superheroes, Wertham wrote: "They do not work. They are not homemakers. They do not bring up a family. Mother-love is entirely absent." He added that "in no other literature for children has the image of womanhood been so degraded." This was partly inaccurate; the alter egos of many female superheroes had jobs, including Wonder Woman. Wertham restricted the notion of proper womanhood to homemaking and child-rearing, which explains his assumption of lesbianism for Wonder Woman and other female superheroes.

To Wertham, a woman was supposed to be a wife and mother and take care of the home. Running off to fight crime was the opposite of being a homemaker and, following his logic, the opposite of being a wife and mother was being a lesbian. Wertham believed that if a woman wasn't actively engaging in or pursuing a domestic, maternal lifestyle, then she just didn't like men or children, and thus she was a homosexual. Wonder Woman's adoption of Jan had lesbian overtones because it was impossible for Wonder Woman to be maternal; because she was a superhero, she was automatically a lesbian and lost any sort of maternal, nurturing potential.

Furthermore, Wertham decried the fact that "Wonder Woman is not the natural daughter of a natural mother, nor was she born like Athena from the head of Zeus." In 1954, the Golden Age Wonder Woman origin story still stood, and she was made of clay and brought to life by the gods. Her lack of a "natural" mother or

father placed her further outside of maternal, familial norms than her fellow female heroes and made her the archetype for Wertham's narrow-minded lesbian deduction.

It sounds ridiculous, but this assumption of lesbianism is the only way to understand Wertham's discussion of Wonder Woman. While he provided extensive evidence and clinical research for his discussion of a homosexual reading of Batman, he seemed to feel that a lesbian reading of Wonder Woman was as plain as the nose on his face. He even wrote that "if it were possible to translate a cardboard figure like Wonder Woman into real life, every normal-minded young man would know there is something wrong with her." This was Wertham at his worst, and it takes away from his interesting arguments and progressive stances on other issues.

Amusingly, while Wertham's baseless suppositions and sexist assumptions about Wonder Woman were terrible, shoddy work, his conclusion inadvertently stumbled onto a fascinating aspect of the character. A close look at Marston and Kanigher's work on *Wonder Woman* shows that a reading of Wonder Woman as a lesbian isn't off base at all.

Suffering Sappho!! Was Wonder Woman a Lesbian?

Marston's key psychological work, *Emotions of Normal People*, didn't mention lesbians, lesbianism, or any derivation of the term, but this was solely an issue of terminology. "Lesbian" suggests exclusivity in sexual preference, namely that you are a female who is attracted *only* to women. The terms "lesbianism" and "lesbian" were well established in psychological parlance by the time *Emotions of Normal People* was written, but Marston, as he was wont to do, used his own terminology.

Marston spent a lot of time discussing sexual relations between women as a part of "female love relationships." He noted that women tended to form very close bonds and care for each other deeply, but he also found "that nearly half of the female love relationships concerning

which significant data could be obtained, were accompanied by bodily love stimulation." By "bodily love stimulation," Marston meant sexual acts. He called this a physical love relationship, but was quick to explain that this was in addition to physical relationships with men.

Marston wrote that "in several cases, well-adapted love relationships with husband and children were not felt to be sufficient, without supplementary love affairs with other women." This wasn't lesbianism, but instead a type of bisexuality where heterosexuality was the default and sexual relations with other women were additional. Marston explained these relationships by referencing his earlier claim that women had twice as many love organs as men. With twice as much love to go around, he suggested, it was only logical that women would engage in sexual relationships with each other.

In the 1920s, sex and attraction outside of heterosexuality was seen as a perversion of the norm, and as a medical and psychological problem. Havelock Ellis argued that lesbians were women with aberrant masculine tendencies and described them as "the pick of the women who the average man would pass by." The notion that nonheterosexual relationships were problematic was widespread and, as evidenced by Wertham in 1954, continued for some time.

Even Marston wasn't immune to these theories; he argued that male homosexuality was a purely dominant relationship and not at all healthy for the participants. But while Marston avoided the term "lesbian," his analysis of the effects of sexual relationships between women bucked the trend of his peers' condemnation. He stated that:

> With regard to the possibly deleterious effect upon women's physical health of this type of love relationship with other women, I have been unable to verify [. . .] that such love affairs between girls were always injurious to their physical health.*

---

*His only exception was a case where two women in a prison experienced weight loss and a general deterioration of health because of "the excessive amount of passion response repeatedly evoked by their female lovers"—or, basically, having too much sex.

From a psychological perspective, Marston found that "girls and women who indulge in this form of love expression appear to feel no abnormality or unnaturalness about it." While not an endorsement of lesbianism, this was certainly an endorsement of sexual relations between women.

Marston's examination of female love relationships may have been reflected in his personal life as well. His polyamorous relationship with his wife, Elizabeth Holloway Marston, and their lover, Olive Byrne, sounds similar to the sort of relationship Marston described in *Emotions of Normal People*. He even opened his discussion of "Woman's Passion" with a preamble about his naïveté when it came to female love relationships, and how he learned much more about them "with the invaluable aid of my collaborators," meaning Elizabeth and Olive. The fact that Elizabeth and Olive stayed together for nearly forty years afer Marston's passing, until Olive's death, suggests that there may have been more to their association than a mutual love of Marston. Marston may have lived in the middle of a female love relationship, and this could have influenced his work.

This, however, brings up a chicken/egg question for Marston. Much like it was difficult to determine whether his enjoyment of bondage led to DISC theory or if his discovery of DISC theory led to his prominent use of bondage, so too is it tricky to determine which came first: Marston's advocacy of female love relationships or his enjoyment thereof. With bondage, we found that the fixation extended past metaphor into fetishism, and the same appears to be true here.

Emotions of Normal People contained many anecdotes about patients Marston had treated and stories he'd heard that illustrated his arguments concerning dominance and submission. These usually took the form of a paragraph that simply laid out the story, but there was one illustration that went above and beyond the rest. It included pages of tables and surveys, as well as pages and pages more of extensive examination of the data. It was one of the most, if not *the* most, detailed portions of the entire book and, perhaps not surprisingly, it involved both bondage and pleasure between women.

This extensive study concerned a "baby party," a sorority initiation where freshmen were dressed as babies, blindfolded and bound, and then given various punishments, including paddling and performing stunts. Olive Byrne and Marston attended such a party at Jackson College in 1925, and Marston found it absolutely fascinating. Marston reported that the event was fun for nearly everybody involved; the initiators experienced the "excited pleasantness of captivation emotion" while for the initiates "about three-fourths of the girls physically made captive to other girls at the Baby Party experienced pure, pleasant passion emotion." Marston ultimately came to the conclusion that:

> it seems undoubtedly to be the fact that girls, acting as inducers, can evoke intense and very pleasant passion emotion from all normal and well-balanced girls [. . .] without administering genital organ stimulation directly or indirectly.

This meant that women didn't need to engage in direct sexual activities with other women in order to evoke a sexually pleasurable response. This pleasure could come from simply submitting to another woman and being made helpless to their power, like in a bondage situation. The great detail of this section of *Emotions of Normal People* is noteworthy, and Marston continued this sorority theme, with the accompanying theme of sexual pleasure between women, in his other work.

In *Venus with Us*, Marston's sex romp novel about the life of Julius Caesar, women engaged in bondage with each other and willingly became each other's slaves. While this is certainly interesting in terms of Marston's inter-female sexual pleasure fixation, an entire chapter of the book, entitled "Ladies' Night in the High Priest's Palace," dealt with initiations remarkably similar to the baby party in *Emotions of Normal People*.

These initiations involved a mystery cult instead of a sorority, but the basic scenario remained the same: a group of women initiated a younger group of stripped down, blindfolded, and bound

women into the ways of their secret society. Their cult worshipped a goddess named Bona Dea, and when Caesar asked if he could attend their initiations, Servilia told him, "Bona Dea is a woman's goddess exclusively. The sacred rites practiced by us initiates would certainly interest you—intensely—if you could only know them. But you can't." The new initiates at the ceremony were "very young girls, some of them still in their early teens, with a few young married women recently converted to the service of the Good Goddess," which was reminiscent of older classmates initiating freshmen.

Although the rituals of the ceremony weren't detailed specifically, it was strongly hinted that they were of an erotic nature. Servilia's teasing of Caesar suggested that something salacious was going on, and the action cut away from a neophyte beginning her initiation with the words "Cassandra felt the hands of several women busy themselves with her garments . . ." That seems to be a rather telling ellipsis.

Marston's continuing fixation inevitably brings us to the Holliday Girls and their sorority, Beeta Lambda. A scene in *Sensation Comics* #3, the second appearance of the Holliday Girls, depicted Etta Candy and her fellow sorority sisters initiating Eve, a new member. The panel showed Etta swinging a piece of candy from a string in front of the blindfolded initiate, who was down on all fours and got paddled every time she missed when she tried to catch the candy in her mouth. Eve's initiation continued in the next issue, where the kneeling initiate was paddled by a hooded girl and then chained to a radiator with a dog collar around her neck. When Eve escaped to attend a previous engagement, Etta and the girls gave chase with Etta calling out, "Woo-woo! Eve got away! Come on, girls! Bring your ropes and paddles."

These initiation rituals were common for the Holliday Girls. In *Wonder Woman* #12, for example, Etta punished two initiates who were late for their duties by sentencing them to be bound, blindfolded, and left in the middle of the Holliday College campus, after which they had to find their way back to the sorority house in their

impaired state. In another issue, an initiate called Etta the "grand mistress of spanks and slams." Since we know that these initiations were always a source of sexual pleasure in Marston's other work, we can conclude that inter-female sexual enjoyment was portrayed in Wonder Woman comics.

As for Wonder Woman herself, she too must have enjoyed female love relationships in a sexually pleasurable manner. Bondage was a regular game on Paradise Island, but we need to build on our previous conclusions. The "erotic element" Marston thought inherent in bondage wasn't just a voyeuristic kink for readers; given Marston's sexual interpretation of sorority initiations, the bondage was sexually pleasurable for the participants as well.

This raises an interesting point, because while female love relationships were always in addition to heterosexual relationships, there were no men on Paradise Island. If the only sexual activities the Amazons engaged in involved women via their bondage games, this would imply that they were, in fact, lesbians. Wonder Woman, on the other hand, was a citizen of both Paradise Island and the world of men. But the Golden Age Wonder Woman regularly rebuffed Steve Trevor's advances and returned home to engage in bondage games, and with enthusiasm. She had a far better time with her Amazon sisters than she ever did with Steve. Marston might have been trying to tell us something.

One of Wonder Woman's signature catchphrases also hinted at lesbianism. She regularly exclaimed "Great Hera!" or "Merciful Minerva!"—referencing deities of the Greco-Roman pantheon like those with a Christian background say "Good Lord!" or "Oh my God!" These deities were some of the most powerful goddesses in the pantheon; Hera was the wife of Zeus, the chief god, and Minerva, the Romanized form of Athena, was the goddess of wisdom and the daughter of Zeus. Wonder Woman had a long list of expressions, and all of them had a similar origin: "Shades of Pluto!" "By Neptune's trident," and "Thunderbolts of Jove!" were just a few of her

favorites, and all of them were connected to Greco-Roman gods.* But another of Wonder Woman's signature catchphrases, "Suffering Sappho!" didn't reference any deity at all.

Sappho was an ancient Greek poet from the sixth century BCE, best known for her poems in which female protagonists extolled their love for other women. Her home, the island of Lesbos, was the basis of the term "lesbian" when it was coined in the late nineteenth century, and the terms "lesbianism" and "sapphism" both referred to an erotic relationship between women until "lesbian" became the commonly used term in the early twentieth century. This was an unusual name for Wonder Woman to reference, to say the least. Hera and Minerva make sense as part of a go-to phrase, but Sappho was best known for poetry concerning love and attraction between women. To mention Sappho was to make a very specific reference to this type of attraction; Sappho wasn't really known for anything else. If Marston or Kanigher were looking for alliteration, they could have referenced Selene, the goddess of the moon, or perhaps Semele, the mortal mother of the god Dionysus. "Suffering Sisyphus!" would have made a lot of sense. Mentioning Sappho only had one connotation and she was mentioned often, though not by Marston.

There's one Sappho reference that was undoubtedly Marston, when he had Wonder Woman exclaim "By Sappho's stylus!" in *Wonder Woman* #6. Sappho wasn't mentioned again until a few years later in some Joye Murchison stories. In *Comic Cavalcade* #12, the Amazons watch a movie in Sappho Hall, and then Wonder Woman said "Suffering Sappho!" for the first time in *Wonder Woman* #20 in November 1946. The expression appeared a few times after this in stories attributed to Marston, but this is a gray area for credits. Marston was very sick at the time, so his scripts

*The Golden and Silver Age Wonder Woman sounded a lot like Ron Burgundy, though I don't think Wonder Woman ever exclaimed "By the beard of Zeus!"—and "Great Odin's raven!" is a whole other pantheon.

were likely coauthored or tweaked by Murchison or Kanigher, if he even wrote them at all.

When Kanigher took over full writing and editing duties for the series with *Wonder Woman* #30, "Suffering Sappho!" became a staple of Wonder Woman's vocabulary. From Kanigher's first issue in 1948 to when he revamped Wonder Woman in 1958, "Suffering Sappho!" was exclaimed over 160 times, or almost 2.5 times an issue.*

You have to dig into Marston's work to see hints of lesbianism in his Wonder Woman, but Kanigher was much more direct. He mentioned Sappho frequently, and decades later in an interview with Trina Robbins he stated outright that all of the Amazons were lesbians. While Kanigher never had Wonder Woman engage in any sort of romantic or sexual relationship with another woman, it's hard to get much clearer than that.

As much as we've been critical of Kanigher, it's possible that he was subverting his own comic book. On the surface, Wonder Woman was all wrapped up in her relationship with Steve and wished she could settle down and become a housewife. However, the constant referencing of Sappho undercuts this heterosexual focus. In fact, the more romantic the comics got, the more Wonder Woman exclaimed "Suffering Sappho!"

Sensation Comics got a makeover late in 1949. The logo switched to a softer, more flowing script, and the series got a new cover artist. Instead of Wonder Woman battling bad guys and deflecting bullets, the covers showed Steve carrying Wonder Woman across a brook or bringing her flowers. *Sensation Comics* suddenly looked like a romance comic more than a superhero book. Before this change,

---

*In *Wonder Woman* #131 in July 1962, Kanigher wrote a story explaining all of Wonder Woman's expressions. Diana Prince said, "Sappho was so sensitive, she couldn't stand the sight of suffering in **any** form," and that's why Wonder Woman says "Suffering Sappho!" However, a) that doesn't make any sense, and b) that's not at all what Sappho was known for.

Wonder Woman said "Suffering Sappho!" occasionally during Kanigher's run on the book, about 0.5 times per issue. After the new romantic style began, Wonder Woman said it nearly three times as often, at roughly 1.4 times per issue. More romance with Steve equaled more references to a lesbian poet. Of course, this could just be coincidental, but maybe this was Kanigher's way of hinting at Wonder Woman's true sexual leanings.

So was Wonder Woman a lesbian? To answer that question we have to go beyond the comic book itself and really read between the lines. Going purely by the comic book, Wonder Woman wasn't a lesbian. There was nothing in the books that specifically identified her as such, and it's unlikely that her young readers were familiar with *Emotions of Normal People*, *Venus with Us*, or Greek erotic poetry from the sixth century BCE. Ultimately, Wonder Woman was a fictional character and her life only consisted of the panels on the page. We can't make any claims about Wonder Woman's sexuality because it just wasn't addressed. If anything, through her flirtations with Steve, and their dating in the Silver Age, the comic books implied that she was simply heterosexual. There were no overt references to Wonder Woman being attracted to women.

What we *can* say is that in light of Marston's other work and Kanigher's later interviews and references to Sappho, it's fairly reasonable to interpret Wonder Woman as either bisexual or lesbian. Based upon the evidence, we can't make any definitive statement about Wonder Woman herself, but we can state that due to Marston's proclivities and the hints in his comic books, there may have been a bisexual or lesbian subtext to the series. It's similar to Wertham's claim that Batman and Robin weren't gay but could be read as gay, except that in this case the evidence is far more compelling; I'm not aware of Batman's creators writing any books that endorsed a homosexual lifestyle. As for Kanigher's time on the book, it seems that he saw Wonder Woman as a lesbian, and he regularly hinted at this fact. In the end, Wertham was inadvertently onto something, in terms of both the Holliday Girls and Wonder Woman herself.

His research was poor and his evidence laughable, but he accidently stumbled upon a conclusion that had some merit.

Regardless of the veracity of his claims, Wertham's allegations and the subsequent fallout prompted great changes throughout the comic book industry, including *Wonder Woman.*

The Changing Content of *Wonder Woman*

One of Wertham's problems with Superman was his invulnerability, which made him an unstoppable agent of violence. It's probably not a coincidence that Kryptonite, an element poisonous to Superman that rendered him powerless, appeared far more often and in different forms in Superman comic books in the years following the publication of *Seduction of the Innocent.* A more blatant example that's been noted by many historians involved Batman's supposed homosexuality. The addition of Batwoman to the Bat-universe in 1956, followed by Bat-Girl in 1961, is often seen as a direct response to Wertham's allegations of homosexuality. These new romantic interests for the Dynamic Duo made the pair part of a nuclear family instead of two single fellows who enjoyed each other's company almost exclusively. The changes *Seduction of the Innocent* prompted in *Wonder Woman* were more subtle, but there were clear shifts after 1954.

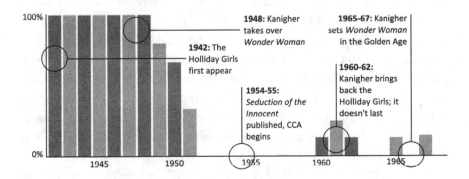

In his very short critique of Wonder Woman, Wertham singled out the Holliday Girls as evidence of Wonder Woman's supposed lesbian nature, but they hadn't been a part of the series for years. The chart on the previous page shows the frequency of the Holliday Girls appearances by year for the entire Golden and Silver Ages. While the Holliday Girls were a staple of Marston's tenure, appearing in every single issue, the beginning of Kanigher's run in 1948 brought a speedy decline, and they disappeared for eight years starting in 1952. The Holliday Girls did come back sporadically after 1960, but never seemed to catch on. Kanigher wasn't one to put a great deal of thought into his comic books, so their disappearance and subsequent reappearances were probably entirely random. The most likely explanation is that he just forgot about them for eight years. We can definitively state that Wertham had no effect on the Holliday Girls whatsoever, even though he mentioned them by name.

Although Wertham didn't mention Wonder Woman's Amazon sisters directly, he talked about Wonder Woman being surrounded by women, so the chart below shows the frequency of the Amazons' appearances. They were a regular part of the Marston years, dropped a bit once Kanigher took over, and then began to appear more frequently once the CCA started and Kanigher kicked off his new direction for the series. Quantitatively, this is the opposite of

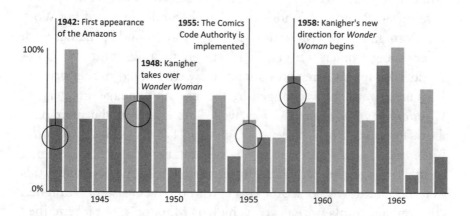

what we'd expect to see. After Wertham's comments about relationships with other women, you'd think that the Amazons would appear less frequently after 1954. But graphs don't always tell the whole story.

Although Amazons appeared more often than they had before, how they appeared had changed. Before 1954, particularly during the Marston years, Wonder Woman associated with many different Amazons, like Mala, the warden of Reform Island. They all had competitions together and played bondage games, and there was an atmosphere of general camaraderie. After 1954, the Amazons became background players who barely said or did anything, and Wonder Woman interacted almost exclusively with her mother, Queen Hippolyta. The other Amazons were around, but Hippolyta was the only one with any dialogue or participation in the stories.

This shift might have been spurred by Wertham. His claim that "mother-love is entirely absent" may have led DC to show Wonder Woman in a more familial environment to counteract Wertham's lesbian accusations. After 1954, many of Hippolyta's appearances involved her giving Wonder Woman advice about what to do with Steve. Similarly, a lot of Kanigher's Wonder Girl stories had scenes where Hippolyta counseled her daughter on love, life, and beauty. Kanigher's "Impossible Tales" teamed up everyone, with Hippolyta, Wonder Woman, Wonder Girl, and Wonder Tot going on fun family adventures. Paradise Island became solely family oriented for Wonder Woman. A nice visit with your mother and bondage games with other young women were two very different things, and after 1954 Wonder Woman's Amazon interactions were limited to the former.

There were stark changes to the use of bondage imagery in *Wonder Woman* after 1954 as well. The chart on the next page shows every issue of Wonder Woman from 1952 to 1958, or *Wonder Woman* #51–102, in terms of the percentage of panels containing bondage imagery in each issue. In the early 1950s, the bondage totals were up and down, as we'd expect from the inconsistent Kanigher. His bondage totals were never as high as Marston's, but it remained

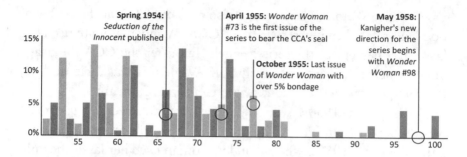

a fairly regular part of the book. The publication of *Seduction of the Innocent* didn't do anything to halt the roller coaster of bondage totals, but things changed soon after the CCA was implemented.

April 1955's *Wonder Woman* #73 was the first issue of the series to have the seal of approval from the Comics Code Authority on its cover. The next issue was the last issue to have a total percentage of bondage higher than 10 percent. Three issues later, *Wonder Woman* #77 was the last issue to have the percentage over 5 percent. Starting with *Wonder Woman* #78 in November 1955, the bondage in the series nearly died out completely. Zero percent was the most common total and, compared to the years before, the use of bondage was almost nonexistent. There were no other notable changes to the book; Kanigher's new direction for the series, with its new artists, origin, and stories, didn't begin until *Wonder Woman* #98, twenty issues and almost three years after the bondage dropped off.

There appears to be a clear connection between the implementation of the Comics Code and the amount of bondage in the series. Wertham never mentioned Wonder Woman's frequent use of bondage, but there were portions of the Comics Code that could be read as applicable to bondage. The Code stated that "suggestive and salacious illustration or suggestive posture is unacceptable" and that "sex perversion or any inference to same is strictly forbidden." It's possible that DC Comics or Kanigher himself, all of whom were well aware of the sexual connotation of Marston's approach to bondage, decided to curtail its use in order to conform to the Code.

Wonder Woman's lasso usage also puts the CCA at the center of bondage-related changes. Before the CCA, Wonder Woman used her lasso in 9 percent of the series' panels, but after the CCA the usage fell to 5 percent, a drop of nearly half. While this was a big decline, the change in how she used it was even more significant.

In the early 1950s, when Wonder Woman used her lasso she roped people about half of the time and roped objects for the other half. In the late 1950s, when Wonder Woman used her lasso she only used it on people about 10 percent of the time and lassoed objects 90 percent of the time.* So not only did Wonder Woman use her lasso less frequently after the CCA, she also used it to tie up people far less often. That's a double bondage drop, with the CCA right in the middle of these significant changes.

The fallout from *Seduction of the Innocent* and the creation of the Comics Code Authority had some influence on the series. A writer would have to go out of his way to avoid bondage to get such a low percentage with Wonder Woman. After all, her main weapon was a lasso! It appears that someone decided to eliminate bondage from the series, and the timing suggests it was because of the Comics Code. There's no smoking gun to prove this claim, no interoffice memo from DC Comics or some such, but the numbers speak for themselves. Wertham, who unknowingly went after Marston's comics with his Holliday Girls outrage and inadvertently stumbled onto

---

*Statistics side note: These numbers are for the percentage of Wonder Woman's lasso usage, not for the overall book. Given the shift to campy, fantastical stories in the Silver Age, you might think that Wonder Woman stopped lassoing people and started lassoing spaceships and giant birds instead. This could account for the difference, not the CCA. But when we look at the numbers per issue, we see that while lassoing people dropped from 5 percent of the panels per issue before the CCA to less than 1 percent after, the percentage of panels where Wonder Woman lassoed objects remained at 5 percent for both periods. Objects didn't replace people; she tied up fewer people but the same number of objects, and the overall drop in the total use of her lasso came from tying up people far less often.

the book's possible lesbian subtext, unintentionally was the catalyst for the death of Marston's favorite metaphor.

The Real World Carries On

The Golden Age Wonder Woman and the typical American woman of the 1940s were different in many ways, but at their core both embarked on a new role for women in a very complicated environment. Wonder Woman was a new kind of hero with several complex subtexts, while women had new wartime jobs and duties while managing their responsibilities at home and the difficulties of the war years. The Silver Age Wonder Woman was better defined by simplicity; over the years, Kanigher undid most of Marston's complexity, resulting in a character who was no longer unique, whose heroic mission was a hassle that stopped her from getting married, who didn't fight real criminals, who let her boyfriend aggressively control their relationship, and who lacked any sort of metaphor or subtext other than the importance of romance and marriage. The Silver Age Wonder Woman retreated to a traditionally feminine role, and the rest of popular culture from this era would have you believe that all American women did the same.

Cold War culture and domestic containment resulted in a focus on women solely as wives and mothers, happy homemakers who spent all of their time caring for their family. The rapid spread of suburbia facilitated this role, and American popular culture perpetuated the image of this ideal woman who found complete contentment in domesticity. Sitcoms like *Leave It to Beaver* and *The Donna Reed Show*, as well as magazines like *Ladies' Home Journal* and *Good Housekeeping*, furthered this message of domestic, suburban bliss. It seemed that everyone was happy in the late 1950s, and if they weren't it was because they were living outside of this ideal life. However, these cheery depictions weren't completely accurate. In reality, the 1950s were a complicated time for women, and the

simplicity of the Silver Age Wonder Woman wasn't at all mirrored in the real world.

The 1950s are often seen as a sort of lost decade for women, an unfortunate period between their new roles during World War II and the emergence of the women's liberation movement in the late 1960s, but this wasn't the case. The progress made during the war didn't disappear altogether when it ended, and second wave feminism didn't suddenly appear out of nowhere two decades later. Throughout the 1950s, women played pivotal roles in social change that improved their position in society. Many women who remained in the workforce after the war were involved in union activities, helping to gain better wages and benefits for all workers. Among these benefits were better hours, maternity leave, and on-site child care for many professions.

Also, women were heavily involved in the civil rights movement, attending protests, marches, and sit-ins across the nation to fight for equal rights and civil liberties. After Martin Luther King Jr., the name most commonly associated with the civil rights movement is probably Rosa Parks, who famously refused to give up her seat on a bus in 1955. Beyond Rosa Parks, innumerable women of all colors and classes were involved in every level of the civil rights movement. In fact, the civil rights movement was both inspiration and a breeding ground for many women who later got involved in the women's liberation movement. The advances made by women in the 1950s improved their quality of life and paved the way for future progress.

The 1950s were also remarkable in terms of women taking control of their sexuality. Many women worked tirelessly in the area of birth control, with great success. Beginning in 1953, Katharine Dexter McCormick funded research on oral contraception that ultimately resulted in the first birth control pill, also known as "the pill," in 1960. McCormick's friend and Marston's aunt Margaret Sanger, the founder of Planned Parenthood, was also a tireless advocate for birth control and worked to educate women about their birth control options and change laws that limited these options.

Although we tend to associate the battle for women's sexual freedom with the late 1960s, the groundwork was laid in the decades before. Women worked together to help each other however they could, from large organizations like Planned Parenthood to secret, local networks where women could procure illegal means of birth control or abortions. The pill wasn't available to all American married women until 1965 or to unmarried women until 1972, while many states had laws against other birth control devices, and abortions were illegal until *Roe v. Wade* in 1973. Because of these prohibitions, women banded together to assist each other and to fight to secure their reproductive rights.

Strides were made in other areas of sexuality as well; the postwar era saw the emergence of a strong and vibrant lesbian subculture. The authorities viewed these women as deviants and tried to harshly repress them, but their efforts were in vain and the subculture continued to thrive. Lesbian feminism was a significant aspect of the women's liberation movement and was, yet again, firmly rooted in the 1950s.

The participation of women in activities outside of the domestic norms showed that many women weren't satisfied with the lives that the dominant Cold War culture had prescribed for them. This dissatisfaction was most famously articulated in Betty Friedan's *The Feminine Mystique*, which hit the shelves in early 1963. Friedan looked at the lives of white, middle-class, suburban women and found that the role society had foisted upon them wasn't fulfilling for many of them. Through surveys, Friedan discovered that women lacked their own identity and that their lives revolved entirely around their families and not around themselves. Friedan blamed the media, like women's magazines and advertising, for causing women to focus solely on housewifery, and she argued that this trapped women in a lifestyle where their efforts were undervalued and their desires and potential were set aside for those of their husbands or children.

The Feminine Mystique was an instant success; within three months of its publication it reached the *New York Times* bestseller

list despite its unknown author and daring subject matter. Many women identified with Friedan's characterization of the "Problem That Has No Name," this dissatisfaction with suburban life, and many historians cite the publication of *The Feminine Mystique* as the spark that brought about the women's liberation movement. It had been building throughout the 1950s and early 1960s, with innumerable women laying the groundwork for its emergence, and in 1963 the lives of American women were about to change forever.

When Rosa Parks refused to give up her seat on a bus in December 1955, Wonder Woman was playing baseball with a gorilla and fighting a robot octopus in *Wonder Woman* #78. When the Food and Drug Administration approved the use of the pill as an oral contraceptive in June 1960, Wonder Woman went to a parade with Steve and fought giant balloon animals brought to life in *Wonder Woman* #114. When *The Feminine Mystique* was published in February 1963, Wonder Woman was at a carnival with Steve and was turned into a giant by nefarious aliens in *Wonder Woman* #136. The world was changing in many ways, but Wonder Woman wasn't changing with it.

If anything, Wonder Woman was sinking further into innocuous story lines and defining herself more and more through her relationship with Steve. In *Wonder Woman* #136, a confident Steve told Wonder Woman what to do and extolled the pleasure of his company, stating, "All you have to do is perform a few feats for charity—and spend the rest of your time with me—enjoying **yourself!**" Steve dictated Wonder Woman's activities and later described her as "my **Wonder Woman.**" The Silver Age Wonder Woman wasn't in tune with the lives of women in the real world, particularly those who were working to improve the role of women in American society. The 1950s saw the gradual undoing of Wonder Woman's complex nature, and by the early 1960s, Wonder Woman was a generic superhero. But the comic book industry was about to change again, and these changes would lead to a radical new direction for Wonder Woman as the Bronze Age began.

INTERLUDE 2

Letters and Advertisements

*W*onder *Woman*'s intended audience over its first few decades is very clear in retrospect. Marston stated several times that he aimed the book at boys, trying to teach them to submit to the loving authority of women. In the 1950s, extra features like "Marriage a la Mode" and "Gems of Destiny" suggested that DC Comics was trying to appeal to female readers. The target audience reveals a lot about *Wonder Woman* and the aims of the creators and editors behind the book, but what it can't show is who actually read the series.

Some fairly safe assumptions can be made about the age range of the audience, since superhero comics in the Golden and Silver Ages were read primarily by kids. In the 1960s, Marvel comics brought in an older crowd of teen readers as well, and by the end of the decade DC was trying to get the same demographic, but there aren't any exact figures. Data about comic book readers in general from the early decades of the industry is fairly minimal, much less for specific series. There are no numbers out there that give a clear idea of who

was reading *Wonder Woman*, but hints of this information can be found in other ways.

Letter Columns

Wonder Woman's letter column changed a lot over the years, going through several titles and a big demographic shift. Initially the column was called "Wonder Woman's Clubhouse," and young kids would write in to Wonder Woman herself. They'd ask Wonder Woman questions about her life or tell her about the fan clubs they'd started. Most of the columns consisted of several short letters, with replies from Wonder Woman.

In 1965, the content changed. Instead of several short letters to Wonder Woman from little kids, there were two or three longer letters addressed to the editor, written by older readers, at least in their early teens. These more substantial missives addressed issues like continuity, mythology, or art and storytelling techniques.* This format became the norm and lasted through many name changes. The column became "Wonder Woman's Readers Write!" in 1967, then "The New Wonderful World of Wonder Woman" late in 1968, followed by "Wonder Woman's Write-In" in 1971, "Princessions" in 1972, and "Wonder Words" in 1974. "Wonder Words" actually stuck, and it lasted well into the 1980s.

The letter column appeared in almost every single issue of *Wonder Woman* once it began, providing an excellent set of data on the series' audience. By tabulating the names by gender and charting them, the broad strokes of how *Wonder Woman*'s readership

---

*Among these writers were several young men who later became famous in the comic book industry, including Marv Wolfman, a noted comic book writer; Mark Evanier, a multiple Eisner award winner; Mark Gruenwald, a writer and editor at Marvel Comics; and Michael Uslan, a producer on all of the modern Batman films.

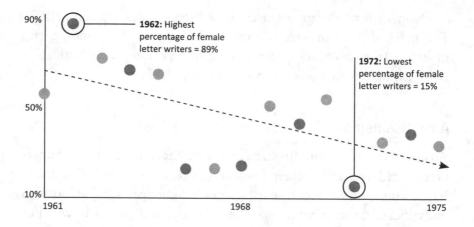

changed from 1961 to 1975 can be seen.* While the numbers by year are somewhat scattered, the trends are clear. Female writers to *Wonder Woman*'s letter column declined fairly steeply over the fifteen years examined, while there was a commensurate growth in male writers.

In terms of reliable information, there's some subjectivity in letter columns. Editors didn't painstakingly craft each column to statistically reflect all of the letters they'd received that month. Rather, a slew of factors likely affected which letters were chosen. For example, in the early 1960s DC encouraged kids to form fan clubs for their characters, so letters about fan clubs probably had a better chance of being published. When "Marriage a la Mode" and other female-directed features dominated *Wonder Woman*, they may have chosen letters from female readers to showcase their intended audience. Similarly, when a feminist outcry led to Wonder Woman's return to her Amazon roots in the 1970s, the editors might've been more likely to publish letters from women.

---

*Every name mentioned in each column was counted as male, female, or unspecified (less than 4 percent of all letters writers were unspecified). The totals for each year were turned into percentages, and then charted with a trend line to show the larger pattern in the data.

Nonetheless, the trends over these fifteen years are compelling. The marked drop in letters from girls and the corresponding rise in letters from boys suggest a change in readership and indicate a diminishing female audience over this period.

Advertisements

Ads from the Silver and Bronze Ages were charming and fun. Super-heroes told you about their favorite Hostess products,* you could buy onion gum or a bald cap for pocket change, get buff after a bully kicked sand in your face at the beach, and own a bowlful of happiness and have instant pets with sea monkeys! There weren't many ads in the Golden Age, but publishers worked hard to maintain the price of comics by lowering page counts for their comics and increasing the number of ads over the course of the 1950s.† By 1960, ads made up a substantial part of every comic book, and a sense of who advertisers thought were reading *Wonder Woman* can be derived by examining the ads' intended audience.

Comic book ads weren't subtle. Many ads proclaimed their intended audience with bolded headlines that read "BOYS!!" or "GIRLS!!" Others showed images of their intended audience using the product, like boys playing with toy cars or girls applying makeup. For ads without those helpful hints, stereotypical assumptions can be made about which gender the product was traditionally associated with. Boy ads consisted of things like toy soldiers, race cars and other vehicles, monsters, guns, and the NFL Punt, Pass, and Kick

---

*Wonder Woman appeared in at least eight different Hostess ads, and her favorite treat by far was Twinkies. Wonder Woman did five Twinkies ads, two for chocolate cupcakes, and one for fruit pies.

†Despite the increase in ads, the ten-cent price rose to twelve cents in 1962. After holding steady at ten cents for twenty years, the twelve-cent price only lasted seven years, and *Wonder Woman* jumped to fifteen cents in 1969. It then leaped to twenty-five cents in 1972, to thirty cents in 1976, and to forty cents in 1978. Three decades later, *Wonder Woman* is $2.99.

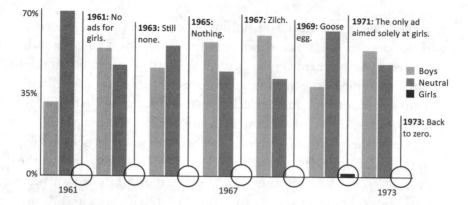

Competition. Girl ads included dolls, hair accessories, makeup and beauty products, jewelry, and helpful books like *How to Slenderize Heavy Legs.** There were also many ads for products that were gender neutral, like records, stamps, amusement parks, televisions and radios, and those classic full-page spreads that showed a variety of items that could be purchased, earned, or won.

The chart above shows a gendered breakdown of the ads in *Wonder Woman* for every second year from 1961 to 1973. Astoundingly, of nearly five hundred ads, only one was aimed at girls. It appeared in *Wonder Woman* #197 from November 1971 and was for Kenner's Easy Care Manicure Set. It was an impressive product that included tools to smooth, shape, and buff your nails, along with two bottles of nail polish. Other than that, it was all boys or gender neutral, and they each averaged out to about half of the total ads examined.

The ads for dolls, hair accessories, and the rest listed above were all from the pages of *Young Love*, one of DC's romance comics, because no examples could be found in *Wonder Woman*. In fact, advertisers seemed to go out of their way to avoid aiming ads only

---

*Along with its counterpart *How to Add Alluring Curves to Skinny Legs*; both offered a "tested and proven method" in "only fifteen pleasant minutes a day."

at girls. Jewelry ads featuring smiling women with rings, bracelets, and necklaces always included a set of cufflinks or a ring for military men, making them gender neutral. The ads for Iverson bicycles featured laughing boys having adventures, but each ad ended with a reminder that they had a model "especially for girls." After a few months, though, Iverson cut any mention of their girls' bicycle.

The furthest that advertisers were willing to go to sell to girls were ads that appealed to both genders. This is largely due to the nature of ad sales at the time. Advertisers didn't buy ads in individual books, but in lots. For example, *Wonder Woman* and *Aquaman* came out on similar schedules, and over the course of the 1960s both titles featured the exact same selection of ads 97 percent of the time.* By grouping *Wonder Woman* with their other superhero titles, it's clear that DC Comics and its advertisers felt that *Wonder Woman*'s readership was akin to DC's other superhero books. And, as evident from the intended audience of these ads, this readership was predominantly male.

DC had another group of series that were aimed at female readers with ads to match, composed of romance series like *Heart Throbs* and *Young Love*. A stark example of this gender divide for ads comes from Marvel comics and an ad for the Wayne School, a way to finish high school at home. In *Fantastic Four*, the ad showed a young man being told by a woman in the personnel department, "Sorry, we only hire high school graduates." In *Millie the Model*, it was the *exact* same ad, except the young man was replaced by a

---

*Having the ads match so closely was quite an impressive achievement. A lot of the ads in the 1960s were a half or a third of a page, so the comic's story would have to end at a certain point on the page for the ad to fit. Corralling the writers and artists of the various comics to all hit the same spots every month must have been quite an editorial feat. With *Wonder Woman* and *Aquaman* specifically, *Wonder Woman*'s letter column was only one page while *Aquaman*'s was often two pages. That's a one-page deficit for *Aquaman* in terms of potential ad space every issue, yet they still fit in 97 percent of the ads that they ran in *Wonder Woman*.

young woman. Both publishers had a boy group and a girl group for ads, and *Wonder Woman* was in the boy group. This choice speaks volumes about her audience.

Not Who, but How Many

The above data has obvious limitations and doesn't provide us any definitive numbers for *Wonder Woman*'s readership, but the trends are quite clear.

An area that's much more definitive, however, is sales. Regardless of how many boys or girls read *Wonder Woman*, there weren't a lot of them. The sales data from the 1960s is fairly solid, showing that *Wonder Woman* was in rough shape. From 1960 to 1969, the book averaged sales of just over 200,000 copies per issue. By today's standards those numbers would be fantastic, but in the 1960s *Wonder Woman* sold barely a quarter of what the top book sold and averaged forty-seventh place on the charts. For a series that had occasionally outsold *Superman* and *Batman* in the Golden Age, this was a big drop. *Superman* and *Batman*, along with the many other titles starring the two heroes, consistently owned the top of the charts, but *Wonder Woman* floundered.

It probably came as little surprise when DC announced a new direction for the series in 1968. The industry was changing rapidly and *Wonder Woman* was very much behind the times, so Robert Kanigher was out and a new, younger team came in to revitalize Wonder Woman and make her a more modern character. The dawn of the Bronze Age brought with it the newly depowered Diana Prince, who caused quite a stir.

The Bronze Age

Wonder Woman No More

By 1968, it seemed that Kanigher was running out of ideas for *Wonder Woman*. He had spent nearly all of 1966 on Golden Age throwback stories, bringing back forgotten characters from Marston's era while Andru and Esposito tried to replicate H. G. Peter's art style. The response in the letter columns was mixed at best, and the fan community seemed bored with Kanigher. Sales dropped as well, so Kanigher was removed as editor and writer and a whole new creative team came onboard.

Denny O'Neil was a fairly new writer who wasn't yet thirty years old when he took over the series with *Wonder Woman #178* in September 1968. He'd done some work for Marvel and Charlton Comics, but *Wonder Woman* was his first big job at DC Comics, an inauspicious beginning to what became a storied career. Joining O'Neil was artist Mike Sekowsky, who had been drawing comic books since the early 1940s. Throughout the 1960s, Sekowsky was a well-known and respected artist, a mainstay on *Justice League of America*. Along with DC's editor-in-chief Carmine Infantino and series editor Jack Miller, the team decided on a new direction for Wonder Woman where she gave up her superpowers and became a

regular, modern woman. The depowered Wonder Woman was one of DC Comics' first attempts to respond to the new tone of the 1960s comic book industry, and it failed spectacularly.

The Marvel Age

The Bronze Age was preceded by a sub-age caused by the rise of Marvel Comics. Formerly known as Timely Comics in the 1940s and Atlas Comics in the 1950s, Marvel introduced a new approach to superheroics that moved the industry away from fanciful beasts and bizarre alien creatures. Although Atlas had tried to publish a few superhero comic books in the early 1950s with poor results, the events of 1954 didn't dramatically affect the company. While DC Comics had its heroes called out by name in *Seduction of the Innocent* and actively attempted to make its books as inoffensive as possible after the Comics Code Authority came in, Atlas was a C-list publisher at best and hadn't been through the wringer like DC. With a new company name and 1954 a fading memory, Marvel didn't create its superheroes with the pro-Code, pro-camp fervor of DC. It had to follow the Code, but DC's swift turn to the innocuous had made superheroes palatable to the general public again, so Marvel could try something new and different without fear of reprisal.

The biggest difference between the two publishers was that Marvel's main writer and editor, Stan Lee, and artists Jack Kirby and Steve Ditko made their comic books more realistic. They set their series in the real world; instead of fictional cities like Metropolis and Gotham, most Marvel heroes operated in New York. They created scientifically based explanations for their heroes' superpowers; instead of power rings from aliens or abilities from the gods, Marvel heroes gained their powers through encounters with radioactivity, gamma rays, or genetic mutation. The alter egos of Marvel heroes were as important, if not more so, as their superhero identity; while the main focus of *Batman* was Batman, the main focus of *The*

Amazing Spider-Man was Peter Parker, who just happened to be Spider-Man.

Marvel's first new series, *Fantastic Four*, debuted in 1961 and was created by Lee and Kirby. The Fantastic Four were led by Dr. Reed Richards, a scientist who constructed a rocket to fly into space before the USSR did. Accompanying Reed was his wife, Sue, her brother, Johnny Storm, and Reed's pilot and friend, Ben Grimm. The four developed superpowers when they were exposed to cosmic rays and decided to use their powers to fight crime and protect the innocent. Reed became Mr. Fantastic, able to stretch his body to incredible lengths; Sue became the Invisible Girl, who could make herself and other objects invisible; Johnny became the Human Torch, bursting into flame and flying through the air; and Ben became the Thing, his skin turned into a hard, rocklike substance that rendered him both strong and nearly impervious to harm.

Fantastic Four was soon followed by *The Incredible Hulk*, created by Lee and Kirby in 1962. Dr. Bruce Banner was a mild-mannered scientist, but after being exposed to gamma rays he developed the ability to turn into the huge and powerful Hulk. This transformation was involuntarily triggered by emotion, most often anger or fear, and so the Hulk was a violent, destructive Mr. Hyde to Banner's docile Dr. Jekyll.

Later in 1962, Lee and Ditko created Spider-Man, who first appeared in *Amazing Fantasy* before moving to his own series, *The Amazing Spider-Man*. Peter Parker was a studious high-schooler bitten by a radioactive spider while visiting a laboratory. He developed superstrength and agility, could climb walls and jump great distances, and created his own web-shooting devices to complete his spider theme. Parker initially tried to make money off his new powers, but when he refused to stop a criminal who later killed his uncle, he decided to use his powers for good.

Other heroes followed these new properties, including the X-Men, a group of powerful mutants; Iron Man, a millionaire with a metal suit that gave him superpowers; Doctor Strange, master of

the occult; Thor, the Norse god confined to a frail human body; and Daredevil, a blind man whose other senses were superhumanly heightened.

What made Marvel superheroes different from their predecessors were their personalities, not their superpowers. Superstrength, invisibility, and elasticity were nothing new, nor was fighting crime, but Marvel comic books focused on their heroes' personal lives as well. Clark Kent, Bruce Wayne, and Diana Prince were all alter egos of convenience who never had any real problems. All they did was allow the heroes to blend into society or fund their vigilante career. The alter egos of Marvel heroes were extremely inconvenient and caused the characters a lot of problems.

For example, the Fantastic Four were a family, who squabbled as most families tend to do. Reed and Sue often had marital spats, Johnny was headstrong and reckless, and Ben was depressed and angry about his bizarre appearance. There was a dysfunctional quality to the Fantastic Four that drove their stories, making the book a superheroic melodrama instead of a simple adventure series where they battled a new villain each month. The height of personal drama at DC was the omnipresent silly love triangles, but Marvel characters had real conflict, personal and otherwise.

Before becoming the Hulk, Bruce Banner had been a normal scientist with a normal life and a girlfriend, Betty Ross. All of that ended after he became the Hulk; the military came after the destructive Hulk, forcing Banner to be secretive, withdrawn, and often on the run. His relationship with Betty suffered and she soon found another man. Peter Parker had a complicated life to juggle as well: he had to attend school, care for his widowed aunt, spend time with his girlfriend, and work as a photographer at the *Daily Bugle*, all while fighting crime as Spider-Man. Plus he had to protect his secret identity lest villains try to get at him through his family and friends. For Marvel heroes, fighting bad guys was the easiest part of their life. Their real-world problems were much more difficult to navigate.

Marvel's realistic approach to superheroes appealed to a different audience than DC's fantastical adventures, and the Marvel readership tended to be older. Teenagers, and even college students, began to read Marvel comic books, likely identifying with the real-world problems they presented. Marvel books were also more socially relevant than those of other publishers. For example, the X-Men faced great persecution and fear for being different, serving as a clear analogue of African Americans and the ongoing civil rights movement. Marvel also had several physically disabled heroes, including the blind Daredevil and Thor, who had a leg impairment as his alter ego, Donald Blake.

In *Comic Book Nation*, comics historian Bradford Wright cites a 1966 poll in *Esquire* magazine where college students "ranked Spider-Man and the Hulk alongside the likes of Bob Dylan and Che Guevara as their favorite revolutionary icons." The rise of Marvel led to the decline of campy, simplistic superhero stories and changed the audience for superhero comic books. By the late 1960s, with Marvel becoming more and more popular, DC had to respond and follow Marvel's lead, signaling the end of the Silver Age and the beginning of the Bronze.

The Bronze Age

While historians generally agree on the start of the Golden and Silver Age of superhero comics, the exact start of the Bronze Age is a matter of some debate. The most commonly cited events and dates include:

- *House of Mystery* #174, March 1968: Horror had been forbidden by the Comics Code in 1955; DC's creation of a new horror series marked the end of the horror-less era and a shift toward comic books for older readers.
- *Green Lantern/Green Arrow* #76, April 1970: The two heroes teamed up to travel America and addressed issues like

crime, race relations, and drug use. The left-leaning Green Arrow showed Green Lantern the real America that he was missing by being up in the stars, and it was the first DC series to really tackle modern social issues.

- *Amazing Spider-Man #96*, May 1971: The federal Department of Health, Education, and Welfare asked Stan Lee to include an antidrug story in one of his series, so he wrote a three-part story where Peter's friend Harry Osborn abused pills. The CCA refused to approve the issues because of the drug use, and so Marvel printed them without the Code's seal. No one was offended and sales were unaffected, and it ultimately led to a revision of the Code that made it far less severe.

The thread connecting all of them was a shift toward stories that were meant for an older audience and the diminishing influence of the Comics Code Authority.

There's no one key moment, so suffice it to say that the transition from Silver to Bronze took place around the late 1960s and early 1970s. DC Comics had spent over a decade strictly adhering to the Comics Code in an attempt to avoid a repeat of the events of 1954, and did quite well revitalizing its superhero line. However, by the late 1960s it wasn't necessary to tell silly, inoffensive stories anymore. Marvel had great success with its more realistic and relevant stories and, perhaps more important for DC, the Silver Age schtick was no longer profitable. Marvel's sales increased steadily over the decade while DC's slowly declined, and Marvel ultimately surpassed DC in total sales in 1967. The stories that had saved DC in the 1950s were now dragging it down, so the company made substantial changes to many of its titles.

At the forefront of two of the most radical and critically acclaimed revamps was Denny O'Neil. Editor Julius Schwartz, the man responsible for many of DC's successful new heroes, took over the Batman line and rid the books of their Silver Age frivolity with O'Neil at the helm. O'Neil found inspiration in the early days of

Batman, and along with artist Neal Adams he turned Batman into an ominous figure who struck terror into the hearts of criminals. The stories had a gothic flavor, pitting Batman against fearsome villains with murderous intentions. Adams's artwork is legendary today; he extended and sharpened the ears on Batman's cowl, making them look almost like fierce horns, and lengthened Batman's cape so it could be a dark shroud when it enveloped him or a frightful, bat-like wingspan when flowing freely. Mood was key to this darker Batman, and Adams made excellent use of shadow and the night in depicting the Bronze Age Batman.

Adams also worked with O'Neil on *Green Lantern/Green Arrow*. While their Batman collaboration rebelled against the Code with its darker stories and often frightening tone, their *Green Lantern/ Green Arrow* work challenged the limits of the Code with its subject matter. In a famous exchange from *Green Lantern/Green Arrow* #76, an elderly African American took Green Lantern to task, stating, "I been readin' about you . . . how you work for the **blue skins** . . . and how on a planet someplace you helped out the **orange skins** . . . and you done considerable for the **purple skins**! Only there's **skins** you never bothered with—the **black** skins! I want to know . . . **how come?!**" The chastised Green Lantern could only hang his head in shame.

This indictment of Green Lantern for neglecting the plight of minorities and the underprivileged can also be read as an indictment of DC's superhero comics as a whole. They spent the 1950s and 1960s battling aliens and strange creatures, not addressing real-life problems at all. *Green Lantern/Green Arrow* marked a turn toward relevance for DC, and the verdant heroes continued to address major societal issues, most shockingly in *Green Lantern/Green Arrow* #85.

The cover depicted Green Arrow's ward, Speedy, sitting next to a needle and drug paraphernalia, and Green Arrow proclaiming, "My ward is a **JUNKIE!**" Speedy was hooked on heroin, and the following issue declared that drugs were "more deadly than the atom bomb" and included an antidrug message from John V. Lindsay, the

mayor of New York City. The series gained a lot of acclaim for its discussion of drug use, including positive profiles in several leading magazines and newspapers, but O'Neil and Adams's tenure only lasted for fourteen issues due to poor sales.

Sales in the 1970s weren't great for anyone, with the lagging DC continuing to decline and even the successful Marvel dipping considerably, but the Bronze Age at least brought a creative renaissance to DC. Apart from Batman and Green Lantern, Julius Schwartz took over the editing duties for the Superman line from Mort Weisinger, ending the era of multicolored Kryptonite and pets like Comet the Super-Horse and Beppo the Super-Monkey. DC also nabbed Jack Kirby from Marvel, who created his famous Fourth World line of comics at DC. The books chronicled the intergalactic war of the evil planet of Apokolips and its cruel lord Darkseid against the good planet of New Genesis and its benevolent ruler Highfather. The books were trippy and epic, reflective of the psychedelic culture of the time, and they remain highly regarded today.

In the midst of all of this creativity and new ideas was *Wonder Woman*, rejuvenated by Denny O'Neil, the architect of DC's two most famous Bronze Age properties. But the new direction for Wonder Woman didn't go over well with anyone.

The End of Wonder Woman

By all accounts, they had the best of intentions. Wonder Woman hadn't been popular for years, so O'Neil and Sekowsky chose to revitalize the character, making her a normal human woman who had to deal with real-world problems. The title of the series changed slightly to *Diana Prince: Wonder Woman*, and a new era for the character began. Unfortunately, it was a mess behind the scenes. After twenty-seven years where *Wonder Woman* had only two editors and two writers, the twenty-six-issue, four-year run of the Diana Prince era had four editors and three writers. Everyone tried valiantly to fit Diana Prince within the hip, contemporary world of

women's lib and mod fashion, but the new direction was met with criticism and cries for a return to the Amazon Wonder Woman. On top of the editorial chaos and general disdain for the book, Diana Prince was a startlingly pathetic depiction of a modern woman.

One of the main goals of this new direction was to appeal to a female audience. Sekowsky later described his approach to the series: "I didn't see how a kid, male or female, could relate to [the Amazon Wonder Woman]. It was so far removed from their world. I felt girls might want to read about a super female in the real world, something very current." The ads for the book made their target audience very clear, declaring, "**Girls!** If you dig **romance**, and we know you **do**—you'll really flip for the new **Wonder Woman!** Yes, **romance**, plus **intrigue**, **high adventure**, and a brand-new kind of story that will bring you a brand-new kind of thrill!" The ad also warned: "Don't dare miss the heroine of the year!"

Making Wonder Woman a normal human in the real world without superpowers could have been fascinating, particularly with the timing. A female perspective in the midst of the burgeoning women's liberation movement and the general social upheaval of the late 1960s offered a wealth of stories and issues to address. But O'Neil and Sekowsky ignored all of that and took a different tack that was rooted in their origin story for the depowered Diana Prince.*

Although the new creative team meant to depict an independent Diana Prince setting out into the world on her own, her origin story and the series that followed were actually all about Steve Trevor. In *Wonder Woman* #179, Steve went on a secret mission to infiltrate a powerful criminal network run by the nefarious Dr. Cyber. After assaulting his superior officer and fighting through a wall of guards as he fled an army base, Steve was branded a traitor and became a

---

*This wasn't a traditional origin story, since it didn't reboot the character and Wonder Woman's previous origin story was still part of her history. Nonetheless, the transition from Amazon warrior to human being was such a huge change for the character that it can be considered a type of origin story.

wanted man. Only Steve and his superior officer knew the truth: this attack was a hoax to let Steve have an in with the criminal underworld. Wonder Woman was understandably shocked when she read a newspaper headline that proclaimed "Hunt Col. Trevor: Army Officer Labeled Spy By Superiors!"

Wonder Woman didn't believe for a second that Steve was a traitor, and she was formulating a plan to help him when she was summoned back to Paradise Island by her mother. Queen Hippolyta told her, "For ten thousand years, we have lived here, performing the mission assigned to us . . . helping mankind find maturity! But now, our magic is exhausted! We must journey to another dimension, to rest and renew our powers!" Paradise Island was about to disappear from the Earth, along with all of the Amazons, and Wonder Woman could either leave with her sisters or stay behind without her superpowers.

She immediately replied, "I love you, mother . . . you and my sister Amazons! But Steve Trevor desperately **needs** me . . . I must stay!" Her decision was swift and not at all difficult; given the choice, she immediately chose Steve. Steve was clearly in a bad spot and was going to need some help, and Wonder Woman, with or without superpowers, was the heroic, helpful type.

Leaving behind her bracelets, star-spangled outfit, and golden lasso, she stated, "I hereby relinquish all mystic skills! I lay upon the sacred altar the glories of the Amazons and willingly condemn myself to the travails of mortals." She bid her mother good-bye and returned to America, and even her invisible plane disappeared once she'd landed in the Lower East Side of New York City. Luckily for her, in less than a page she found a commercial space for rent with an apartment on top and decided to open a fashion boutique. Diana was Marvelized, established in an actual city with an apartment, a job, and other real-world problems. By the issue's end, she'd found Steve and was ready to embark on a new life without Wonder Woman.

Diana gave up her superpowers for heroic reasons, sacrificing her family and her abilities to rescue Steve. However, *Wonder Woman* #179 can be viewed in a different light due to the events in *Wonder Woman* #178. This alternate reading casts Diana's ostensibly heroic sacrifice in a more problematic, self-serving light.

The issue began with Steve's arrest for murder after a man he had a scuffle with one evening turned up dead later that night. Steve's explanation was that he was at a hippie club called the Tangerine Trolley, but he was found guilty because the girl he was talking to had disappeared and couldn't confirm his alibi. Wonder Woman decided to ingratiate herself within the hippie community via her Diana Prince alter ego to find the missing girl and exonerate Steve, but first Diana had to abandon her usual square appearance so she would fit in. She ditched her glasses and her dowdy military uniform in favor of a new, flowing hairdo and modern, psychedelic fashions with bright colors and bold prints. In the end, she found the girl and saved Steve, but Diana's mod new appearance added a twist to Wonder Woman and Steve's relationship.

Wonder Woman #178 ended with the freed Steve and Wonder Woman relaxing together on a sofa; Wonder Woman was nestled in close to Steve, who had his arm around her. Steve mentioned that he could never forget what Diana had done for him, stating, "She's so much more than what I thought she was—in fact, I think I'll ask her out one of these days and really get to know her." This was a huge new development in how Steve saw Diana. For nearly three decades, Steve had barely noticed her, instead dedicating all of his time to Wonder Woman. Diana had just saved him from a long prison sentence, but she had saved Steve many times before. The only difference was that she'd changed from a plain wallflower to a trendy, attractive woman. This change in Steve's attitude toward Diana prompted Wonder Woman to think, "Why, this is silly . . . I can't be jealous of myself—**can** I? If he can fall for Diana like this, he can fall for any woman! And I'll lose him forever if I don't do **something** to

keep him interested in **me**!" The issue ended with Wonder Woman thinking, "Wonder Woman must change . . ."

Reading between the lines of her rapid decision to give up her superpowers, the fact is that Diana didn't need to be Wonder Woman to be with Steve anymore. If Queen Hippolyta had summoned Wonder Woman home before Diana's mod makeover, the depowered wallflower Diana Prince would have been all alone, because Steve didn't care about her at all. But now Steve was interested in Diana and, if mentioning asking her out while on a date with Wonder Woman was any indication, he seemed to like Diana more than Wonder Woman. Not only could she remain behind and date Steve as Diana Prince, but she would be giving Steve the woman he preferred. No wonder she was so quick to decide to stay behind. It was a win-win situation for the man she loved. This reading sends an interesting message about this independent, modern heroine; letting the desires of her boyfriend dictate her choices was hardly in keeping with the spirit of the women's liberation movement.

This interpretation perhaps reads too much into O'Neil and Sekowsky's desire to get rid of the Amazons and move onto their new direction as quickly as possible. The speed of Diana's decision may have been solely because of the limited space given the departure of the Amazons, since the whole thing only took two pages. Regardless of intention, the implication that Steve now preferred Diana over Wonder Woman can be easily read. In either case, Diana stayed behind because of Steve Trevor and became a normal woman, getting an apartment, opening a shop, and even learning kung fu.

Right after she arrived in New York and secured her new shop and apartment, Diana saw an old, blind man being attacked in a back alley. She ran to help him, but he dispatched his attackers by himself. The man was I Ching, a martial arts master and enemy of Dr. Cyber, who sought out Diana after he deduced that she was really Wonder Woman. Finding her powerless, he taught her karate, kung fu, and several other fighting forms, and together they scoured the criminal underworld for any information about Steve. Ultimately, Steve

showed up on Diana's doorstep, having just been gunned down by Dr. Cyber's thugs when they found out he really wasn't a traitor to America. Steve was rushed to the hospital in critical condition.

In the following issue, Diana set out to find his assailants, but Steve was kidnapped and killed right in front of her. Holding his dead body, a distraught Diana cried out, "I've lost **everything!** Without family . . . without **Steve** . . . my life is **worthless!**" After Steve died, the main plot of the series became Diana's quest to find Dr. Cyber and avenge his death. Diana and I Ching traveled the globe, battling their way through scores of henchmen and leaving destruction in their wake. The real-world aspects of the mod Diana Prince and her new life in New York running a boutique took a backseat to this pursuit of vengeance.

O'Neil and Sekowsky's goal was to turn Wonder Woman into a realistic woman whom readers could identify with, but the end result was that Diana's entire life was centered around Steve. The decisions that led to her losing her powers were based on what was best for him, not for herself, and her life became a quest to avenge him. Basically, everything about the new Diana Prince was defined by Steve, and she didn't have her own identity outside of him.

Although the era of female comic book characters striving to be subservient housewives was now past, Diana embodied that old mind-set where a man was a woman's sole reason for existence. Elsewhere in superhero comic books, female characters had moved beyond this limited depiction of womanhood. Rather than being an independent, liberated woman, the new Diana Prince represented everything that real-world independent, liberated women rallied against.

Behind the Times

We can call Marston's comics kinky, or label Kanigher's stories as silly, but neither is a commentary on the quality of the comic books. Each creator had a particular take on Wonder Woman, and we've

delved into these differences and the evolution of the character without making a value judgment. Certainly both creators thought that they were doing fine work. This was not the case with the mod era of *Wonder Woman*. Every time Denny O'Neil is asked about his time on the series, he talks about how bad the book was and how many glaring missteps he made, and he often apologizes for his work. These were not good comics.

The mod *Wonder Woman* suffers further when placed in the context of the Bronze Age. Marston's *Wonder Woman* had problematic quirks, but comparatively it was rather progressive and, at the very least, completely different from the other books being published at the time. Kanigher's *Wonder Woman* was campy, but so was everything else in the Silver Age. The mod *Wonder Woman* was regressive at a time when comics were getting good. Great strides were made in depicting the role of women in superhero comic books, while simultaneously women battled for new rights and fair treatment in the real world. Wonder Woman lagged behind everyone, to such a degree that Gloria Steinem and other feminists took it upon themselves to call for a return to the original, Amazon Wonder Woman. The world was moving forward while Wonder Woman moved backward.

8

Doin' It for Themselves

The Bronze Age marked the end of the marriage-obsessed, damsel-in-distress monopoly in comic books. There were still many characters that fit that mold, and there still are today, but that wasn't the only option anymore. A shift began, and many women in superhero comics broke away from their old ways to become more independent.

This change happened everywhere in popular culture as the women's liberation movement gained momentum, and in most fields, this change was gradual. In *America on Film*, Benshoff and Griffin write that "films of the late 1960s and early 1970s did slowly begin to deal with contemporary issues facing women [and] tentatively celebrate women's independence and touch on other feminist issues." The film industry didn't turn completely feminist all of a sudden, but a steady change was set in motion. The old model was fading away.

It was a slow turnaround for teen romance novels too. Linda Christian-Smith finds that in this era more female lead characters wanted some control of their lives. They were frustrated with traditional gender roles and keen for more independence. These characters became increasingly assertive with their boyfriends, no longer

catering to their every whim. The change wasn't profound, but there was a definite shift nonetheless.

In science fiction, the changes were substantial and began earlier. Throughout the 1950s, letter columns and editorials in pulp magazines argued for more female characters in science fiction. By the late 1960s, female characters weren't just poor damsels in distress to be rescued or evil foes to be vanquished; they were heroes. In fact, one of the most popular subgenres of science fiction in this period was stories about female utopias, most of which had harsh critiques of patriarchal society and gender inequality.

While the depiction of many of DC Comics' female characters changed in the late 1960s, Marvel beat DC to the punch. With its more realistic superhero stories and teen fan base, Marvel had its ear to the ground for social change. Case in point: Sue Storm, the Fantastic Four's Invisible Girl.* Initially, Sue was a classic Silver Age damsel in distress. She was a devoted wife and "mother" of the Fantastic Four's pseudo-family. Sue was also the weakest member of the team and was captured often. Mr. Fantastic was brilliant and could do impressive elastic feats, the Human Torch could fly and shoot flames, and the Thing had superstrength and nearly impenetrable skin; the Invisible Woman could only disappear.

This all changed in January 1964's *Fantastic Four* #22, when Sue found out that she had a secondary superpower. On top of turning invisible, she could also create powerful force fields and project them to protect objects and other people. Not even the Thing could break the force field, which made Sue the most powerful member of the Fantastic Four. She broke free of her damsel in distress and den mother roles and became an equally formidable member of the team.

Another noteworthy shift occurred in the pages of *The Amazing Spider-Man*. Originally, Peter Parker's girlfriend was Gwen Stacey, a

---

*Having a character named the "Invisible Girl" was a spectacular, unintentional metaphor for female characters in the Silver Age.

wholesome, blonde, all-American girl who embodied the virtues of a traditional "good girl" character. Gwen was sweet and studious and keen to marry Peter and settle down. In fact, Stan Lee's long-term plan was for Peter to ultimately end up with Gwen. However, comics need dramatic tension, so in 1966 Peter and Gwen had what was intended to be a momentary breakup.

During the breakup, a new character was introduced as a blind date for Peter in *The Amazing Spider-Man* #42 in November 1966. Her name was Mary Jane Watson, and her first words are one of the most famous lines in comic book history; when Peter met Mary Jane and was momentarily stunned by the vivacious redhead's beauty, she proclaimed, "Face it, Tiger . . . you just hit the **jackpot!**" The confident and free-spirited Mary Jane was the complete opposite of Gwen Stacey. She was all about having a good time and wasn't interested in marriage or babies, and she broke off any relationship that began to get serious lest she be tied down. Mary Jane and Peter dated briefly, and she continued to be flirtatious with him after they broke it off. Despite Stan Lee's original plans, the hipper Mary Jane became a fan favorite, and Gwen Stacey was eventually killed off in 1973. Gwen's lack of popularity showed that comic book readers wanted modern, independent female characters, and Marvel Comics was happy to oblige.

DC Comics caught up to Marvel as the Bronze Age began, and started to embrace the shift away from traditional roles for women. While Diana Prince languished in stereotypes and violence, flitting from man to man, other female characters at DC reflected the changing role of women in the real world, and in popular culture generally.

Diana Prince as the New Wonder Woman

While Marston's and Kanigher's versions of Wonder Woman had many differences, the mod Diana Prince was a complete contradiction of her predecessors. Most of the unique characteristics of

Wonder Woman that had carried over from the Golden to the Silver Age were reversed with the new Diana, and intentionally so. Denny O'Neil and Mike Sekowsky made a clean break from her past depictions to take the character in a new direction. It was a bold approach, but the end result was the undoing of everything progressive and special about the character without replacing these qualities with anything new or exciting. It seemed that the only things salvaged from Wonder Woman's earlier incarnations were the lovestruck dopiness of Marston's Diana and the romantic troubles of Kanigher's. Diana compares poorly to her fellow female characters, but she comes off even worse in comparison to her past selves.

Wonder Woman was a founding member of the Justice League in the Silver Age, the only woman on the team's regular roster. She was an equal, contributing member and one of the most regular characters in the team's rotating cast. Having a female superhero front and center in one of DC's bestselling books went a long way to countering the male dominance of DC's line. Most of the male members of the Justice League had their own books that outsold *Wonder Woman*, but her presence on the team showed that super-heroics weren't the exclusive domain of men.

Soon after she gave up her powers and her identity as Wonder Woman, Diana resigned from the team in *Justice League of America* #69, written by Denny O'Neil. She announced, "I'm no more than an ordinary mortal now . . . much as I admire the **Justice League**, I feel I no longer have a place in it!" Batman told her that she was welcome back anytime and Superman refused to accept her resignation, instead calling it a leave of absence, but she was gone. A letter from reader Scott Fader in "The JLA Mail Room" column a few issues later made an excellent point about the situation:

> As Don Rickles might say, "YOU DUMMY!" You blew a perfectly good non-super-heroine! If Batman and Green Arrow (both non-super) can be in there, why can't Wonder Woman? I

think you dum-dums have a few things to learn about ousting Justice Leaguers.

It appeared that while men could be in the Justice League without superpowers, a woman had to have superpowers to merit membership. Diana's fellow heroes thought that her resignation was a rash decision, but rash decisions were a hallmark of the mod era.

For over twenty-five years, Wonder Woman had been kindhearted and peaceful, using force only when her diplomatic solutions were rejected. This all changed with the mod Diana Prince; her anger perpetually boiled just below the surface and erupted with any sort of provocation. Violence was her response to nearly every situation. Her only motivation was avenging Steve's death, and she fought through anything that stood in her way. A typical panel read: "Then—there is **fury**! Like an avenging goddess, Diana leaps forward, feeling nothing—nothing except a consuming hate . . . with inhuman strength and swiftness, she sweeps through her enemies." The art on this page showed a silhouetted Diana punching and kicking Dr. Cyber's agents with reckless abandon, sending them flying through the air. The book became little more than a series of elaborate fight scenes and explosions, with Diana at the center of each one.

The violence wasn't limited to brawling. In an issue ominously titled "Red for Death!" Diana traveled to China and ended up strafing Chinese fighter jets with a massive machine gun. Another story arc had Diana trapped in the interdimensional kingdom of Chalandor, where she killed at least twenty men with blazing sword work before she was captured. Diana later escaped, joined a local rebel group, and taught them to make gunpowder. She and her fellow rebels then shot down the enemy's air ships with cannons, blowing up the gas-filled and heavily manned flying machines. Diana's solution for any problem was to hit it or blow it up or, more often than not, kill it.

She was also reckless and regularly ran into dangerous situations despite the warnings of I Ching and her other companions.

No matter how many thugs were in her way, Diana dove right in, half-crazed. Her emotions replaced her common sense, and anger dictated her actions. It seems that traits like calmness and rationality didn't fit O'Neil and Sekowsky's concept of a normal, identifiable woman. At times, Diana was downright hysterical. The mod revamp was meant to offer a new version of the character, but an irrational woman ruled by her emotions was just a cliché.

O'Neil and Sekowsky continued to hit all of the stereotypical bases in *Wonder Woman* #182. Diana was trying on clothes in London with a new beau, and the narration read: "Happiness for any healthy, red-blooded young gal, is bedecking herself in the latest fashion finery . . . and our **Wonder Woman** just happens to **be** a healthy, red-blooded young gal." Then, overhearing her fellow shoppers discuss a party they were attending that evening, Diana thought, "Imagine me in the same room with London **high society!** It's as though I were suddenly dropped into a **Cary Grant** picture!" Diana Prince, former Amazon princess, charter member of the Justice League of America, and personal friend of the Olympian gods, was ecstatic to be trying on new clothes in the same room as two women on their way to a fancy party. Fashion, and the doors that being fashionable opened to her, was of paramount importance to Diana.

Diana's new look brought her a lot of attention. Not only did Steve take an interest in Diana instead of Wonder Woman for the first time, but her new look caught the eyes of many other men as well, who were glad to give her information or buy her gifts. Later, she was able to hobnob with high society and travel the globe on the dime of these new suitors. The attention her new look brought her went over very well with Diana, who found all of it terribly exciting. This focus on her appearance and the many benefits it brought was a big change for the series. As Wonder Woman, the subtext was always that it was good to be strong and caring and heroic; as the mod Diana Prince, the subtext was that it was good to be pretty because boys would like you and you'd be treated better.

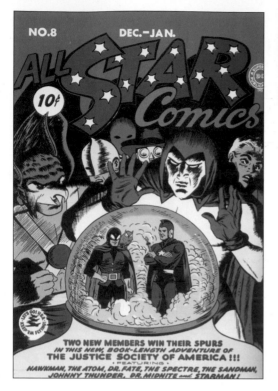

TOP LEFT: *All Star Comics* #8, cover by Everett E. Hibbard, All-American Comics, 1941

The first appearance of Wonder Woman, though she's not on the cover. She continued to costar in *All Star Comics* as the secretary of the Justice Society.

TOP RIGHT: *Sensation Comics* #1, cover by H. G. Peter, All-American Comics, 1942

Wonder Woman's origin story continued here, launching her new series. Wonder Woman starred in the lead story and on the cover of *Sensation Comics* every month.

BOTTOM RIGHT: *Wonder Woman* #1, cover by H. G. Peter, All-American Comics, 1942

Wonder Woman's solo series. She starred in every story in each issue, which came out quarterly during the Golden Age.

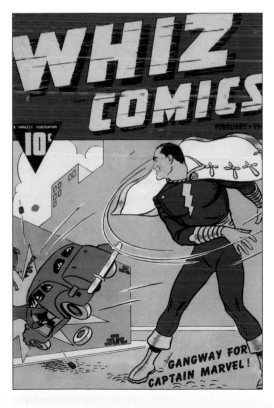

TOP LEFT: *Action Comics* #1, cover by
Joe Shuster, Detective Comics Inc., 1938
The first appearance of Superman, the
hero who started the superhero craze.
Many imitators followed, which led William
Moulton Marston to create Wonder Woman
as a counter to the genre's "blood-curdling
masculinity."

TOP RIGHT: *Captain America Comics* #1,
cover by Jack Kirby, Timely Comics, 1941
The first appearance of Captain America,
an American super soldier, punching Hitler
before America even entered World War II.

BOTTOM LEFT: *Whiz Comics* #2, cover by
C. C. Beck, Fawcett Comics, 1940
The first appearance of Captain Marvel.
He was less violent than other heroes but
enjoyed demonstrating his superior strength,
while Wonder Woman only used force as a
last resort.

TOP: Wonder Woman sketch by H. G. Peter, 1941

An original design of the character, with notes by Marston and Peter. The skirt was soon replaced by briefs, and the sandals became boots. H. G. PETER; IMAGE COURTESY OF HERITAGE AUCTIONS (WWW.HA.COM)

BOTTOM: Etta Candy vs. the Cheetah sketch by H. G. Peter, 1943

Etta Candy, the stalwart leader of the Holliday Girls, boxes with the felonious Cheetah.

H. G. PETER; IMAGE COURTESY OF HERITAGE AUCTIONS (WWW.HA.COM)

LEFT: The Wonder Woman team, from *Wonder Woman* **#2, All-America Comics, 1942**
From left to right, writer William Moulton Marston, artist H. G. Peter, editor Sheldon Mayer, and publisher Max Gaines.

BOTTOM: The Marstons and friends at home, 1944
From left to right, Marston's live-in lover Olive Byrne (note the large bracelets), occasional Wonder Woman writer Joye Murchison, Marston's wife Elizabeth Holloway Marston, and Marston himself. IMAGE COURTESY OF PETE AND CHRISTIE MARSTON

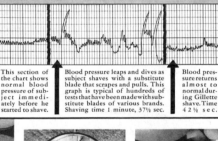

Ad for Gillette razors, *LIFE* magazine, October 24, 1938

Marston shows how the lie detector proves Gillette's superiority. Though a Harvard-educated psychologist, Marston was a bit of a huckster as well.

LEFT: Alice Marble, from _Wonder Woman_ #1, All-American Comics, 1942
The former tennis star and associate editor of _Wonder Woman_, enjoying the series' first issue. Marble worked on sixteen issues of the series and wrote the regular "Wonder Women of History" feature.

BOTTOM LEFT: _Sensation Comics_ #13, cover by H. G. Peter, DC Comics, 1943
Wonder Woman strikes against Hitler, Hirohito, and Mussolini in this wartime issue.

BOTTOM RIGHT: _Wonder Woman_ #10, cover by H. G. Peter, DC Comics, 1944
Wonder Woman halts an alien invasion, ultimately ending the conflict by negotiating a trade agreement between Earth and Saturn.

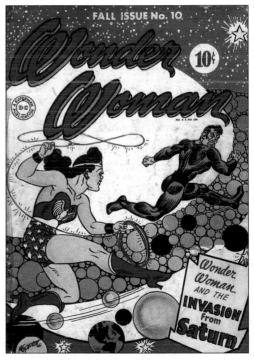

RIGHT: *Venus with Us* by William Moulton Marston, Sears Publishing, 1932

The classier, original cover for Marston's sex romp novel about Julius Caesar.
IMAGE COURTESY OF THE BOOK COLLECTOR'S LIBRARY (WWW.TBCLRAREBOOKS.COM)

BOTTOM: *The Private Life of Julius Caesar* by William Moulton Marston, Universal, 1952

Venus with Us retitled and recovered as a pulp novel featuring scores of nude women to better reflect the lascivious story inside. IMAGE COURTESY OF HANG FIRE BOOKS (WWW.HANGFIREBOOKS.COM)

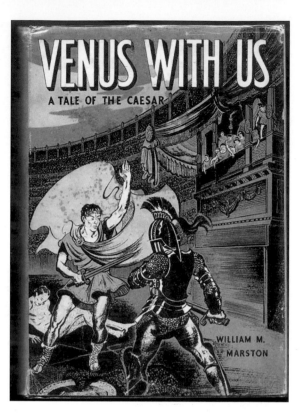

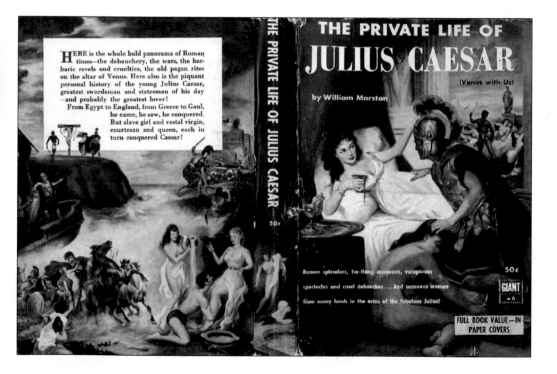

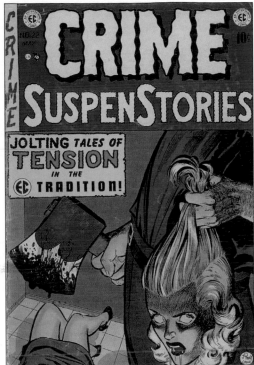

TOP LEFT: *Wonder Woman* #103, cover by Ross Andru and Mike Espositio, DC Comics, 1959

New artists updated Wonder Woman's look in the Silver Age, replacing Peter's classic style with a more conventional aesthetic and a tweaked costume design.

TOP RIGHT: *Crime SuspenStories* #22, cover by Johnny Craig, EC Comics, 1954

The cover that doomed William Gaines's testimony before the Senate Subcommittee on Juvenile Delinquency when he had to declare that it was "in good taste."

BOTTOM LEFT: The seal of the Comics Code Authority

The mark of the organization that monitored comic book content for decades.

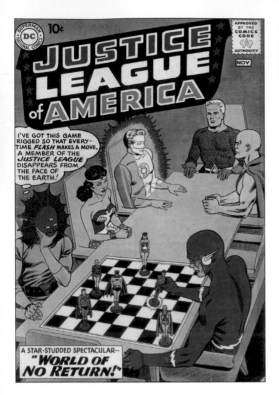

TOP LEFT: *Justice League of America* #1, cover by Murphy Anderson, DC Comics, 1960

For a decade, Wonder Woman was the only female member of DC's superhero team— now a full member and not just the secretary.

TOP RIGHT: *Wonder Woman* #105, cover by Ross Andru and Mike Esposito, DC Comics, 1959

Robert Kanigher loved fantastical creatures, and giant birds were a common foe for Wonder Woman during the Silver Age.

BOTTOM RIGHT: *Wonder Woman* #125, cover by Ross Andru and Mike Esposito, DC Comics, 1961

Steve Trevor and Mer-Man fight over Wonder Woman. Her refusal to choose between them constantly agitated both suitors.

TOP LEFT: *Superman's Girl Friend Lois Lane* #16, cover by Curt Swan and Stan Kaye, DC Comics, 1960

In the Silver Age, Superman pretends to be hurt by Lois's Kryptonite vision to teach her a lesson. Every female character in the Silver Age, including Wonder Woman, had to put up with a domineering boyfriend.

BOTTOM LEFT: *Sensation Comics* #94, cover by Arthur Peddy, DC Comics, 1949

The comic may look like a stereotypical romance on the outside, but inside Wonder Woman constantly made Sapphic references.

BOTTOM RIGHT: *Wonder Woman* #124, cover by Ross Andru and Mike Esposito, DC Comics, 1961

Queen Hippolyta, Wonder Woman, Wonder Girl, and Wonder Tot often teamed up as the Wonder Family.

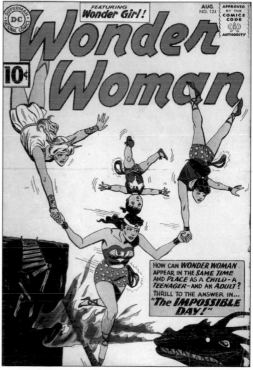

TOP: Ad for "The New Wonder Woman" in *Superman's Girl Friend Lois Lane* **#92, DC Comics, 1969**
DC Comics' in-house ads for a revamped *Wonder Woman* targeted female readers directly, promising romance and intrigue.

RIGHT: *Wonder Woman* **#178, cover by Mike Sekowsky and Dick Giordano, DC Comics, 1968**
The Bronze Age Wonder Woman abandoned her superpowers and her classic costume in favor of a new, mod look.

TOP LEFT: *Wonder Woman* #180, cover by Mike Sekowsky and Dick Giordano, DC Comics, 1969

A weeping Diana Prince, a common occurrence throughout the mod era.

TOP RIGHT: *Wonder Woman* #203, cover by Dick Giordano, DC Comics, 1972

Samuel Delany's muddled "Special! Women's Lib Issue," the series' only attempt to address the women's liberation movement.

LEFT: Mike Sekowsky and Joyce Miller, DC Comics Publicity Photo, 1969

Sekowsky uses a fashionable model as inspiration for his *Wonder Woman* art.

TOP RIGHT: *Wonder Woman* #189, cover by Mike Sekowsky and Dick Giordano, DC Comics, 1970
Diana Prince strafes a Chinese fighter jet with a machine gun, one of her many uncharacteristically violent escapades in the mod era.

BOTTOM LEFT: *Superman's Girl Friend Lois Lane* #109, cover by Dick Giordano, DC Comics, 1971
The Bronze Age Lois Lane has had quite enough of Superman. They broke up a few issues later, and the newly independent Lois stood in stark contrast to Diana Prince's chronic need for male attention.

BOTTOM RIGHT: *Detective Comics* #359, cover by Carmine Infantino and Murphy Anderson, DC Comics, 1967
The first appearance of Barbara Gordon as Batgirl. As a nonsuperpowered crime fighter, Batgirl was the feminist heroine Diana Prince should have been.

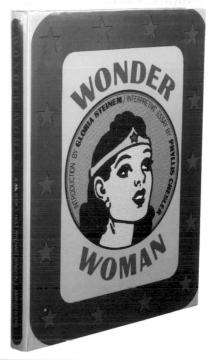

TOP LEFT: *Ms. #1*, 1972
Wonder Woman graces the cover of the first issue of *Ms.* magazine. The issue reprinted a portion of her Golden Age origin story.

TOP RIGHT: *Wonder Woman*, **with an introduction by Gloria Steinem, 1972**
A collection of Golden Age Wonder Woman stories published by *Ms.* magazine to celebrate her return to her Amazon roots.
IMAGE COURTESY OF HERITAGE AUCTIONS (WWW .HA.COM)

BOTTOM LEFT: *Wonder Woman #204*, **cover by Don Heck and Dick Giordano, DC Comics, 1973**
After four years as a normal human without superpowers, the Amazon Wonder Woman returned.

TOP RIGHT: *Sister: The Newspaper of the Los Angeles Women's Centre*, **cover by C. Clement, 1973**
A cartoon in a feminist paper had Wonder Woman advocating for women's sexual health.

BOTTOM LEFT: *Wonder Woman* **TV show publicity photo, 1977**
Lynda Carter as TV's Wonder Woman. Carter's portrayal became the definitive version of the character, cementing Wonder Woman as a pop culture icon.

BOTTOM RIGHT: *Wonder Woman* #1, **cover by George Pérez, DC Comics, 1987**
Wonder Woman was relaunched as a brand-new series with a premier artist and a strong feminist slant.

TOP LEFT: *Wonder Woman* #190, cover by Adam Hughes, DC Comics, 2003
In one of the biggest Wonder Woman stories of the Modern Age, she got a haircut.

TOP RIGHT: *Justice League* #12, cover by Jim Lee, DC Comics, 2012
In another big Modern Age Wonder Woman story, she hooked up with Superman.

BOTTOM LEFT: The cast of *The Big Bang Theory* as superheroines, publicity photo, 2010
Howard (Simon Helberg) as Batgirl, Sheldon (Jim Parsons) as Wonder Woman, Leonard (Johnny Galecki) as Supergirl, and Raj (Kunal Nayyar) as Catwoman. SONJA FLEMMING / CBS

The boys certainly did like Diana, and Diana liked them back, adding fickleness to the growing list of the mod Diana's new traits. In her fascinating book *Reading the Romance*, Janice Radway surveyed women who were regular romance novel readers and used their responses to create a template for the ideal romance novel. This ideal romance begins with the destruction of the protagonist's identity, after which she embarks "on her quest for a new self and new connection." A key part of this quest is meeting a man who transforms her into "a passive, expectant, trembling creature who feels incomplete without the attention of the hero." This is a perfect description of Diana Prince.

After she lost her Wonder Woman identity, Diana constantly had to have the attention of a strong man. Just one issue after Steve's death, Diana was attracted to her new associate, Tim Trench. Lying in her bed and unable to sleep, she thought, "I'm becoming fond of Tim . . . **very** fond! He's crusty . . . but he's also strong, decisive . . . a **man!** At times he makes me forget Steve . . . **almost!** I wonder if being **human** means being **fickle!**"

Tim was soon replaced by Reginald Hyde-White, who paid for Diana's London shopping spree. Afterward, Reggie professed his love for her, saying that "in the few hours since we met, you've become **everything** to me!" Diana bought the line and kissed him, but noted afterward that "as an Amazon princess—as **Wonder Woman**—I had perfect control of my emotions! As plain Diana Prince, I'm human—too **darn** human!" If Diana was still an Amazon she'd have been able to resist Reggie's advances and wouldn't have kissed him scant hours after meeting him, but as a normal human woman she was powerless to control herself.

Reggie was followed by Patrick McGuire, a pilot who assisted Diana and I Ching on their mission to China. Then came Ranagor, leader of the rebels in Chalandor. The next was Baron Anatole Karoli, an ambassador from Koronia whom Diana protected while he was visiting America. Last was Jonny Double, a private detective. Counting Steve, Diana was involved with seven different men in the

twenty-six issues of the mod era. And that's not including *World's Finest* #204, where Diana almost kissed Superman after he saved her from a group of armed goons.* By her own admission, Diana was fickle, as apparently all human women were supposed to be. It was as if she couldn't exist without the affection and attention of a man, and her reaction to betrayal demonstrated how important having a man was to her.

The closer Diana got to a man, the more likely it was he would turn out to be a villain. A few of the guys were nice, but it often ended horribly. Baron Kanoli was an assassin sent to kill the president, while Tim turned on Diana for a fortune in diamonds. Tim's shocking betrayal sent Diana into the arms of Reggie, but Reggie owed Dr. Cyber a substantial debt and had been working for her to capture Diana. A tearful Diana cried out, "You **lied** to me! You said you **loved** me!" and began to beat Reggie ferociously. I Ching had to pull her off because he was afraid she would cripple Reggie, to which she replied, "I **want** to hurt him . . . I want **him** to feel what **I'm** feeling!" Distraught, Diana ran off into the night as the issue ended.

The following issue began with narration that read, "Diana (**Wonder Woman**) Prince, hurt, bewildered, angry—no longer insulated (by her renounced super-powers) to shock and emotion, reacts violently! Not a **Wonder Woman**—but a heartbroken girl runs into the night." The panel showed a montage of Diana beating Reggie and fleeing the scene, ending with the heartbroken Diana exclaiming, "This being a **human HURTS!**" Reggie had only been in the series for one issue. In terms of the comic book's timeline, Diana had

---

*The issue included stirring dialogue, with Superman declaring, "Diana . . . in another second or so, I'll feel like kissing you—and we both know I **shouldn't!**" and Diana responding, "Right you are—darn it!" Superman always knows best. It's another Denny O'Neil issue, by the way, not to pick on the poor guy. Seriously, he's done a lot of excellent comic books. Just not any with Wonder Woman in them.

known Reggie for maybe twelve hours, yet she was so wounded by his betrayal that she was prepared to cripple him.

Diana's other significant relationship was with her martial arts master I Ching, and she was regularly shown to be inferior to her blind mentor. While brawling with villains in a ski lodge, Diana was impressed with her new martial arts skills, thinking, "**Karate . . . judo . . . kung-fu** . . . whatever I **need** . . . I've **got**! I'm as effective as a person **can** be . . . without **Amazon powers!**" However, observing her blind master she then thought, "Still, Ching fights **better** even though he's **sightless!**"

More important, I Ching always had far better judgment than Diana. When faced with the evil witch Morgana, Diana's first inclination was to fight, but her physical skills couldn't handle the metaphysical powers of her opponent. Throughout the battle, I Ching repeatedly attempted to get Diana's attention, saying, "Diana, wait—I can—" and "Diana—will you listen—" only to be interrupted by Diana again attacking Morgana. Finally Diana stopped and I Ching quickly disabled the witch with his own magical powers, saying, "I tried to tell you, Diana, I could have spared you all this trouble." I Ching even got top billing on the series' covers for a short while when for six issues the title read *The Incredible I-Ching! And . . . the New Wonder Woman.*

Acclaimed science fiction author Samuel Delany wrote the last two issues before Wonder Woman got her powers back, and he tried to inject the series with some modern feminist discussion in *Wonder Woman* #203. The cover declared "SPECIAL! Women's Lib Issue," and the story began with Diana's friend Cathy, all fired up from a women's lib meeting, attacking a group of men who were trying to hit on Diana. Later, one of those same men offered Diana a job as a spokeswoman for Grandee's department store, which she gladly accepted despite Mr. Grandee referring to her as "little girl" and "little lady" throughout their meeting. However, Cathy took issue with Diana accepting a job there because Grandee was underpaying his female employees. Diana defended Grandee by spouting this

random bit of legalese: "You can't pay less than minimum wages except in businesses not involving interstate commerce!" As everyone knows, the best way to teach kids about feminism is with long discussions about interstate commerce law.

When Cathy asked her to attend her women's lib group, Diana stated, "I'm for equal wages, too! But I'm **not** a **joiner**. I wouldn't **fit** with your group. In most cases, I don't even **like** women." An argument followed, culminating in an upset Cathy declaring, "Perhaps I'm incompetent and unsure, but I'm **conscious** of it and enraged at anyone who says I must **stay** that way!" and daring Diana to "walk away from my anger!" Diana couldn't, and the two went to Cathy's women's lib meeting. Grandee's goons soon burst into the meeting to rough up the women because they planned to take action against Grandee's unfair wages policy. The attack resulted in the city shutting down the store and Diana thinking, "Now I feel I've **really** accomplished something for women's image!" But then, a group of angry women came into the meeting and accused the group of taking 250 jobs away from women. The victory was tempered with the loss of jobs, and the story was never resolved, because the Amazon Wonder Woman returned in *Wonder Woman* #204.

Delany was clearly trying to present a nuanced, thoughtful look at the women's liberation movement that represented both its possibilities and its difficulties. His intentions were good, but the results were muddled. Superhero comic books don't do nuance well; they rely on good guys and bad guys and victory and defeat. The issue's ambiguous ending doesn't provide this at all, and Delany certainly could have benefited from having another issue to finish his story. As it is, the ending casts the story in a new light.

For the entire issue, our hero, Diana, was disinterested in and dismissive toward the women's liberation movement. Women's libber Cathy was rash and, by her own admission, incompetent. The discussion of the issues surrounding equal pay was technical and legalistic, and most readers likely glossed over it. Ultimately, Diana did side with the activists, only to have their actions questioned

because of the job loss that ensued, and Delany made clear that the upset women had a justifiable point.

The sum total of the issue was that Diana actively opposed women's lib and its impetuous supporters for most of the issue, and then discovered that it was as likely to harm women as help them. Delany's issue was the mod era's sole attempt to engage with the women's liberation movement, and it was not a success.

It's no wonder that Gloria Steinem and other feminists took issue with the mod Diana Prince and rallied for a return to her Amazon roots. Compared to her past incarnations, the rash and fickle Diana was a poor example of the power of women, and compared to her fellow female comic book characters she was very much behind the times.

Lois Lane

While sales of *Wonder Woman* slumped during the 1960s, *Superman's Girl Friend Lois Lane* was one of the industry's bestselling comic books. It sold more than 482,000 copies per issue, averaging an impressive fifth place for the decade. In April 1970, the series put out its hundredth issue, quite a feat for a series based on a secondary character.

Lois Lane was a huge success, on the newsstands and in her stories as well. In *Superman's Girl Friend Lois Lane* #80, we learned that Lois had won the Pulitzer Prize, journalism's highest award. However, while 1968 marked the beginning of a new era for Wonder Woman, for Lois it was just more of the same old. Superman continued to submit her to elaborate ruses to teach her lessons, and she still fell in love with every strong man who crossed her path. Nonetheless, there was a subtle shift in Lois's interactions with Superman, and she became increasingly displeased with his treatment of her. In one issue, she told Superman, "You've ignored me, hurt me, humiliated me **too many times!**" In another, she said, "You've had me on the string for **years**. Now I'm **calling off** this hot and cold

romance!!" Lois always came back to Superman in the end and the old formula remained intact, but cracks were beginning to form.

In 1970, instead of spending all of her time coming up with schemes to get Superman to marry her, Lois became interested in social issues, particularly race relations. In *Superman's Girl Friend Lois Lane* #106, Lois wanted to learn more about Metropolis' black community, Little Africa, but was called "whitey" and an enemy when she visited.* Undeterred, Lois used a machine to transform herself into a black woman so she could experience firsthand the racism and poor living conditions the community faced. Ultimately, Lois even became friends with Dave Stevens, an outspoken young black man who had shamed her into leaving when she first visited.

This racial theme continued a few issues later when Lois and Clark visited Santa Fe, New Mexico, where a group of local Pueblo Indians protested a new dam that would block off their sacred river and drown their land. Superman got permission to remove the dam, and Lois ended up adopting a newly orphaned Pueblo baby named Little Moon. When Lois returned to Metropolis, she became the object of slanderous gossip for raising a Native American child, but she defiantly responded to her critics, stating, "It's **you** who are **blind! My heart** and **Little Moon's** are the **same color!**"†

In the following issue, Lois advocated for Metropolis's Latino community, who told her, "Por dios, señorita! We all want to help make a better life for our families! But . . . unless we have day centers to care for our muchachos . . . children . . . we cannot go to work!" In *Superman's Girl Friend Lois Lane* #114, Lois stood up

---

*The title of this story was "I Am Curious (Black)!"—an obvious homage to director Vilgot Sjöman's Swedish art house film *I Am Curious (Yellow)*, which addressed social issues and included a brief interview with Dr. Martin Luther King Jr. The film was also fairly sexually explicit and was banned or protested in several American states after being labeled pornographic.
†In the end, the baby's father was found alive in a Viet Cong prison camp, and when he came home Lois returned Little Moon to him.

for women's rights, giving some tough talk to her black friend, Dave, when she said, "**You** don't want to be down-graded because you're **black! Don't** down-grade **us** because we're **women!**" Dave thought that was an excellent point, and the two worked together on improving conditions in Little Africa; the issue also included a two-page spread with biographies of notable black leaders.*

In April 1972, *Superman's Girl Friend Lois Lane* #121 marked the arrival of a new writer, Cary Bates, and a new editor, Dorothy Woolfolk.† In the previous issue, Lois's sister Lucy died tragically, leading Lois to reevaluate her life. Newly returned to Metropolis after six weeks of soul searching, Lois declared to Superman, "Now that my **sister's gone**, I'm going to live my life for her and me . . . to make up for her death by doing **twice** as much in my lifetime . . . and to do my best to help a world so tangled with problems it's **falling apart!**" When Superman asked what that meant for their relationship, Lois said, "Sorry, **Superman!** I'm no longer the girl you can come back to between missions! I can't live in your **shadow—**I've got things to do!"

Lois broke up with Superman and quit her job at the *Daily Planet* to become a freelance reporter and focus on the social justice stories that were important to her. This resulted in a big pay cut, so Lois moved out of her luxury apartment to share a more affordable place with three other women. All four of them worked together on Lois's dangerous assignments, fighting villains and uncovering

---

*There's a reason that people talk about *Green Lantern/Green Arrow* instead of *Superman's Girl Friend Lois Lane* in terms of race relations in the Bronze Age. The stories were somewhat hackneyed and contained racial stereotyping despite their attempt at a progressive message. It may not be surprising to learn that these four issues were written by Robert Kanigher. Still, this was a significant shift for the series that had Lois spending time on real-world problems instead of obsessing over marrying Superman.

†Dorothy Roubicek, *Wonder Woman*'s assistant editor during the Golden Age bondage situation, went on to marry William Woolfolk and return to DC Comics as a full editor.

stories. They called each other "sister" and refused to abandon Lois, no matter what precarious situations her reporting got them all into. Lois had become a strong and independent woman, and this time it stuck for more than an issue.

Lois dumping Superman was nothing new, but for the first time it was handled in an intelligent and thoughtful way. It was clear that Lois still loved Superman and that it was hard for her to end things with him, but that she had to do so because her relationship with Superman was holding her back. Superman's initial understanding response to the breakup soon wore off, and when Lois later restated her desire to do twice as much in her lifetime, Superman replied, "You're only being twice as **stupid!**" As he flew off, Lois called out, "Goodbye, **Superman!** And take your **super-male ego** with you!" Superman frequently tried to rekindle things with Lois, but she was adamant that nothing would happen unless his attitude toward her changed.

When Superman told Lois to be a good girl and stay out of trouble while she covered the Olympic Games, she thought, "Be a **good girl** . . . oooo! Sometimes he is so **conceited.**" In another issue, Superman tried to help out Lois and her roommates, but Lois brushed him off, saying, "I'm tired of your **super-interfering!** We girls are hardier than you think! Leave us alone!" Superman and Lois remained friends, but any hint of male chauvinism from Superman brought a strong response from Lois. She loved Superman, but she knew that so long as he didn't treat her, and other women, equally, they could never be together. It was a groundbreaking new direction for Lois, though short-lived; the book only lasted another seventeen issues before DC Comics rolled *Superman's Girl Friend Lois Lane* and several other titles into one new book, *The Superman Family*, in 1974.*

---

*The Lois Lane adventures in *The Superman Family* were mostly old reprints from *Superman's Girl Friend Lois Lane*, but occasionally there were new stories. The first of these involved Lois working alongside the S.I.A. (Secret Intelligence Agency) to track down a dangerous assassin, but within a few issues Lois was back to her old reporting job. Her romance with Superman was back as well, rekindled even before the *Superman Family* merger.

In *Superman's Girl Friend Lois Lane* #93, published in July 1969, Lois had actually met the mod Diana Prince. Fearing that Diana was trying to steal Superman from her, Lois learned karate and judo so she could fight Diana and win back Superman. In a dream sequence where she defeated Diana, Lois said, "I-I'm sorry, Diana! But **Superman's** my whole **life**! I-I had to beat you—so you would give him up!" This scenario represented the old Lois Lane in a nutshell: Superman was her world, and she would do anything, however ridiculous, not to lose him.

The new Lois didn't need a man at all. While Diana's entire life was dictated by her desire to avenge Steve and she flitted from man to man, Lois did what Diana couldn't. She realized that wrapping up her self-worth and her life's meaning in a man who didn't treat her well just wasn't worth it, no matter how much she loved him.

Batgirl

The name "Batgirl" suggests a very subordinate, sidekick role. Her symbol was borrowed from a male hero, and she was called "girl" while he was called "man." You'd expect her to be a female Robin or, even worse, another poor Supergirl, but Batgirl was the most independent and self-reliant female character in DC Comics at the dawn of the Bronze Age. Batgirl first appeared in *Detective Comics* #359 in January 1967, created by Gardner Fox and Carmine Infantino.* There had been a Bat-Girl in the 1950s, Bette Kane, but this Batgirl was an entirely new character.

Her real name was Barbara Gordon, and she was the daughter of Commissioner James Gordon, Gotham City's head of police. Even without her crime fighting, Barbara was an impressive character. She had a PhD from Gotham State University, where she graduated

---

*While it's commonly believed that Batgirl was brought into the comic books because of the popularity of Yvonne Craig's Batgirl on the *Batman* TV show, her comic book debut actually predated her television debut.

summa cum laude, had a brown belt in judo, and was the head librarian at the Gotham City Public Library. With her old-fashioned reading glasses and her double bun hairdo, Barbara said, "Everybody thinks of me as a 'Plain Jane'—a colorless female brain." Well aware of the image she projected as a librarian, she used her demure appearance and position as cover for her adventures as a vigilante. Barbara also made the most of her library job by using its contents to research crime-fighting techniques and solve cases.

Although she was inspired by Batman and borrowed his name, Batgirl didn't rely on Batman for anything. She made her own costume and got her own supplies, all without the benefit of Bruce Wayne's vast fortune. Furthermore, she was no sidekick; she worked independent of the Dynamic Duo, crossing their paths only when their cases coincided. This independence might have been due to the fact that Batman and Robin didn't exactly take a shine to Batgirl right away.

In her first appearance, both Batgirl and the Dynamic Duo separately attempted to track down the villain Killer Moth. Unbeknownst to Batgirl, Batman had set a trap for Killer Moth, which Batgirl inadvertently stumbled upon. As Batgirl fought Killer Moth and his goons, a hiding Robin declared, "Holy interference! She's ruining all our plans!" To which Batman replied, "We can't let **Batgirl** fight our battles now, can we?" Batman and Robin jumped out of hiding to join the fight, but in the chaos Killer Moth escaped. Batgirl chastised Batman for interfering with her work, but Batman angrily retorted, "No, **Batgirl! We** didn't spoil anything . . . **you did!!**" When she asked to help them track down Killer Moth, Batman said, "No, **Batgirl!** This is a case for **Batman** and **Robin!** I'm sorry—but you must understand that we can't worry ourselves about a girl." Robin echoed Batman's opinion on female crime fighters in a later issue; when Batgirl wasn't at the scene of a robbery, Robin declared, "That suits me fine! Nabbing crooks is **man's** work!"

Batgirl eventually won Batman and Robin over by proving herself to be a smart and capable crime fighter. After Batgirl nabbed

Killer Moth when Batman couldn't, the trio of vigilantes delivered him to police headquarters and Batman said of Batgirl, "I'll welcome her aid, Commissioner Gordon—when and where the occasion arises! From what I've seen, she doesn't have to take a backseat to anybody!" The commissioner was even more impressed and, not knowing his daughter was actually Batgirl, told Barbara that "**Batgirl** sure is tops in my book!"

Not only was Batgirl strong, independent, and well educated, she also addressed and flipped stereotypical female traits head-on. In a story entitled "Batman's Marriage Trap," the women of Gotham City decided Batman should get married and formed a protest group called the W.E.B., Women to End BATchelorhood. Batgirl quickly joined, carrying a sign that read "Batman Unfair to Gotham Girls" amidst similar signs of "Pair Power!" and "Down with Singles!" Although Batgirl looked like a Silver Age marriage junkie, she'd actually infiltrated the organization to root out the mob agent who was using the W.E.B. to try to take out Batman. Batgirl's marriage enthusiasm was an elaborate ruse so she could save the day.

In another issue, Batgirl dealt with vanity and personal appearance. While chasing bank robbers, Batgirl noticed that her mask was crooked and stopped to adjust it, and this pause almost allowed the criminals to escape. Frustrated with herself, she said, "My vanity betrayed me!" and later clarified that "It wasn't personal vanity that made me adjust my headgear—it was an instinctive female reaction!" Batgirl saw her femininity as a weakness but was determined to turn it into a strength. Later, she pretended to stop chasing criminals to fix a run in her stocking, showing off her leg to distract them. As the lawbreakers stared, whistled, and called out, "What a pair of gams!" Batgirl and the Dynamic Duo capitalized on their distraction and apprehended them. While the idea of vanity as an instinctive female trait wasn't particularly enlightened, this clumsy beginning took an intriguing turn as it became a crime-fighting aid.

Batgirl starred in her own semiregular backup feature in *Detective Comics*, which became permanent in June 1970; she appeared

in every issue of the series for the next two years. Having a separate feature further established Batgirl as her own hero. Although the Dynamic Duo occasionally appeared, Batgirl was the undisputed star of the stories, developing her own cast of characters while investigating her own cases. She was popular elsewhere in the DC Comics universe as well, guest-starring in series such as *Adventure Comics*, *Justice League of America*, *Superman*, and *World's Finest*.

Her backup feature only ran regularly for two years but it ended on a high note, with Barbara Gordon's election to the US House of Representatives. Commissioner Gordon was asked to run for Congress but didn't really want the job, while Batgirl was increasingly frustrated with the limits of vigilantism. She revealed her secret identity to her father and asked to run in his stead, asserting, "It's the **only** way I can really fight crime—**prevent** it—through **prison reform! Legislation—law** that creates **order** . . . not **disorder!**"

Barbara took her campaign to the streets of Gotham, holding rallies and calling for change in Washington. In one impassioned speech, she asked, "Will **they** clean up the slums? Create new jobs . . . ? Stop dope-traffic . . . ? I say they **won't!** I say—**boot the rascals out—elect me!**" She became known as "Babs the Boot" and ultimately won the election by inspiring massive turnout from young voters. Her vigilante adventures in *Detective Comics* ended, but Congresswoman Barbara Gordon soon starred in *The Batman Family*, where she was glad to set aside her legislative duties and dig out her Batgirl costume if the need arose.*

Before she even became Batgirl, Barbara Gordon was more impressive than Diana Prince. She earned her doctorate with highest honors, ran the library system of one of the biggest cities in America,

---

The Batman Family was published from 1975 to 1978, when it was merged with *Detective Comics*. Barbara Gordon remained a congresswoman until 1980, when she lost her bid for reelection. She returned to Gotham City and became a member of the Humanities Research and Development Center, where she led the social services department.

and was a judo expert on the side. Diana Prince beat people up and very occasionally ran a small clothing boutique. Once Barbara became Batgirl, she quickly became the equal of her peers, while Diana was regularly shown to be inferior. Batgirl flipped traditional stereotypes, while Diana embodied them.

Much like Diana, Barbara was also the victim of betrayal. She sponsored the rehabilitation and parole of a criminal she'd locked up as Batgirl, only to have him turn around and steal valuable books from the library. Barbara was livid, but instead of trying to cripple him and get vengeance, this betrayal made her decide to run for Congress and attempt to reform the prison system. Betrayal brought out the worst in Diana and only added to her quest for personal revenge, but for Barbara it created a desire to work for the betterment of society as a whole. Barbara was a modern, empowered woman, capable of achieving anything she set her mind to. She was exactly what a superpowerless Wonder Woman should have been.

Emerald Empress

The Legion of Super-Heroes was a club of teenage superheroes from the thirtieth century. Created in 1958, the Legion was made up of teens from a variety of planets with a wide range of superpowers, including a time-traveling Superboy.* The Legion first encountered the group that would become their chief villains, the Fatal Five, in *Adventure Comics* #352 in January 1967. This group of nefarious criminals included Mano, who used his antimatter touch to destroy his home planet; the Persuader, whose atomic axe could cut through almost anything; Tharok, a powerful cyborg; Validus, a dull-witted giant easily controlled by his teammates; and the fiendish Emerald Empress.

---

*The team wasn't only diverse in terms of planet of origin, but in gender too; Lightning Lad, Cosmic Boy, and Brainiac 5 fought alongside Saturn Girl, Shrinking Violet, and Phantom Girl.

Her real name was Sarya, and she came from the planet Venegar, the former home of the ancient Ekron civilization. Sarya found the Emerald Eye of Ekron, an ancient object of near limitless power, and took over her home planet in a matter of hours, becoming the Emerald Empress of Venegar. When her people revolted, she left her home world to raise an army to someday return and again subjugate the planet. The Legion's database called Emerald Empress "the most wanted female criminal in the history of the universe! She is guilty of every crime from murder to space-piracy!"

Facing the threat of a Sun-Eater and lacking the firepower to stop it, the Legion assembled the Fatal Five to help them save the galaxy and offered them pardons in exchange for their help. They did stop the Sun-Eater, but afterward the Fatal Five decided to join forces and try to conquer the galaxy. The Emerald Empress was a key part of this team of supervillains and was often the most capable member of the group.

Tharok's cyborg brain gave him superintelligence, and so he led the team and controlled the mighty Validus, but the Empress was clearly second in command. She was also vitally important to the team because the Emerald Eye teleported the Fatal Five wherever they needed to go, allowing them to get the jump on the Legion or escape them. While her teammates regularly clashed, the Empress was the most reasonable member of the team and did her best to keep her hot-headed associates focused on fighting the Legion instead of each other.

Quarreling with the Emerald Empress rarely went well for her teammates. When Mano suggested that he and the Empress join together and ditch the rest of the Fatal Five, she rejected his offer. An angry Mano tried to attack her with his antimatter touch, but the Empress used the Emerald Eye to bind him in energy handcuffs. Mano scoffed at the restraints, declaring that he would burn through them in seconds, but before he could do so the Empress blasted him out of the room, ending their discussion. Similarly, when the Persuader and Mano were arguing over who was more powerful, the

Empress separated the two with large energy bonds and incapacitated them so their fighting wouldn't destroy the ship.

When battling the Legion, the Emerald Empress was as capable a warrior as her teammates, if not more so. One blow from the Persuader's atomic axe, one touch from Mano's antimatter hand, or one punch from Validus would mean certain death, making those three (and, by extension, Validus's controller Tharok) generally useless in combat. The crafty Legionnaires deftly avoided each villain's sole dangerous move, leaving them ineffective, while the Empress had a whole array of possible attacks with her Emerald Eye.

In a fight scene in *Superboy and the Legion of Super-Heroes* #231, Shadow Lass kicked Mano and Colossal Boy punched Validus, while the Persuader was just swinging at air against Mon-El and Ultra Boy, but the Empress handled Brainiac 5, Element Lad, and Sun Boy with ease. The Empress was also especially good at fighting the Legion's most powerful member, Superboy. She hammered the Boy of Steel with her energy blasts and in one issue encased him in a force field that put him in a state of suspended animation. Aware of his one weakness, the Empress wisely carried around a piece of Kryptonite; her ultimate plan was to control Superboy with the Kryptonite and use him to reconquer Venegar. The Empress may have lacked the death blow powers of the rest of the Fatal Five, but her many abilities made her a more effective fighter than anyone else on the team.

What's most striking about the Emerald Empress is that her portrayal had nothing at all to do with her being a woman. Female villains tended to use their sexuality against their opponents, be betrayed by some sort of inherent compassion, or use villainy only as a way to try and marry the hero. The Empress did none of this. Her only concern was power. She gained amazing powers with the Emerald Eye, took power on her home planet in a swift coup, and saw her union with the Fatal Five as a means to regain power over Venegar and then the entire galaxy.

Using her sexuality was unnecessary because she had such immense strength at her disposal. Compassion or emotion never

came into play either; she was completely ruthless and focused. In fact, her teammates were far more emotional than she: Validus was a cauldron of rage, while the Persuader and Mano were constantly angry and often lost sight of the mission at hand because of it. Only Tharok was as even-keeled as the Empress, and he was half-robot. The Empress was strong, rational, and cunning and lacked any of the stereotypes associated with female characters. At her core, the Emerald Empress was first and foremost a villain, and everything else was secondary. Being a woman didn't define her; it didn't even come into play.

For Diana Prince, her gender was at the heart of the character. Everything about Diana was rooted in an attempt to make her a modern, normal woman. This was Diana's defining quality, to such an extent that she didn't actually have a personality, particularly in the early issues of the mod era. The story wasn't ruled by the author considering what Diana would do, but rather by an attempt to depict a character who acted as a male author thought a woman would: loving clothes, falling in love, and being emotional. The result was one-dimensional; Diana was a combination of stereotypical female reactions and feelings instead of an actual, fleshed-out character. There was no Diana the person, just Diana the generic woman.

Lagging Behind the Times

Despite the best of intentions, the mod Diana Prince paled in comparison to her fellow female characters. Once ahead of her time, the times had left her behind. The idea of stripping the genre's strongest, oldest, and most famous female character of her superpowers ran contrary to the contemporary movement toward female empowerment. Diana engaged in all of the stereotypes and clichés that other female characters had escaped and real-world women denounced. Ultimately, it was so bad that the depowered Wonder Woman resulted in feminists leading a campaign for a return to the feminist heights of the Golden Age.

Restoration and Re-creation

The novelty of a new Wonder Woman initially gave the series a slight sales bump, but the book soon returned to its unimpressive numbers. O'Neil and Sekowsky's attempted portrayal of a modern woman didn't go over well, particularly with modern women. Chief among those disappointed with the comic was Gloria Steinem, a writer and political activist who had become the face of feminism in America. She had been a fan of Wonder Woman as a child and wanted her to return to her Amazon roots. Steinem was also friends with DC Comics' owner Steve Ross, and occasionally stopped by the DC offices in New York City. She lobbied for the old Wonder Woman to return, and DC soon announced that the mod era would end with January 1973's *Wonder Woman* #204; Diana Prince would be Wonder Woman again. Pleased by the news, Steinem splashed the return of Wonder Woman across her new project.

The women's liberation movement was growing rapidly, and Steinem wanted to introduce its ideas and values to a mainstream audience, so she and her associates launched *Ms.* magazine in 1972. Most women's magazines at the time were of the *Ladies Home Journal* and *Good Housekeeping* variety, focused on recipes and

197

cleaning products and how to keep a proper home. *Ms.* was an alternative to these magazines and discussed women's issues, politics, and the feminist lifestyle. It was an instant success, and when the first issue hit the newsstands in July 1972, Wonder Woman was on the cover.

She was a giant, striding forward, with half of her body in an average American street on the left and the other half in a Vietnam War scene on the right. The image suggested that Wonder Woman could be a force for good in both worlds; in one hand, she rescued a group of buildings with her golden lasso, and with her other hand she swatted a fighter plane out of the sky. A sign in the town read "Peace and Justice in '72" while the magazine's headline declared "Wonder Woman for President." The issue included an article by Joanne Edgar about the history of Wonder Woman that ended with the news that she would soon return to her Amazon roots. They also reprinted a few pages from William Moulton Marston and H. G. Peter's first Wonder Woman story from *All Star Comics* #8.

Ms. also had a book-publishing division, which put together a collection that reprinted twelve Golden Age Wonder Woman stories.* The book was prefaced by an article on the history of the Amazons by Phyllis Chesler and a lengthy introduction by Steinem. The comics were divided into four sections: "Origins," "Sisterhood," "Politics," and "Romance," and Steinem provided a brief introduction for each as well.

After years of decline and increasing irrelevance, Wonder Woman teamed up with the women's liberation movement to restore the character to her former glory. The editors at *Ms.* were fans of the original Wonder Woman and saw her as a feminist icon. Edgar wrote that she hoped the new direction for the series would "return our heroine to the feminism of her birth," and Steinem echoed these sentiments,

---

*It was simply titled *Wonder Woman* but will here be referred to as the *Ms. Wonder Woman* book to avoid confusion with the comics series.

writing that she wanted to see "the feminism and strength of the original Wonder Woman—*my* Wonder Woman—restored."

However, when the women at *Ms.* talk about "the feminism of her birth," they're referring to the Marston era. His feminism was complicated, filled with contradictions and some troubling fixations. With their celebration of the original Wonder Woman, Steinem and her friends glossed over the more problematic bits of the character and focused on the areas that reflected their own modern feminist beliefs. Their depiction of Wonder Woman restored parts of the original, but ultimately they re-created Wonder Woman in their own image for a new generation.

The Liberal Feminism of *Ms.* Magazine

Ms. magazine has rightly been called "the most widely recognized publication of liberal feminism." At the core of feminism is the idea that women deserve the same social and political rights and privileges as men, but the women's liberation movement grew rapidly and branched off in innumerable directions. "Liberal feminism" is a term that described a wide range of these many branches. Words like "liberal" can be tricky because yesterday's "radical" is today's "liberal" is tomorrow's "conservative" as more and more radical voices emerge. It's a term with shifting meanings. But for the early 1970s, "liberal feminism" is a good description for Steinem and *Ms.* magazine, especially in contrast with more radical feminist beliefs.*

Many radical groups thought that patriarchy was so pervasive that every aspect of society was rooted in male dominance, and so they'd have to tear it all down to accomplish anything for women.

---

*"Radical" is just as shifty a term as "liberal," and the two make up a bit of a false dichotomy. There are many books about feminism cited in the bibliography, so please consult those for more information on the wider array of feminism.

Working with the government or participating in things like marriage and traditional child rearing was seen as colluding with the enemy. Instead, radical feminists banded together to come up with ways to fix society on their own.*

Some thought that marriage was a way to keep women down and that traditional romantic love was just a fantasy; some decided that lesbianism was the way to go. Others looked to science and hoped that artificial reproduction could free women from the shackles of the nuclear family and domesticity and maybe even eliminate the need for men altogether. Whatever the specifics of the plan, the overarching theme among radical feminists was that society was rigged against women and that true liberation could only come from escaping the existing structures. It wasn't women who needed to change, but the world as a whole.

Liberal feminists were not as extreme. Rather than replacing oppressive societal structures, they tried to work within existing systems to improve the lives of women. One of the first groups to come out of the women's liberation movement was the National Organization for Women (NOW) in 1966. NOW's Statement of Purpose, written by Betty Friedan, declared: "The purpose of NOW is to take action to bring women into full participation in the mainstream of American society now, exercising all the privileges and responsibilities thereof in truly equal partnership with men." The Equal Rights Amendment was of paramount importance to NOW and liberal feminists, and notable leaders including Friedan and Steinem appeared before Congress to support it. Equality was the ultimate aim, and both Friedan and Steinem led a march through New York City in 1970 as part of the Women's Strike for Equality.

---

*"Banded together" actually meant "banded together for a little while until someone got angry and formed their own splinter group." Radically changing society was a complicated job, and it led to many heated debates and divisions. This constant splintering may be part of the reason that the patriarchy has yet to be overthrown.

Alongside their legislative efforts, liberal feminists focused on self-improvement. Mary Peacock, an editor at *Ms.* from 1972 to 1977, said that the magazine's version of feminism was based on "self-esteem and independence." "How-to" articles dominated the magazine, based on the editors' belief that their average reader wanted to take more control of her life by doing things for herself. Women's health issues were a common topic, most notably sexual health; there were articles with information concerning birth control, abortion, and the value of owning one's own speculum. There were also practical home repair tips in the regular "Populist Mechanics" column, as well as detailed instructions about how to start a women's caucus in the workplace or a feminist group in your home.

Instead of looking outward at the problems of patriarchy and wanting to tear down the system, *Ms.* advocated looking inward to improve oneself. There was a critique of patriarchy inherent in this approach: the implied message was that it was more beneficial for a woman to be independent and take care of herself than to rely on a man.

Self-improvement was a substantial task, and it required some inspiration. The sisterhood of the women's liberation movement offered support and encouragement, but there was another aspect of liberal feminism that many women found empowering. This hope for a new, more equal future was actually rooted in a powerful past.

Originary Matriarchy

A major difference between radical and liberal feminism was their preferred historical text. The radicals tended to favor Simone de Beauvoir's *The Second Sex*, first published in 1949. De Beauvoir famously wrote that woman

> is defined and differentiated with reference to man and not he with reference to her; she is the incidental, the inessential as opposed to the essential. He is the Subject, he is the Absolute— she is the Other.

This is why radical feminists were so leery of existing social structures. The entire history of the world was rooted in the idea of men as the default, and thus everything was stacked against women.

Liberal feminists didn't hate *The Second Sex* by any means. It was a classic, and it well described the current predicament of women in society. For the origins of humanity, though, many liberal feminists turned to Elizabeth Gould Davis's *The First Sex*, which was first published in 1971. Clearly a response to de Beauvoir, Davis argued that male domination hadn't always been the default. Instead, matriarchy was the original state of humanity and patriarchy later took over. The theory is known as originary matriarchy, and it quickly became popular.

The First Sex started at the beginning of our existence and argued that humanity was first female, not just figuratively but literally. The first human beings were women who reproduced through parthenogenesis, a form of asexual reproduction where an egg doesn't need to be fertilized by an outside source. Parthenogenesis occurs in several plant species as well as a few types of insects, lizards, and other creatures. It's never been observed naturally in any sort of mammal, much less in humans, but accuracy wasn't at the core of *The First Sex*. Davis also wrote that "the first males were mutants, freaks produced by some damage to the genes caused perhaps by disease or a radiation bombardment from the sun. Maleness remains a recessive genetic trait like color-blindness and hemophilia."

Matriarchies ruled human society after the males arrived. Davis cited worship of a Great Goddess as evidence of these matriarchies, as well as snippets of myths and histories of early civilizations. However, matriarchy was later overthrown when men, resenting their inferior role, took over and suppressed women. This marked the shift from "the previous age of peace and non-violence to the barbarism of the patriarchal age." Female deities became male, and history was rewritten to remove any evidence of female rule. Thus, only these snippets remained to allow Davis to formulate her theories.

Similar theories predated *The First Sex*, and two historians are particularly key figures. The first was Helen Diner, the English pseudonym of Austrian author Bertha Eckstein-Diener. Diner began her book *Mothers and Amazons* with the declaration that "in the beginning, there was woman"; she argued for parthenogenesis as well. The second was J. J. Bachofen, a student of mythology and ancient history who argued that matriarchy was the most important cultural stage of every society. The maternal values of matriarchy, or what he called "mother right," led to order, religion, and morality, creating a strong foundation for these societies before men took over.

Ever since these theories first appeared, historians, biologists, and all manner of other educated experts, male and female, have pointed out the many inaccuracies behind originary matriarchy and *The First Sex* specifically. There are sporadic instances of female-led societies in human history, but the idea of some universal matriarchy at the dawn of all things just doesn't hold up, nor do Davis's biological ideas. Nonetheless, Davis was very popular. Women could now view themselves as more than an oppressed Other; they were the inheritors of the original, utopian state of humanity.

Some of the principal proponents of Davis and originary matriarchy could be found in the offices of *Ms.* magazine. When Davis died in 1974, *Ms.* ran an obituary that glowingly praised her work. Rhoda Lerman summarized Davis's core arguments and declared, "The true history of woman was rewritten in *The First Sex*." Also, *The First Sex* regularly appeared on suggested feminist reading lists compiled by *Ms.* magazine.

In a 1973 issue, *Ms.* published Jane Alpert's manifesto "Mother Right: A New Feminist Theory" with an introduction by Steinem. Alpert referenced Bachofen with her title, and she discussed originary matriarchy at length in the article. Like Bachofen, Alpert believed that the maternal nature of women was the power behind past matriarchies, and the power that feminists should harness now. The article was controversial. Many feminists criticized Alpert for

reaffirming the qualities that the patriarchy used to limit women, i.e., the loving, motherly role, a role that often kept them in the home and out of the workplace. Steinem and *Ms.* stood by Alpert, taking a lot of heat for doing so.

Part of this outrage came from some issues with Alpert herself, who had a rather checkered past, but a lot of it came from a growing stance against anything that referenced originary matriarchy.* Many radical feminist groups thought that a past matriarchal age was pure fantasy and that by rooting women's liberation in some sort of fairy tale, the real-world potential of the movement became nonexistent. Despite these criticisms, originary matriarchy remained a popular theme among Steinem and her cohorts.

It's ironic that the camp that believed in past matriarchies was the camp that was least interested in directly overthrowing the patriarchy and instituting female rule. Originary matriarchy implies a sort of superiority for women, but equality was the watchword of *Ms.* and liberal feminism. Rather than looking to their matriarchal past as a blueprint for the future, they saw it as a source of inspiration to restore dignity and pride to womanhood. Rediscovering their history was empowering; it told women of an inherited strength and nobility that they didn't know they had. It also reinforced the importance of sisterhood by showing that women who worked together could achieve great things. All of this came together in *Ms.* magazine's adoption of Wonder Woman as a feminist mascot.

The Amazon Connection

While there were massive divisions and differences among the many branches of feminism in the 1970s, there was one thing everyone

---

*Alpert was involved with some radical leftists, including the Weather Underground, and conspired in the bombings of several federal buildings. In fact, she was on the lam when she wrote this piece for *Ms.* magazine, sending it unsolicited and with a copy of her fingerprints to prove her identity.

agreed on: they all loved the Amazons. For instance, Ti-Grace Atkinson, a radical feminist and the founder of the creatively named group the Feminists, called her 1974 collection of essays *Amazon Odyssey*. Jill Johnston, a sort of flower child/lesbian feminist and author of *Lesbian Nation: The Feminist Solution*, titled one of the book's chapters "Amazons and Archedykes." Amazons were everywhere in the women's liberation movement, and nowhere were they more popular than among the advocates of originary matriarchy.

If you believed in past matriarchies, clearly the Amazons would have been of great interest to you. And if you were keen on the Amazons, then Wonder Woman would most definitely be your kind of heroine. When Steinem and her friends adopted Wonder Woman as a feminist mascot, they merged her Amazon heritage with the theories of originary matriarchy to make her a representative of womankind's lost past. Steinem wrote that Wonder Woman was "just one small, isolated outcropping of a larger human memory. And the girl children who love her are responding to one small echo of dreams and capabilities in their own forgotten past."

Chesler was even more thorough than Steinem. Her essay in the *Ms. Wonder Woman* book was called "The Amazon Legacy" and addressed the universal reach of originary matriarchy. It began with an imagined meeting between herself, Diner, and Bachofen.* All three were in conversation with an incredulous fictional interviewer, who stated that the Amazons were merely myths. Chesler, Diner, and Bachofen disagreed, saying that the myths were more than mere stories and that women once ruled the world.

In her original work, Diner saw the ancient Greek wars with the Amazons as a pivotal turning point in history, casting it as a battle over whether patriarchy or matriarchy would shape European society. Bachofen believed that the extremism of the Amazon culture

---

*Diner and Bachofen were both long dead by 1972, so although the conversation wasn't described as fictional in the book, it couldn't have been real.

was "a step forward to a purer form of life" and that warrior women were an important part of all developing matriarchies.

For Chesler, it wasn't just the Amazons of Greek myth that were important but the concept of Amazonism generally. The takeover and suppression of matriarchies by patriarchal forces was a universal occurrence, and there were Amazons of all types now long forgotten across the world. Turning to Marston's Wonder Woman, Chesler found that "many genuine Amazon and matriarchal themes are portrayed," making Wonder Woman the heiress of this matriarchal past. She even read Hippolyte sculpting baby Diana out of clay as a form of parthenogenesis. Chesler hit all of the originary matriarchy bases with her essay.*

Steinem and her friends made the connection between Wonder Woman and originary matriarchy very explicit, and others picked up on this theme. A letter in *Wonder Woman* #212, eight issues into the restored Amazon Wonder Woman era, read, "*Wonder Woman* is an important symbol to me, since we contemporary women are now beginning to realize our great matriarchal Amazonian heritage." Originary matriarchy seeped through all of these discussions of Wonder Woman, and it explains why Steinem and her cohorts were so drawn to her and keen for her to return to her Amazon roots. Wonder Woman was more than just a character they liked when they were children; she was a symbol of the lost power of women they were trying to restore. Not surprisingly, their feminist values had an influence on how they read the early adventures of Wonder Woman.

Revising Wonder Woman

As a young girl, Steinem had loved the heroism and humanity of Wonder Woman; she wrote, "her creator had also seen straight

---

*As problematic as these theories are, this is a well-written piece. Chesler makes a very interesting, although ultimately fruitless, case for originary matriarchy.

into my heart and understood the secret fears of violence hidden there." William Moulton Marston's aim for the series hit home with Steinem, and she wrote glowingly of his creation of a superhero who relied on love more often than force. However, despite the celebration of Marston's Wonder Woman that prefaced the *Ms. Wonder Woman* book, less than half of the stories were actually written by Marston.

Of the twelve stories in the *Ms. Wonder Woman* book, only five were Marston's. There were four by Robert Kanigher, two by Joye Murchison, and one that was credited to H. G. Peter.* This mistake certainly isn't the fault of Steinem or anyone associated with the book. All of the comics said "By Charles Moulton" and were from the 1940s, and in 1972 they didn't have access to the records we have now. In fact, Steinem probably would've been delighted to know that a woman wrote two of the stories in the book. Regardless, the lack of Marston is the least of the *Ms. Wonder Woman* book's issues.

Although Steinem wrote that she wanted to see the "the feminism and strength of the original Wonder Woman" restored when the mod era ended, the portrait of Wonder Woman that emerged from the *Ms. Wonder Woman* book was noticeably different from the Golden Age Wonder Woman. While looking back at the early stories, Steinem and her friends didn't see Marston's complicated feminism. Instead, they saw Wonder Woman through their own feminist lens, focusing on the aspects of the character that reflected their modern values and downplaying the aspects that didn't. The

---

*It seems unlikely to me that Peter wrote a story, but that's what the Grand Comics Database says. The story is from *Sensation Comics* #81 in September 1948, which is a bit of a gray area—after Marston's death but before Kanigher officially took over. Kanigher seems the most likely author, and it could also be a posthumous Marston script. The GCD credits Peter with a few other writing gigs in the 1940s, but with question marks, so I'm incredulous about Peter's supposed writing career.

result was a new take on Wonder Woman with a decidedly liberal feminist bent.

This kind of revision was common among believers in originary matriarchy. Discussing the liberal feminist focus on past matriarchies, Joanne H. Wright states that this past offered "a glorified image of woman on which a new identity could be based." She continues:

> The new identity being forged has little to do with past matriarchy, but is rather a construction, one which is then read back into the past and sanctified for the future.

In the few snippets of myths and ancient history that referred to female rule, liberal feminists built a history of universal matriarchy that reflected, and in turn legitimized, their own values. The details of the actual past were revised or, as Wright says, sanctified to allow the modern values to shine through.

Steinem and her friends did the same with Wonder Woman. They transferred their own values onto the original Wonder Woman stories, creating a historic icon that reflected their own beliefs instead of accurately depicting her original feminism. They were interested in the similarities between Wonder Woman and themselves, not the differences. As such, their image of the Golden Age Wonder Woman was based on selective readings and, at times, inaccurate discussions of the character's history.

One of the ways the original Wonder Woman was reconciled with modern values was by downplaying parts of the comics that a modern audience might find offensive. Coming on the heels of the civil rights movement, the women's liberation movement was very concerned with racism. Like most comic books in the 1940s, *Wonder Woman* often portrayed nonwhite characters in stereotypical and racist ways. Case in point: the sinister Japanese soldiers Wonder Woman regularly faced, with their savage appearance and exaggerated dialogue, like: "So the gr-reat **Wonder Woman** is-ss pris-soner at las-st! Will be pleas-sure to s-see you die s-sslowly!"

Steinem and Edgar both addressed the problem, with Edgar mentioning "the distorted and villainized Nazis and Japanese" and Steinem discussing "highly jingoistic and even racist overtones." However, this was quickly tempered with excuses. Steinem put the blame on the artist, writing that "Wonder Woman's artists sometimes fell victim to the patriotic atmosphere of World War II." After discussing the problematic art of these stories, Steinem began the next paragraph by stating that "compared to the other comic book characters of the period, however, Wonder Woman is still a relief." While they acknowledged the problems, the immediate downplaying swiftly brushed them aside as inconsequential.

It was a similar situation with Wonder Woman's nationalism and participation in the war effort. With America in the midst of the wildly unpopular Vietnam War, peace and nonviolent conflict resolution were prevalent trends. Again, Steinem acknowledged Wonder Woman's involvement in the war, writing that "some of the Wonder Woman stories preach patriotism in a false way," and that these stories contained "superpatriotism." However, she downplayed these problems by arguing that "much of the blame rests with history" and "a nation mobilized for war is not a nation prepared to accept criticism."

However, Wonder Woman fought in World War II more than any other DC Comics superhero, both on the front lines as Wonder Woman and in the defense department as Diana Prince. Many in the 1970s were upset about a war in Vietnam to depose a leader with anti-American beliefs, but Wonder Woman did that often in the 1940s. She regularly ousted local leaders across the globe who worked with the enemy or promoted un-American ideals, replacing them with American-style democracies and leaders who supported the Allies. The Golden Age Wonder Woman was more than patriotic; she was a bona fide agent for the American military, fighting its wars and spreading its values.

After running through the potentially problematic aspects of Marston's Wonder Woman, Steinem wrote that "all these doubts

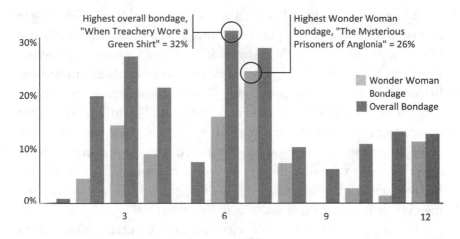

Highest overall bondage, "When Treachery Wore a Green Shirt" = 32%

Highest Wonder Woman bondage, "The Mysterious Prisoners of Anglonia" = 26%

Wonder Woman Bondage

Overall Bondage

paled beside the relief, the sweet vengeance, the toe-wriggling pleasure of reading about a woman who was strong, beautiful, courageous, and a fighter for social justice." Troublesome aspects of the past could be downplayed because there were so many better things to talk about. To be fair, the degree of racism in early Wonder Woman comics is debatable and her superpatriotism, however prevalent, really wasn't the main point of the character. However, this tendency to dismiss parts of Wonder Woman's past put Steinem and her friends on a slippery slope to missing Marston's message entirely.

Racism and superpatriotism were at least mentioned before being downplayed, but there was no discussion of bondage in any of the celebratory Wonder Woman articles, despite the fact that there was a fair bit of bondage in the *Ms. Wonder Woman* book. Overall, 15 percent of the panels in the book had bondage imagery. The chart above also shows some impressive individual numbers, with someone tied up in 32 percent of the panels in "When Treachery Wore a Green Shirt" and Wonder Woman herself tied up for 26 percent of "The Mysterious Prisoners of Anglonia."

The *Ms. Wonder Woman* book well represents Marston's use of bondage, ranging from the fun binding games of Paradise Island with Wonder Woman tied to a pole to the brutality of Dr. Psycho

ripping the soul from her body and chaining it to a wall.* Even though they didn't directly address bondage, Steinem and her group nonetheless showcased it, but omitting bondage from their discussion led to ignoring submission as well. The heart of Marston's feminist theories, submission was the thread that connected nearly everything he ever wrote. He was an advocate of the loving authority of women and the world peace that it would bring, but no one mentioned submission, DISC theory, or his utopian vision of the future.

This omission may have been intentional. Both Steinem and Edgar quote Marston's distaste for the "blood-curdling masculinity" of other superhero comics, a line from an article he wrote for the *American Scholar*. In the next paragraph of that very article, Marston talked about the appeal that a strong heroine had for boys, writing, "Give them an alluring woman stronger than themselves to submit to and they'll be *proud* to become her slaves!" Neither Steinem nor Edgar brought up that bit.

Having left out bondage and submission, there was no groundwork laid for Marston's message of female superiority. Steinem saw traces of such a message but was unsure about it. She wrote that "females were sometimes romanticized as biologically and unchangeably superior" and that the comics "hint that women are biologically, and therefore immutably, superior to men," but "sometimes" and "hints" are hardly strong terms. Ultimately, Steinem asked incredulously, "Is the reader supposed to conclude women are superior?"

---

*Amusingly, some of the most well-known Wonder Woman bondage images come from the *Ms. Wonder Woman* book. Until the late 1990s, when the Archive editions started to come out, the only way to read Marston's stories was in expensive back issues. Thus, most of the many discussions of Wonder Woman and bondage from scholarly journals to Internet forums used images from the *Ms. Wonder Woman* book. While there are more extreme images of a bound Wonder Woman than are shown in the book, there are few, if any, that are more widespread.

The answer, of course, is yes. That was the entire point. The superiority of women was the core message of the book, and Steinem kept missing it. She concluded that Wonder Woman was so busy stopping bad guys and saving the world that she "rarely has the leisure to hint at what the future social order ought to be," but the entire purpose of Wonder Woman comics was to prepare young readers for the inevitable coming matriarchy. It was squarely focused on the future social order, and everything Marston said about his comics reinforced that point.

An important component of this disconnect between Marston and *Ms.* was who they believed the book was for. Marston was writing for boys, to get them used to strong, loving women and to prepare them for the transition to matriarchy. For Steinem, Chesler, and Edgar, however, Wonder Woman was meant to be for girls.

The most prominent theme that ran through all three women's essays was that Wonder Woman was a role model for female readers. Reflecting on reading Wonder Woman comic books as a young girl, Edgar asked, "Who could resist a role model like that?" Chesler wrote that "the comic also underlines the importance of successful female role models in teaching women strength and confidence." A huge portion of Steinem's essay was about reading Wonder Woman comics as a young girl and how much Wonder Woman meant to her growing up. She called Wonder Woman a "version of the truisms that women are rediscovering today: that women are full human beings; that we cannot love others until we love ourselves; that love and respect can only exist between equals." When Steinem put Wonder Woman on the first cover of *Ms.* and adopted her as a feminist icon, it wasn't because the mod Diana Prince desperately needed some feminism. It was because women and girls needed the Amazon Wonder Woman as a role model. As originary matriarchy shows, liberal feminists were always in search of a feminist past; with Wonder Woman they found an established role model who could be a symbol for everything they were trying to become.

Steinem listed the values that Wonder Woman represented; not surprisingly, they were the core tenets of liberal feminism:

- "Strength and self-reliance for women"
- "Sisterhood and mutual support among women"
- "Peacefulness and esteem for human life"
- "A diminishment both of 'masculine' aggression and of the belief that violence is the only way of solving conflicts"

Sisterhood and self-reliance were especially emphasized in the *Ms. Wonder Woman* book. The largest section of the book was titled "Sisterhood," and in her preface Steinem wrote that "Wonder Woman's final message to her sisters almost always contained one simple and unmistakable moral: self-reliance." Which is true. However, Marston's focus on self-reliance was because women were superior and could do a better job than men. For Steinem and her friends, self-reliance was a key part of their belief in self-improvement. It was to make them less dependent on men, not to ready them to take over the world.

This association of Wonder Woman with the liberal feminist focus on self-improvement caught on quickly. For example, in the July 1973 issue of *Sister: The Newspaper of the Los Angeles Women's Center*, a cartoon showed Wonder Woman snatching a speculum from a male doctor and announcing, "With my speculum, I **am** strong! I **can** fight!" Taking control of your sexual health was an important principle in liberal feminist self-reliance, and Wonder Woman was right there, a role model leading the way.

Self-reliance and sisterhood were important components of Marston's Wonder Woman as well. The liberal feminist version of Wonder Woman wasn't a radical reinterpretation of the character; she was a modern update, building on certain aspects of the old while setting aside others. Compared to Kanigher's Wonder Woman or the mod Diana Prince, this incarnation of the character probably had the most in common with Marston's vision.

It's quite impressive that Steinem and company were able to translate Marston's particular feminism into something that resonated with a modern audience. It was a fascinating evolution of the character, and one that made Wonder Woman relevant for the first time in decades. While it may have been an inaccurate depiction of Marston's Wonder Woman, what's more significant is that Wonder Woman meant so much to these women and that they were able to remake her into a massively popular feminist icon. Authorial intent is important, but writing isn't a one-way street. What resonates with readers and what they see in a character is just as relevant, and Steinem and her friends saw a fantastic role model in Wonder Woman.

However, one problem remains: the articles were written as if these liberal feminist beliefs were Marston's actual intent. They celebrate the "original" Wonder Woman but are fairly inaccurate in that respect. What's happened since is that the *Ms.* take on Wonder Woman has overwritten Marston's actual intent for Wonder Woman.

The *Ms. Wonder Woman* book has been the premier resource for the history of Wonder Woman for some time. For decades, there was nowhere else to see the old comics, and Marston's other writings were largely unknown. As such, the articles by Steinem and her friends are often viewed as definitive accounts of the early years of Wonder Woman. This cleaned-up, role-model Wonder Woman has become the only Wonder Woman. Much like Steinem and her friends read Wonder Woman comics through the lens of their own feminism, many since have read the same comics through the lens of Steinem. Marston's brand of feminism is largely forgotten, and it is often quickly dismissed or downplayed when it comes up.

Epic Comic Book Fail

Steinem and Edgar both had high hopes for Wonder Woman's return to her Amazon roots. They were well aware of her recent comic book

RESTORATION AND RE-CREATION

history; Edgar noted that "like many of us, she went into a decline in the fifties," and Steinem decried the mod Diana Prince era and its depowered heroine. Both were excited to have Wonder Woman back as a fully powered superhero and were particularly pleased that a woman, Dorothy Woolfolk, would be editing the book.

The Amazon Wonder Woman returned in January 1973 in *Wonder Woman* #204, but it didn't start well. A sniper was loose in the city and his first victim was "Dottie Cottonman, women's magazine editor." Starting off the issue by killing off a women's magazine editor after a women's magazine had enthusiastically endorsed this new direction for the book was an odd choice. That the editor's name was an obvious analogue for Dorothy Woolfolk was just in poor taste. Despite being announced as the book's editor, Woolfolk wasn't at the helm for *Wonder Woman*'s relaunch. She'd been replaced by another editor. What editor could have possibly had the short-sighted, imbecilic idea to simultaneously disrespect a colleague and offend any new liberal feminist readers who bought the book because of *Ms.*?

It was Robert Kanigher, back in the *Wonder Woman* fold again, writing and editing the series.* His four years away from the book hadn't changed his style at all. Kanigher's first issue did achieve the goal of ending the mod era and reestablishing the Amazon Wonder Woman. I Ching was killed by the sniper four pages in, and after developing amnesia due to a blow to the head, Diana was drawn back to Paradise Island, where her memories and powers were

---

*Woolfolk was replaced as editor on all of her series in the fall of 1972. There are reports that Woolfolk's outspoken feminism didn't go over well with the many men who ran DC, so she may have been removed or forced out because of that. However, she soon became the author of the Donna Rockford teen detective series from Scholastic, so she might have left DC to pursue her own writing. As for Kanigher taking over the book, he was the only person at DC with any experience writing or editing a superpowered Amazon Wonder Woman, which may explain why he got the job.

restored. Her origin was retold through this memory restoration, a combination of Marston and Kanigher's origin tales. It included both the despondent women who had lost their husbands and the Hercules story, and Hercules was still the source of a quarter of Wonder Woman's abilities despite the inclusion of his villainous actions. Ultimately, Wonder Woman returned to America where her alter ego, again Diana Prince, got a job as a translator at the United Nations.

In the next two issues it was revealed that Nubia, a mysterious black Amazon, was Diana's sister, and they fought each other before teaming up to fight a dragon and then Mars, the god of war. After that, the series became rehashes of old Kanigher stories. Kanigher slightly rewrote one of his old ideas, and a new artist would draw it. For example, "The Chessmen of Doom!" from *Wonder Woman* #55 became "Chessmen of Death!" in *Wonder Woman* #208, though Kanigher didn't even bother to change the title for most of the stories. Kanigher's second tenure on *Wonder Woman* only lasted eight issues, likely due to the fact that he only wrote three original scripts. He was replaced by Julius Schwartz as editor and a team of new writers with *Wonder Woman* #212.

The book wasn't doing well in sales, so Schwartz decided to add regular guest stars by having Wonder Woman perform twelve tasks in order to be readmitted to the Justice League of America. Thus, a Justice League member could be in the book each month to supervise her tasks. The idea of Wonder Woman having to prove herself to a bunch of men was a problematic plot, and it likely lost most of any remaining new feminist readers. If the letters page was any indication, very few women were reading the book.

Schwartz edited the book until *Wonder Woman* #227, when it again switched hands, this time to Denny O'Neil. The book went through two more editors before the decade ended, including Ross Andru, *Wonder Woman*'s penciller during the Silver Age. Incidentally, all of them were men, as were all of the writers and artists.

Whatever hopes Steinem, Chesler, and Edgar had for the series were quite thoroughly dashed.*

Moving off the page and into television, Wonder Woman starred alongside Superman, Batman, Robin, Aquaman, and others in the animated series *Super Friends*. The program premiered in 1973 and was part of ABC's Saturday morning cartoon lineup until 1986, and it's been shown in reruns ever since.† The animated Wonder Woman, voiced by Shannon Farnon, didn't particularly embody any sort of feminist values, apart from being a female hero on a mostly male team. Superman did the heavy lifting, while Batman and Robin did the investigating. Wonder Woman's tasks often involved her invisible plane, which she used to scope out dangerous areas or to fly Aquaman to the ocean so he could summon an aquatic beast to help the Super Friends. Her animated self was bland, but there was another version of Wonder Woman that proved to be both popular and powerful: the live-action TV show starring Lynda Carter.

In Her Satin Tights, Fighting for Her Rights

In February 2008, the cover of *Playboy* magazine featured model and reality "star" Tiffany Fallon as Wonder Woman. Apart from the boots, Fallon was completely nude and a Wonder Woman costume

---

*If the data we saw in interlude 2 is any indication, by the early 1970s DC seemed much more interested in male readers than female readers. After all of the publicity surrounding the original Wonder Woman's return, things likely settled back into the old status quo at the DC offices and appeasing feminists was no longer a concern. Not a lot has changed since then.

†Another animated version of Wonder Woman actually predated her *Super Friends* incarnation when she guest-starred on an episode of the cartoon *Brady Bunch* spinoff, *The Brady Kids*, in 1972. Wonder Woman was sent back in time with the Brady Kids, and they all attended the Olympics in ancient Greece while learning a valuable lesson about cheating and brains versus brawn.

was painted on her body. Reaction to the cover was passionate, and the blogosphere was outraged with this depiction of a feminist icon as a sex object. Interestingly, what many bloggers took issue with wasn't the picture itself but the blurb on the inside of the cover that called Fallon "a modern-day Lynda Carter." Heidi Meeley of *comics fairplay* wrote: "What bothered me more then [sic] the ass shot was the comparison of the woman on the cover to Carter." A comment to a post by blogger Rachel Edidin asked: "How exactly did Tiffany Fallon earn the right to be called a modern-day Lynda Carter? Ugh." Lisa Fortuner of *Newsarama* argued that comparing Fallon to Carter was ridiculous, stating that "when [Carter] put on that uniform in the 70s she was a role-model for little girls. She was their superhero, [. . .] a symbol of idealism and power and capability." In contrast, Fallon was simply "a reality TV Queen they thought looked hot in the costume."

For many women today, Lynda Carter *is* Wonder Woman, and her version of the character is the definitive take on their feminist hero. One of those women is Tiffany Fallon herself, who said, "I grew up watching the TV show with Lynda Carter and I just always admired her." The *Wonder Woman* TV show is by far the most well-known version of the character, and it was strongly rooted in the liberal feminist take on Wonder Woman.

Warner Bros. had tried to bring Wonder Woman to the small screen twice before Lynda Carter took the role, but neither version did well. First, in 1967 a Wonder Woman sitcom inspired by the live-action *Batman* show was written, but it didn't even shoot a full pilot before it was scrapped. Then in 1974 a Wonder Woman TV movie was made with Cathy Lee Crosby as a blonde Wonder Woman. The movie didn't much resemble the comic books; it was a spy adventure with Wonder Woman working on behalf of the government in a star-spangled jumpsuit to track down a stolen list of undercover agents. She had gadgets rather than magical items; for example, instead of a lasso she had a golden rope hidden in her belt that combined with one of her bracelets to create a grappling line for

scaling walls. The TV movie didn't perform well enough to warrant a further series.*

Trying to capitalize on the current popularity of Wonder Woman as a feminist mascot, producer Douglas Cramer put together a new television movie in 1975. Likely influenced by *Ms.*'s focus on the Golden Age Wonder Woman, the movie was set during World War II. It starred Lyle Waggoner as Steve Trevor, Cloris Leachman as Hippolyta, and former Miss World USA Lynda Carter as Wonder Woman / Diana Prince. The movie aired on ABC in November 1975, and after two more specials in April 1976 it premiered as a series the following fall. The entire first year of the show was set during World War II.

The initial TV movie was a fairly faithful adaptation of Wonder Woman's origin story from *All Star Comics* #8 and *Sensation Comics* #1. In what was probably not a coincidence, these were the two stories that opened up the *Ms. Wonder Woman* book too. The first year of the series followed the same basic setup as Marston's comics: Steve Trevor was a pilot and Diana Prince was his secretary who would turn into Wonder Woman whenever danger arose. The show even borrowed some characters from the original comics, with Etta Candy becoming a coworker of Diana's and Paula von Gunther showing up as a villain for an episode.

Carter played her dual role with the same contrast as the Marston years. Her Wonder Woman was vibrant and bright, a brave and confident heroine, while her Diana Prince was a meek and dowdy wallflower. Carter captured both sides well, especially in a scene where she explained her life in America to her sister, Drusilla. As Wonder Woman, she nobly declared, "If the Nazis win, the whole world would be subjected to slavery. I feel that by staying here, I can help in some small way towards preventing this catastrophe." She then pulled the classic spin change, and in her Diana garb she

---

*Though it did have Ricardo Montalban in it, which is always fun.

giggled and said that working for the military "allows me to stay close to Steve . . . Major Trevor. I work for him." Carter's Wonder Woman focused on being a hero and her Diana was a doe-eyed gal in love with Steve.

Marston's utopian message made it into the initial TV movie as well, but it was soon undermined. Queen Hippolyta exclaimed, "I named this island 'Paradise' for an excellent reason: there are no men on it. Thus it is free of their wars, their greed, their hostility, their barbaric, masculine behavior." She added, "We are stronger, wiser, and more advanced than all those people in their jungles out there. Our civilization is perfection!" This sounds like Marston on paper, but the way it was played on screen told a different story. Cloris Leachman's Hippolyta was more feminazi than feminist, slightly crazed and full of hatred for men. These words weren't said with the peace and serenity of a noble queen but with a sneer of contempt.

Furthermore, Wonder Woman soon found herself disagreeing with her mother's take on humanity, and on men in particular. Throughout the first season, Hippolyta wanted her daughter to come back to Paradise Island for good and get away from the corrupting influence of man's world, but she always refused. Wonder Woman saw the good in men, American men like Steve Trevor in particular, and didn't find them barbaric like her mother did. Just like Steinem downplayed Marston's focus on the superiority of the Amazons, so did the TV show, and the similarities with *Ms.*'s take on Wonder Woman continued from there.

While Steinem and Edgar downplayed the racist elements in Golden Age Wonder Woman comics, the TV show just eliminated race altogether. Almost everyone on the show was white, even in the background. The show also changed the focus of the war. The original Wonder Woman fought the Japanese more than the Germans, but on the TV show the war was solely between the Americans and the Nazis. The Pacific front didn't come up. This made the show even whiter, eliminating Asians from the equation. They avoided the

issue of racism entirely by not having any other races on the show, which in itself is rather racist.

Steinem and Chesler also expressed concerns about Wonder Woman's warmongering and "super-patriotism," but the Wonder Woman TV show reframed the entire war. By turning World War II into a fight just between America and the Nazis, the war became a battle between the forces of ultimate good and the forces of ultimate evil. No villains in the history of the modern world were more evil than the Nazis. It wasn't just a fight between warring nations but, as Wonder Woman told Drusilla, this was freedom versus slavery, with the fate of the entire world in the balance.

Bondage was ignored as well. Wonder Woman got tied up from time to time, and used her lasso on the occasional villain, but it didn't amount to much. Batman and Robin got into far more elaborate bondage situations each week on their TV show. While Marston's *Wonder Woman* was an intentionally kinky book, the only thing remotely titillating about the TV show was Wonder Woman's outfit.

The net result was a show that lacked nuance. Steinem and her friends portrayed a cleaned-up, modernized Wonder Woman that sidestepped a lot of the complexities of Marston's tenure, but the Wonder Woman TV show erased any potential problems entirely, presenting an ideal version of the character. The good versus evil, freedom versus slavery version of the war was a simplified setting, and within this setting Wonder Woman became the representative of the ultimate good. She was a hero who was powerful, independent, and virtuous, but who was *only* powerful, independent, and virtuous. Wonder Woman wasn't just cleaned up; she was, to borrow Wright's term for past matriarchies, sanctified. Lynda Carter's Wonder Woman was heroic and wholesome, with nothing impeachable about her character, making her an excellent role model.

Helping other women was a big part of the show, and anytime a female character was poorly treated by a man, Wonder Woman would speak up. For instance, when she was interrogated by a

female Nazi agent who was constantly insulted by her male commanding officer, Wonder Woman told her, "Fraulein Grabel, you are a woman of great intelligence and should not be taking orders from that man." Wonder Woman later declared, "Women are the wave of the future and sisterhood is stronger than anything."

Even though Wonder Woman regularly encouraged women to be more self-reliant, it was made abundantly clear that normal women could never be as impressive as Wonder Woman. That point was hammered home in this exchange:

STEVE: She is a wonder. Strong and fearless, and still compassionate. All the virtues of femininity with none of the vices.

ETTA: You're right. Sometimes I wish I was like Wonder Woman. . . . Most of the time I wish I was like Wonder Woman.

STEVE: (laughs) There's only one Wonder Woman, Etta.

DIANA: Etta, I think the most we can do is be the best women we can possibly be.

STEVE: Sound advice, Diana.

The TV show didn't demonstrate the superiority of women but instead focused on the uniqueness of Wonder Woman herself. While liberal feminists looked to Wonder Woman as an inspiration for the traits they wanted to develop in themselves, the program made Wonder Woman an unattainable ideal, a role model that no woman could ever hope to match.

Wonder Woman the TV show wasn't intended to be feminist propaganda. TV was a business, and the show was meant to appeal to a wide audience and make money for the network. *Wonder Woman*, like *Charlie's Angels, The Bionic Woman,* and several other 1970s female-led action shows, combined snippets of feminism for female

viewers and pretty girls for male viewers. Tellingly, producer Douglas Cramer said of casting Carter: "We needed a large woman, a statuesque woman, a buxom woman, and an angelic face." As an afterthought he added, "Beyond all that we needed someone that could play it, that could act and sustain a television movie." With cup size and beauty as the primary criteria, it's clear that the TV show was motivated by more than promoting feminism.

Replacing the Past

In the 1970s, William Moulton Marston's approach to Wonder Woman slipped by the wayside. As did Robert Kanigher's, and Denny O'Neil and Mike Sekowsky's. Marston was overwritten by Steinem and her friends, so while the Golden Age Wonder Woman became a hero for liberal feminists, it wasn't actually his messages that were being celebrated. With the "original" Wonder Woman now a feminist icon, the work of Kanigher, O'Neil, and Sekowsky is often dismissed for not being true to the "original" version of the character and deemed inconsequential.

Of course, there is no "true" version of Wonder Woman. Wonder Woman was a character who evolved and changed in fascinating ways, but our modern perception of her is fairly generic. She's loved for being a female hero in a male-dominated genre, but outside of that she doesn't have much of an identity, nor has she had much of a presence in the years since the TV show ended.

10

The Mundane Modern Age

By the late 1970s, Wonder Woman was rather popular. Her TV show ran for three years with decent ratings, and she costarred in the animated series *Super Friends* with the rest of the Justice League. You could see Lynda Carter as Wonder Woman on CBS at 8:00 PM on Fridays and then watch her in cartoon form on ABC's Saturday morning cartoons. You could also buy her comic book every month, but not many people did. Nor were they buying anyone else's comics either. The comic book industry hit a big slump in the 1970s, and in some ways it has never come back from it.

The industry faced a perfect storm of problems in the 1970s, starting with the rise of the direct market. Interest in comics had started to dwindle, in part due to price increases. Newsstands and drugstores made less and less on comics, and the big distributors weren't particularly concerned when orders started to drop, because they made the bulk of their money in magazines. After decades of spinner racks being a fixture at corner stores, comics became a niche product available primarily in specialty comic shops. Retailers bought the books directly through smaller, more amenable distributors instead of from major distribution conglomerates. This new

system had its advantages and kept the industry alive, but it also limited the availability of comic books.

Marvel remained more popular than DC Comics, so DC attempted a big push to gain ground on its competitor. It rolled out its poorly timed "DC Explosion" in the mid-1970s, premiering several new series and increasing the page count of all of its books. Soon after, America slipped into a recession, so money was tighter for customers; inflation and rising paper costs cut into DC's profits; and huge blizzards in 1977 and 1978 wreaked havoc with distribution. Nothing was going well for DC. The "DC Explosion" was followed by what became known as the "DC Implosion" in 1978. Over twenty series were canceled and several other books merged together. It was a massive contraction of DC's comics line and the company limped into the new decade. In 1970, its average monthly circulation had been about 6 million; by 1980 it was under 3 million. Marvel wasn't spared either, sliding from 7.5 million in 1970 to about 5 million in 1980.

Things slowly improved as the direct market caught on and the rise of comic book shops led to an increased interest in back issues. Old comics were suddenly worth money, and many fans started to see new comics as an investment, thinking that a $1.50 comic could be worth hundreds or thousands of dollars down the road if it was well preserved. Inevitably, this bubble burst spectacularly in the mid-1990s. With collectors stockpiling comics, nothing was rare and worth never increased. Things got so bad that Marvel declared bankruptcy, and it took almost another decade for the comics industry to return to any kind of stability. Today, DC and Marvel are relatively solid, but they are also kept alive by the corporations that own them (Time Warner and Disney, respectively) and which are interested in them primarily for their film, TV, and licensing prospects.

Superhero comic books aren't terribly relevant these days. There's a lot of great work being done by fantastic creators, but their range of influence is a far cry from the days when kids bought *Superman*, *Batman*, and *Wonder Woman* in the millions and exchanged them

on the playground. Comics are a niche market and have been for some time. Things like Senate hearings and spotlights from national feminist magazines are long past. The characters are doing well on TV and in the movies, but the general public isn't all that concerned about what's going on in the funny books.

This is especially true for Wonder Woman. In a time when comics aren't all that popular to begin with, *Wonder Woman* has averaged about sixty-fourth on the monthly sales charts over the past two decades. Many other superheroes have stayed in the public eye on the big and small screens, but not Wonder Woman. Batman has had seven major motion pictures, and Superman has had six movies and two TV shows, while Wonder Woman has only made sporadic appearances in cartoons.

Wonder Woman still comes out every month, but there's been nothing as unusual or fascinating as the adventures of her early incarnations, good or bad. For the past thirty years, Wonder Woman has been an afterthought in the comic book world.

The George Pérez Era

In 1985, DC began *Crisis on Infinite Earths*, a twelve-issue miniseries that amalgamated its various fictional universes into one unified whole. After nearly fifty years of comics, continuity was muddled and complicated, and *Crisis on Infinite Earths* streamlined the many different characters and worlds into a single, new universe. The agent of this reorganization was the evil Anti-Monitor, and all of the heroes came together one last time in the final issue to save the new world. Wonder Woman was hit by the Anti-Monitor's antimatter blast and disintegrated into nothingness, but instead of dying, she regressed back through time, de-aging and ultimately reverting back to the clay from which she was formed back on Paradise Island. Wonder Woman was about to be reborn.

The only problem was that DC wasn't sure what to do with her. *Crisis on Infinite Earths* #12 had a cover date of March 1986,

and it was almost an entire year before a new *Wonder Woman* #1 debuted.* As *Crisis* wound down, *Wonder Woman* was DC's worst-selling series, and the company wanted a strong, exciting take on the character for the relaunch. Several creators pitched ideas, most of which resembled Wonder Woman in name only. Finally Greg Potter came in with a proposal that retained most of Wonder Woman's classic elements, and even then DC was unsure. Knowing the book was having trouble getting off the ground, *Crisis on Infinite Earths* artist George Pérez stopped by the DC offices to pitch his take on the character and offer his artistic services. Most high-profile creators didn't want to touch Wonder Woman, with her checkered history and decades of tangled continuity, but Pérez saw potential for something new. He got the job right away.

A lot of Potter's proposal was used, and he stayed on the new series as scripter and co-plotter for a few issues, but *Wonder Woman* soon became Pérez's book. While he'd only planned to help launch the series and stick around for six months or so, Pérez ended up staying on the book for five years.

Pérez's new origin story for Wonder Woman had a framework that was similar to her Golden Age origin and retained a feminist message, but it was also more involved. The story began in 1200 BCE, when the Olympian goddesses finally had enough of the constant war and violence of mankind. They proposed a new female race of humans who would be "strong . . . brave . . . compassionate" and set an example for the rest of mankind. Ares, the god of war, was fiercely opposed to this because all of his power came from mankind worshipping war. Ultimately, Zeus refused to pick a side and the female goddesses, with the help of Hermes, set about creating the Amazons.

---

*Though in between there was a four-issue miniseries called *The Legend of Wonder Woman*, written and illustrated by Trina Robbins, along with cowriter Kurt Busiek, and set primarily in the Golden Age.

They journeyed deep into Hades to the womb of Gaea, the mother of the Earth itself. In this most secret part of Hades, Gaea had hidden the souls of women who had been killed by men, their lives cut short by violence and hatred. Artemis released the souls and they became the Amazons, bursting forth as fully formed women in a new land. Hippolyte was the first to emerge, and she became their queen. The newly born Amazons were visited by the goddesses, who told them that they were a "sacred **sisterhood**," a "**chosen race**— born to lead humanity in the ways of **virtue**."

Then came Hercules, goaded on by an irate Ares. Hercules tricked the Amazons, they were captured, Athena freed them, and they left for a new home far away from the world of men. The Amazons hadn't succeeded in their mission to change the world, but the goddesses were playing a long game. Something great would come from the Amazons.

The bearer of Hippolyte's original soul was pregnant when she died, and so the queen felt a yearning for a daughter. The oracle of the Amazons told her to form a baby out of clay and then "open yourself to fair **Artemis**—that the **mid-wife of all Olympus** may enter you." There was one soul remaining in the womb of Gaea, specially saved for this moment, and it gave life to the clay baby. The goddesses also granted the baby gifts: power and strength from Demeter, great beauty and a loving heart from Aphrodite, wisdom from Athena, the eye of the hunter and unity with beasts from Artemis, "sisterhood with fire—that it may open men's hearts to her" from Hestia, and Hermes gave her speed and flight. The baby was named Diana, and she soon became the champion of the Amazons.

Borrowing the Hercules story and the clay from Marston and the gods bequeathing powers from Kanigher, Pérez continued the post-Marston trend of Diana being unique among the Amazons but he also made the goddesses the source of the majority of her powers. The Pérez origin was a hybrid, referencing the past with an eye to the future.

Soon grown, Diana won a tournament in disguise and became Wonder Woman, saved Steve Trevor and returned him to America, and then she saved the world from a great evil, but these familiar elements had new twists. Steve was older, a pilot near retirement age forced to fly a secret mission by a cult of Ares that had gained power in the American military. Ares, still upset about the Amazons, was about to start World War III and wanted to eliminate the champions of the goddesses who would oppose him. Steve unknowingly flew the secret passage to Themyscira, the home of the Amazons, and his possessed copilot tried to blow up the island. Not surprisingly, Wonder Woman lassoed the missile, saved Steve, and, once she arrived in America, foiled Ares's master plan.

She did so with a new supporting cast. Etta Candy was a lieutenant in the air force, a nod to her military role in the TV show, and Etta and Steve soon became a couple. Wonder Woman's main companion was Julia Kapatelis, a professor of Greek history at Harvard, and her teenage daughter, Vanessa. They became her surrogate family in America. Wonder Woman also had a publicist, Myndi Mayer, who helped her establish herself and her message of peace and compassion in the world of men.

The Amazons were more fleshed out as well, with characters like Epione the healer, Hellene the historian, Menalippe the oracle, Philippus the captain of the guard, and many more. Themyscira was no longer a generic all-female utopia; it housed women with varied personalities and different ideas of the Amazons' role in the world. This came to a head when Wonder Woman wanted to open up Themyscira to the rest of the world. There was much debate, and it came to a vote. The majority decided to rejoin the world, and the isolationism of past incarnations of the Amazons ended. Instead of barricading themselves to maintain some sort of superiority and purity, they became part of the world again. Themyscira welcomed visitors, male and female, and Hippolyte even traveled to the United Nations to speak.

Wonder Woman faced challenges from patriarchal forces, both mortal and divine. She spent most of her time battling rogue gods and mythological beasts, but Pérez kept the series planted firmly in the real world and he tackled some heavy topics. Myndi Mayer died of a drug overdose, and an issue explored alcohol and drug abuse. In another issue, Vanessa's cheery friend Lucy Spears committed suicide, and the book dealt with depression and the loss of a loved one. Wonder Woman's human friends kept the series grounded and relevant to a modern audience.

Wonder Woman was also notable for its many female creators. Janice Race developed the book before handing the editorial duties to Karen Berger, who remained editor for Pérez's entire run.* Women were involved in *Wonder Woman* at every level while Berger was in charge. Mindy Newell cowrote twelve issues with Pérez, while Jill Thompson penciled most of the last third of Pérez's tenure and did occasional covers. When Thompson needed a breather, Colleen Doran and Cynthia Martin took over illustration duties. Tatjana Wood did the coloring for the early issues of the book, and Nansi Hoolahan was the regular colorist by the end of the Pérez era.

While the Pérez relaunch is well regarded, the book wasn't without its problems. The series continued the depiction of Wonder Woman as an unattainable ideal, and other female characters weren't empowered by knowing Wonder Woman so much as they felt bad about themselves in comparison. For example, Vanessa was concerned her boyfriend wouldn't like her anymore once he got a look at Wonder Woman, and Wonder Woman's lithe figure made Etta Candy feel sensitive about her weight.

Nonetheless, the Pérez era revitalized Wonder Woman, however briefly. He combined elements of her Golden and Silver Age past

---

*Berger was also the editor of Neil Gaiman's *Sandman*, and she would go from *Wonder Woman* to running the wildly successful Vertigo imprint at DC.

into a new, modern take on the character that retained her feminist leanings and also established Wonder Woman as a champion of global peace and cooperation. For the first time in decades, Wonder Woman was relevant and the book was selling well. This didn't last for long.

Background Player

After George Pérez left *Wonder Woman* in the early 1990s, the series remained stagnant for the next two decades. William Messner-Loebs replaced Pérez as writer and took Wonder Woman in a new direction. She became a space pirate for a while, then got a job at the Mexican fast food restaurant Taco Whiz when the Amazons disappeared and left her homeless.

Messner-Loebs was soon joined by artist Mike Deodato Jr., whose style sexualized the book. Wonder Woman had impossibly long legs, a minuscule waist, breasts that jutted out like torpedoes, and a perpetual sexy glare. She and her fellow Amazons were always positioned so as to best emphasize their features, and Wonder Woman's briefs turned into a painful-looking thong that pulled up past her waist, while Hippolyta wore what can only be described as dual breast hammocks. Deodato's artwork was a far cry from Pérez's more classic, tasteful style.

John Byrne took over as writer and artist after Messner-Loebs left and largely ignored everything that had happened before. He moved Wonder Woman to the fictional Gateway City, gave her a new supporting cast, and even killed her for a few issues. The book wasn't terrible, but nor was it particularly good. By the mid-1990s, the series had settled into a middling quality with middling sales, and it never came back in any lasting way.

There were some good moments: Phil Jimenez's run on the book as writer and artist is very well respected; writer Greg Rucka was twice nominated for an Eisner, the comics industry's biggest award, while writing *Wonder Woman*; and Gail Simone became the series'

first regular female writer.* There were occasional sales jumps, but they quickly petered out. Another relaunch in 2006 lit up the sales charts briefly, but delays and a tie-in to *Amazons Attack*, a poorly executed miniseries in which the Amazons invaded America, soon dragged the book down. When *Wonder Woman* was renumbered to mark its 600th issue overall, J. Michael Straczynski came onboard as writer and sales rose initially until Straczynski abruptly left the book. Then sales plummeted again.

DC Comics often refers to Superman, Batman, and Wonder Woman as its "Big Three" or the "Trinity," its three heroes who have been around the longest and are most well known. However, while Wonder Woman spent most of the Modern Age trucking along in the middle of the pack with her one series, the men were much busier. Batman and Superman didn't just have their own starring books; they were a brand. Along with their own titles, their sidekicks and associates had titles of their own, all tagged with the bat symbol or the S-shield to show they were part of a larger family of books. Wonder Woman just had *Wonder Woman*.†

The chart on the next page shows a timeline of select ongoing series that starred or were closely related to the Big Three.‡ Wonder

---

*The Eisners were occasionally good to *Wonder Woman*. Brian Bolland and Adam Hughes both won for their cover art, while colorist Trish Mulvihill was nominated four times and finally won in 2004. Mulvihill was the series' most prolific creator, coloring over 100 issues of *Wonder Woman* in the Modern Age.

†Wonder Woman began costarring in a new series in October 2013 titled *Superman/ Wonder Woman*. The two heroes are dating in the new DC universe, and the book is about their adventures as a superpowered couple. Wonder Woman gets second billing, and the book may as well be called *Superman's Girl Friend Wonder Woman*.

‡These aren't all the Bat-books and Super-titles, just the longer-running ones. Also, the chart doesn't show miniseries; with miniseries, this chart would be an eight-page foldout and the Wonder Woman books would still be barely noticeable at the bottom. Off the top of my head, while I can think of maybe five or six Wonder Woman–related miniseries that came out in the past twenty-five years, I can also think of five or six Batman-related miniseries that are coming out this *month*.

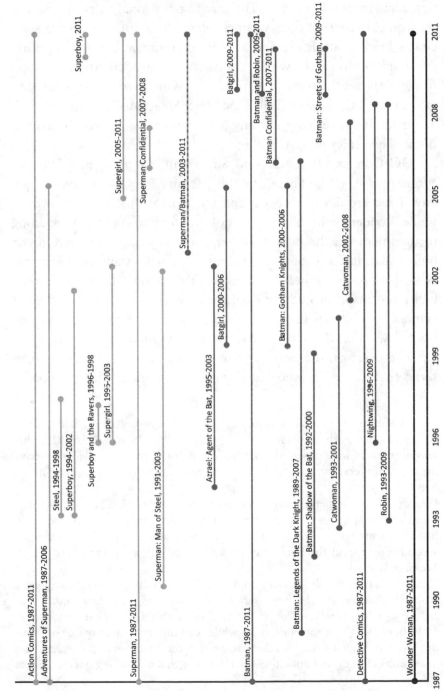

Woman costarred in Justice League books and is involved in big, line-wide events with everyone else, but she and her supporting cast have only had one book of their own for the entire Modern Age while Superman, Batman, and their many associates have had scads of titles. Wonder Woman hasn't been a priority at DC, and so she's faded into the background.

Part of this is due to a lack of iconic stories. Batman has books like Frank Miller's *Batman: Year One* and *The Dark Knight Returns* that invigorated Batman in the late 1980s, and later books like *The Long Halloween* and *Hush* that continue to sell well. Superman has classic shorter stories from the 1980s, like Alan Moore's "Whatever Happened to the Man of Tomorrow?" and "For the Man Who Has Everything," along with later successes like *Superman for All Seasons* and *All Star Superman*. All of these books have been reprinted in various editions over the years, and the Batman and Superman sections in bookstores are always jam-packed.

Wonder Woman doesn't really have any iconic stories. The Pérez issues were collected once, and her new issues come out as graphic novels twice a year, but those don't stay in print for long. One of her only standalone graphic novels, Greg Rucka and J. G. Jones's *Wonder Woman: The Hiketia*, was a critical success in 2003, but it's out of print now too. Wonder Woman's back catalog is very thin. In May 2013, DC Comics put out the *DC Entertainment Essential Graphic Novels and Chronology 2013* guide, a comprehensive handbook of its extensive backlist catalog. Batman had eighty-four titles listed and Superman had fifty-three, while lesser-known heroes like Green Lantern and the Flash had forty-six and fifteen titles, respectively. The Wonder Woman section listed only six titles.

Batman and Superman have also had huge event stories that were key moments in the DC Comics universe. The villain Bane broke Batman's back in *Knightfall*, and that story along with Batman's return has been a touchstone for Batman comics since. Furthermore, Bane became a regular villain in the DC universe, and

he and the breaking of Batman were a key part of the blockbuster movie *The Dark Knight Rises*.

Causing even more of an impact was the death of Superman, which received international press attention. The issue where the monster Doomsday killed Superman is one of the bestselling comic books of all time, and the collections have been extremely successful and are constantly reissued. Doomsday remains a key part of the DC universe, as do characters created in the wake of Superman's death, like Steel and a new Superboy. The story hasn't been on the big screen yet, but it was turned into an animated movie that launched DC's direct-to-DVD line.

Both Superman and Batman had catastrophic events with ramifications still felt in comic books today that are known even outside of the comic book world. Over the same period, Wonder Woman died twice and lost the title of Wonder Woman, and no one particularly cares or remembers. She died very briefly during the Pérez era in the crossover story *War of the Gods*, lost her title to the upstart Amazon Artemis during the Messner-Loebs/Deodato era, and then died and was replaced by her mother before coming back to life as the goddess of truth during the Byrne era. All of those stories have been out of print for years, and their lasting effects are practically nonexistent. They've certainly not inspired new characters or been adapted into movies.

For the vast majority of the Modern Age, Wonder Woman has been an afterthought. Batman and Superman have had innumerable comic books, several movies each, live-action TV shows, and cartoon TV shows. Wonder Woman has had her comic book, and that's about it. Other DC properties have been expanded into brands and found success elsewhere. Green Lantern was turned into a live-action movie and a cartoon show, and there are five titles in the Green Lantern comics family right now. Lesser-known teams like the Teen Titans and Legion of Super-Heroes have had Saturday morning cartoon shows. Marvel has put nearly all of its characters in its many movies. There have been rumors of Wonder Woman movies and TV

shows over the years, but they haven't come to fruition yet. All she's had is her one comics series and a few costarring, background roles elsewhere on cartoons like *Super Friends* and *Justice League.**

The Fridged Women of DC Comics

Wonder Woman has been relegated to the background for quite some time, in a comic book limbo where she's there each month but not really doing anything good or bad, fascinating or controversial. However, given how things have gone for a lot of the female characters at DC Comics over the past couple of decades, limbo might not be the worst place to be.

Though not for Lois Lane, who's had a decent go of it for the most part. Clark Kent told her that he was Superman and they eventually got married, and she continued working hard as the world's foremost journalist.† Sometimes this got her into trouble, like when she was shot while embedded with troops in wartorn Umec as she tried to help an injured soldier, but even that didn't keep her down for long. She hasn't had her own ongoing series since *Superman's Girl Friend Lois Lane* was canceled in 1974, but she's costarred in most of those Superman-related series and remains a fixture at DC.

She's also far and away the Modern Age's most prominent female character outside of the comics. Lois was played by Margot Kidder in the Christopher Reeve Superman movies, then by Teri Hatcher in the TV show *Lois and Clark: The New Adventures of Superman.*

---

*A 2009 direct-to-DVD animated film starred Keri Russell as Wonder Woman. It premiered poorly but has sold steadily since. Gal Gadot will play a live-action Wonder Woman in the *Man of Steel* sequel in 2016, in a tertiary role behind Superman and Batman. A solo Wonder Woman film has yet to be announced.
†They're not married anymore, though. DC Comics relaunched their entire line in September 2011, and the Clark/Lois marriage never happened in the new universe, along with several other notable marriages like Barry Allen (the Flash) and Iris West, and Oliver Queen (Green Arrow) and Dinah Lance (Black Canary). Everyone's young and single now. It's a happening scene.

She was excellently voiced by Dana Delany in *Superman: The Animated Series*, then portrayed by Erica Durance in *Smallville*, Kate Bosworth in *Superman Returns*, and multiple Oscar nominee Amy Adams in *Man of Steel*. No female comic book character has been onscreen more often than Lois Lane. Wonder Woman had one live-action TV show in the 1970s. Since then, a live-action Lois has costarred in two shows and six movies.

In fact, the movies have been good for a lot of female characters in the Modern Age. Catwoman was played by Michelle Pfeiffer in *Batman Returns*, by Halle Berry in her own eponymous film, and by Anne Hathaway in *The Dark Knight Rises*. Sue Storm, the Invisible Woman, was portrayed by Jessica Alba in two Fantastic Four movies, while Natasha Romanoff, the Black Widow, has been played by Scarlett Johansson in several *Avengers*-related movies. Mary Jane Watson was played by Kirsten Dunst in three Spider-Man movies, and now Emma Stone stars as Gwen Stacey in the franchise's reboot. Supergirl had her own movie starring Helen Slater, and Batgirl was played by Alicia Silverstone in *Batman & Robin*. Even Carol Ferris, a.k.a. Star Sapphire from the Silver Age, made it to the big screen, portrayed by Blake Lively in *Green Lantern*. It seems that everyone has made it to the movies except for Wonder Woman.

These successes for women on the big screen didn't continue in their monthly print adventures. The dominant trend for female characters in the Modern Age can be defined by this seemingly nonsensical phrase: "Women in Refrigerators." First coined by Gail Simone, this term is a reference to *Green Lantern* #54 when Kyle Rayner, the Green Lantern, returned home to find that a villain had killed his girlfriend, Alex DeWitt, and stuffed her in the refrigerator. Simone argued that a disproportionate number of female characters were killed, seriously injured, or sidelined, often in a sexualized manner, in the service of furthering a male character's story. It's a plot device used to create emotional turmoil in the narrative of a male character, often at the expense of ending a female character's very existence.

The theory gained a lot of traction and even inspired a new verb. To be "fridged" is to be dispatched in such a manner.

One of the most famous fridgings involved Barbara Gordon, the Bronze Age Batgirl. In Alan Moore and Brian Bolland's 1988 graphic novel *Batman: The Killing Joke*, the Joker showed up at the home of Barbara's father, police commissioner James Gordon, and shot her through the spine when she opened the door. The Joker then undressed her and took nude pictures of her as she lay on the floor, bleeding. Barbara was paralyzed and wheelchair bound for the next two decades.*

Barbara wasn't shot because she was Batgirl, or because she was out stopping a crime of some sort. She was shot because she was the commissioner's daughter and the Joker wanted to upset him and Batman. The Joker displayed her nude photos in a carnival meant to drive Commissioner Gordon insane, and her injury prompted Batman to be even more determined in his quest to track down the Joker. Crassly, the book ended with the Joker and Batman laughing at a dumb joke, with nary a mention of Barbara.

Another notable fridging involved Supergirl, when she sacrificed herself to save Superman while battling the Anti-Monitor during *Crisis on Infinite Earths*. One of her last thoughts was "I may never be as good as he is, but Kal always taught me to do my best." She died so Superman would be around to lead the charge to save the universe, and the story made it clear that his life was far more valuable than hers. When the universe rebooted, she was wiped from existence entirely because DC wanted Superman to be the only surviving Kryptonian. It would be almost twenty years before a Kryptonian Supergirl returned to DC Comics.

---

*She became Oracle, a computer whiz who coordinated communication and information for most of the DC heroes. She starred in *Birds of Prey* for years before recovering and returning as Batgirl in DC's recent relaunch, written by, wait for it, Gail Simone.

Continuing with sidekicks, Stephanie Brown became Batman's new Robin in 2004. After patrolling Gotham City for years as Spoiler, Steph was promoted when the current Robin, Tim Drake, quit. She was Robin for three whole issues before she was brutally tortured and killed by Black Mask during a massive gang war. In fact, the only reason she got to be Robin was to raise her profile before they killed her. Her death was going to be the emotional climax of the Bat-books' massive "War Games" crossover, and the editors decided that her death would hit readers harder if she was Robin. And, in typical Women in Refrigerators fashion, it spurred the male characters into action. Both Batman and Tim, now Robin again, took to the gang war with new fervor and ended it.

As Spoiler and then as Robin, Steph had developed a sizeable, and largely female, fan base, and her brutal death wasn't well received. Nor was DC's response to the fans' displeasure. When asked why Steph didn't have a memorial in the Batcave like Jason Todd, a former Robin who had been killed by the Joker, DC's executive editor Dan DiDio told them that she wasn't really a Robin. A memorial eventually came, but it took some time.*

In terms of villains, familiar characters haven't been fridged but they've been rather sexualized. Catwoman got a new origin as a prostitute in Frank Miller's *Batman: Year One* and was drawn ludicrously proportioned by Jim Balent throughout the mid-1990s. When her series relaunched in 2011, the entire first page of the new

---

*As with most deceased comics characters, Steph was later brought back via retcon. Dr. Leslie Thompkins, a close confidante of Steph's and family friend of Batman, had faked Steph's death to teach Batman a lesson about employing teenagers as sidekicks. She became Batgirl in 2009 in a new series by Bryan Q. Miller and Lee Garbett. The series didn't light up the sales charts, but it sold steadily and was a critical favorite. When DC relaunched its superhero line in 2011, Barbara Gordon returned as Batgirl and Stephanie Brown disappeared from the DC universe, much to the consternation of fans. After more than two years of heavy campaigning by fans, Steph returned as Spoiler in *Batman: Eternal* in spring 2014.

Catwoman #1 was panels of her breasts, and she infiltrated a strip club before finishing the issue by straddling Batman in a sex scene of astoundingly awkward posing. Carol Ferris has appeared frequently in recent Green Lantern stories and has been sexualized as well. Her Star Sapphire outfit has a neckline that dips below her navel, with grasping bits of fabric that barely contain her breasts.

Fridging and sex merged together memorably in one of DC's biggest events of the past decade, *Identity Crisis*, and the murder of Sue Dibny, the Elongated Man's wife. The Justice League had to track down her killer while covering up a terrible secret. The second issue revealed that years before her murder, Sue had been raped by the villainous Dr. Light, an event illustrated in some detail. Sue was graphically murdered and raped to provide the start of a story for the predominantly male Justice League; the terrible secret the league had to protect was that they'd erased Dr. Light's memory of the event, and that they were now worried he'd remembered and returned to kill Sue. But he wasn't the murderer.

Another popular trend of the Modern Age was formerly good women becoming bad guys. The culprit was actually Jean Loring, the ex-wife of the Atom. She thought that by attacking another superhero's wife, her ex-husband might be worried and come back to her, but things quickly got out of hand and Sue died. They corrupted one female character to murder another female character, all because the first female character just missed her husband so much. It's a laughable stereotype. Even as the archvillain of a big comic book event, the female villain's motive boils down to a woman needing a husband.

Soon after *Identity Crisis*, Wonder Woman became a murderer as well, but this time for wholly justified reasons. Nonetheless, she was still vilified and ostracized. When Max Lord took control of Superman's mind and forced him to fight his friends, Batman and Wonder Woman teamed up to stop him. Wonder Woman captured Lord, and he swore that as soon as she let him go he'd take control of Superman again. Under the truth-compelling power of the lasso,

Lord said that the only way to stop him from controlling Superman was to kill him. So Wonder Woman snapped his neck.

It was an absolutely necessary killing. Superman was too powerful to let a madman control him, and Lord would've used him to go on a murderous spree. Wonder Woman made the hard decision and killed Lord. She was shunned for it. The event was played on screens across the planet and the world turned against her. Batman was disgusted, and even Superman disapproved. Wonder Woman may as well have been Jean Loring for the way she was treated, all because she made the difficult decision that none of the boys could.

Maybe it was better that Wonder Woman faded into the background for most of the Modern Age. Whenever a woman took center stage in a DC comic, she was killed or turned evil or sexualized. The choices were death, scorn, or objectification. While there were several good moments for women at DC over the years, the "women in refrigerators" plot device best encapsulates the era. Women were disposable and malleable, and everything revolved around male characters and their stories. The Modern Age could have used a strong Wonder Woman to counter this approach to women, but it's hard to make much of an impact with only one series. Considering what happened when Wonder Woman stepped up to end the Max Lord situation, the background was the safest place to be. At least she's still alive.

CONCLUSION

Wonder Woman, Known but Unknown

Superheroes have been in the news regularly throughout the Modern Age. In terms of comics, events like the death of Superman or President Obama appearing in *Amazing Spider-Man* received global coverage and resulted in huge sales for the books. On the big screen, superheroes have been setting box office records for more than thirty years. Comic book heroes are used to headlines like SPIDER-MAN AND BARACK OBAMA: "AMAZING SPIDER-MAN" #583 TEAM-UP HITS FIFTH PRINTING or *THE AVENGERS* SHATTERS BOX OFFICE RECORDS.

Wonder Woman has received press attention in recent years too, with eye-catching headlines like:

- WONDER WOMAN'S NEW HAIRDO CAUSES A STIR
- JOSS WHEDON DISCUSSES HIS DEFUNCT "WONDER WOMAN" MOVIE
- WONDER WOMAN FINALLY GETS A PAIR OF PANTS
- DC REVEALS SUPERMAN'S NEW LEADING LADY . . . AND IT'S A DOOZY

Entertainment Weekly didn't even mention Wonder Woman by name in that last one, an exclusive announcement about Wonder Woman and Superman getting together. Notice that it's not DC REVEALS WONDER WOMAN'S NEW LEADING MAN either. Wonder Woman's big headlines haven't been momentous events so much as a series of fashion changes, failed projects, and a romance where she takes a backseat role. She's faded into the background in comics, and she hasn't done anything particularly newsworthy in a long time.

And yet, despite these past few mundane decades, Wonder Woman is everywhere. On *The Big Bang Theory*, Sheldon Cooper had to dress as Wonder Woman after losing a bet to his archnemesis, Wil Wheaton. On *30 Rock*, Liz Lemon sang part of the *Wonder Woman* theme song in a recordable birthday card for her boss, Jack Donaghy. On *The Simpsons*, Homer mentioned that he wouldn't mind Wonder Woman tying him up in her lasso. Wonder Woman is a cultural touchstone, and she is referenced often.

Everybody knows of Wonder Woman, but not many people know much about her. It's common knowledge that Superman is Clark Kent and that he's from the planet Krypton, and most people know that Batman is Bruce Wayne and he lives in Gotham City. But it is unlikely that many people could tell you that Wonder Woman is Diana Prince and she's from Paradise Island. To most, their knowledge of Wonder Woman is limited to memories of Lynda Carter's spin change and bullet-deflecting bracelets. Wonder Woman is well known and beloved, but few have little more than a passing familiarity with the character herself. She's a powerful, vibrant woman in a sea of male superheroes, and for this she is loved, as she should be. But there's so much more to Wonder Woman.

That Wonder Woman is the most well-known female superhero is more than enough for legions of fans. Because most people don't know much about her outside of a generic concept of "female superhero," Wonder Woman becomes a blank slate to which we attach our own modern ideas. When a woman wears a bedazzled Wonder Woman shirt from Walmart or Target, she's probably not trying to

say, "I'm a big fan of this Jose Luis Garcia-Lopez artwork from the 1970s post-mod era." The message is more likely "I am a strong woman" or "I am a feminist."

When Wonder Woman is viewed only through a modern lens, the fascinating and important things she's represented for decades are easily missed. Wonder Woman has been a symbol of feminism and what it means to be a strong woman, but these aren't concrete ideas. Feminism in the 1940s was much different from feminism in the 1970s, and the role of women in 1950s America was a far cry from the role of women today. Wonder Woman has always dealt with these ever-changing concepts, whether she was embracing them or reacting against them. When we look at the history of Wonder Woman, we can see the history of American women as a whole, from new opportunities during World War II to the limited, domestic roles of Cold War culture to the assertion of rights and the power of women that brought about the women's liberation movement. Very few female characters have had the longevity of Wonder Woman, in comic books or any other medium. She's weathered every crisis that the comic book industry faced and has endured for seven decades in a constantly changing American society. The story of Wonder Woman is a meaningful history, one that deserves to be known.

Every version of Wonder Woman has been simultaneously progressive and problematic. The Golden Age Wonder Woman flipped typical gender roles and was a powerful heroine who cared about everyone, even her foes. The psychological theories that made the original Wonder Woman so uniquely feminist were tied to an often sadistic fetishism, and the comics both valorized and sexualized women and their powerful traits.

By the Silver Age, Wonder Woman more resembled her fellow female characters, but she was undisputedly the strongest and most courageous female character in comics. She survived being called out in *Seduction of the Innocent*, and she might have secretly been a lesbian the entire time.

245

Female characters began to assert themselves and step out on their own in the Bronze Age, while the mod Wonder Woman fell back as everyone else stepped forward. The human Diana Prince painted a poor portrait of modern womanhood, but amidst the violence and the heartbreak, Diana remained a force to be reckoned with.

Outside of comic books, the 1970s brought new interpretations of Wonder Woman. Cast as a feminist icon and imbued with the tenets of liberal feminism, *Ms.* modernized the character and the *Wonder Woman* TV show made her a household name.

The blank slate Wonder Woman of today is an icon, but by focusing on only that, her history and her humanity are lost. While Wonder Woman has always been a mess of contradictions, she has persevered. For every villain she rehabilitated, she was copiously bound. For every time she kowtowed to Steve Trevor, she defeated an alien giant bent on destroying the planet. For every man she fell in love with, she mastered a new martial art. She isn't a great character despite her contradictions but because of them. Wonder Woman has so many facets and incarnations, and within them lies a character who is both bizarre and brilliant. To forget her past is to miss what makes Wonder Woman such a great hero.

Acknowledgments

*O*ne thing you learn when writing your first book is that while writing is a rather solitary activity, a book is very much a group project.

This book began as an essay during my undergraduate degree in history at Dalhousie University, which was generously funded by a scholarship from Fred Fountain. As that essay grew into my master's thesis, funded by the Social Sciences and Humanities Research Council of Canada, I received great help and advice from my advisor, Dr. Todd McCallum; my thesis committee, Dr. Jerry Bannister, Dr. Claire Campbell, and Dr. Anthony Enns; and Saman Jafarian and the other grad students and staff at the Dalhousie history department.

Along the road from thesis to book, I had research assistance and general help from Janelle Asselin, Geoffrey C. Bunn, Jon B. Cooke, Calum Johnston of the world's best comic book store, Strange Adventures, Lauren Kalal from Rotary International, Alan Kupperberg, Trina Robbins, Jennifer K. Stuller, Kirsten van der Veen at the Smithsonian, and most likely many others I'm rudely forgetting.

The many books listed in the bibliography were invaluable to me, but in particular I should single out Bart Beaty's *Fredric Wertham and the Critique of Mass Culture*, Gerard Jones's *Men of Tomorrow: Geeks, Gangsters and the Birth of the Comic Book*, Amy Kiste-Nyberg's *Seal of Approval: The History of the Comics Code*, and, most important, Les Daniels's *Wonder Woman: The Complete History*. Daniels's book provided a solid background for all of the bizarre directions I took things in my own history of Wonder Woman, and I am indebted to his years of fantastic research in superhero comics across the board.

In compiling the images for the book, I had wonderful assistance from Kate Leth (www.kateordiecomics.com), Christie and Pete Marston (www.wonderwomannetwork.com), George W. Maschke (www.antipolygraph.org), Barry Sandoval at Heritage Auctions (www.ha.com), Robert and Sharon Schulman of the fine rare books shop the Book Collector's Library (www.tbclrarebooks.com), William Smith of the excellent pulp novel bookstore Hang Fire Books (www.hangfirebooks.com), and Roy Thomas (www.twomorrows.com).

Early drafts of the book were read by Drew Hanley, Wendy Hanley, Dr. Krista Kesselring, and Lindsay Pickrem, and their thoughts and comments were much appreciated.

I've also received a great deal of support for my writing online from Rich Johnston, who publishes my monthly "Gendercrunching" column at *Bleeding Cool* (www.bleedingcool.com) and the many guest posts Sue has let me write for the fantastic *DC Women Kicking Ass* (http://dcwomenkickingass.tumblr.com). Other folks like Susanna Baird, Brian Cronin, Alexa Dickman of *Ladies Making Comics*, Jill Pantozzi and Susannah Polo at the *Mary Sue*, Vaneta Rogers, Kelly Thompson, and yet again more people I'm rudely forgetting, have also been great with links, interviews, and the like.

I wrote the vast majority of this book in the study carrels at the Tantallon Public Library, which is a quiet, pleasant place with a great staff and an excellent comics section for when I wanted to take home something to read.

My agent Dawn Frederick of Red Sofa Literary took a chance on a new author when this book was a rough, unwieldy manuscript, for which I will be forever grateful. Yuval Taylor of Chicago Review Press bought it when it was somewhat less rough but still not there yet, and Michelle Hegarty of Modified Editing did most of the heavy lifting to turn it into the readable book it is now.

My best friend Lori read pretty near every draft of the book and endured me blathering on about Wonder Woman for years, and always had great insights and ideas. Huge chunks of the book are worlds better because of her input.

Finally, my parents, Lester and Darlene, my sister, Kate, my grandparents, and all of my family generally have been beyond supportive with this book. It's been a long process, and they've had my back every step of the way.

Source Notes

Introduction

"Wheeee! I'm a butterfly . . ." *Wonder Woman* #182 (May/June 1969).

1. The Utopian Alternative

Wonder Woman comics from the Golden Age are collected in two formats. *Wonder Woman* and *Sensation Comics* are reprinted chronologically in seven hardcover *Wonder Woman Archives* editions thus far, through to *Sensation Comics* #58 and *Wonder Woman* #18. There are also three softcover *Wonder Woman Chronicles* collections thus far, which also include Wonder Woman stories from *Comic Cavalcade*, through to *Sensation Comics* #18, *Wonder Woman* #5, and *Comic Cavalcade* #2. Both include Wonder Woman's first appearance in *All Star Comics* #8 in their first volumes. Select issues are also available digitally online through Comixology. There are various Superman *Archives* and *Chronicles* collecting *Superman* and *Action Comics*, along with Batman *Archives and Chronicles* collecting *Batman* and *Detective Comics*. DC uses *Archives* and *Chronicles* for its Golden Age collections, while Marvel uses *Masterworks*. Comics will be cited here with their issue number and publication date, and you can use those to find them in one of the collections listed above, unless the comic is from an unusual source, in which case that source will be cited as well.

The Golden Age

Information concerning the dawn of the Golden Age came primarily from *Superhero: The Secret Origin of a Genre* by Peter Coogan, *Men of Tomorrow: Geeks, Gangsters and the Birth of the Comic Book* by Gerard Jones, and *Comic Book Nation: The Transformation of Youth Culture in America* by Bradford Wright, though most books on the history of superheroes provide similar information.

"champion of the oppressed . . ." Action Comics #1 (June 1938).
"criminals are a superstitious . . ." *Detective Comics* #33 (November 1939).
regularly outsold Superman . . . See Ben Morse, "Thunderstruck," *Wizard Magazine* 179 (September 2006).

Tragic Genesis and Violence

For the tragic, violent nature of Golden Age superheroes, I relied on Dan Heggs's "Cyberpsychology and Cyborgs" in *Cyberpsychology*, and Jeffrey S. Lang and Patrick Trimble's "Whatever Happened to the Man of Tomorrow? An Examination of the American Monomyth and the Comic Book Superhero" in the *Journal of Popular Culture* 22, no. 3 (1988). Information about Jewish comic book creators came from *Disguised as Clark Kent: Jews, Comics, and the Creation of the Superhero* by Danny Fingeroth, *From Krakow to Krypton: Jews and Comic Books* by Arie Kaplan, *Men of Tomorrow: Geeks, Gangsters and the Birth of the Comic Book* by Gerard Jones, and *Up, Up, and Oy Vey: How Jewish History, Culture, and Values Shaped the Comic Book Superhero* by Simcha Weinstein.

Alan Scott became Green Lantern . . . First appeared in *All-American Comics* #16 (July 1940), created by Bill Finger and Martin Nodell.
The Human Torch was an android . . . First appeared in *Marvel Comics* #1 (October 1939), created by Carl Burgos.
special two-page spread . . . "How Would Superman End World War II?" reprinted in *Superman Sunday Classics: Strips 1–183, 1939–1943*, 187–190.
"You see how effortlessly . . ." *Action Comics* #2 (July 1938).
"I swear I'll follow you . . ." Ibid.
"nothing left of him but charred ashes . . ." *Captain America Comics* #1 (March 1941).

"I'm not talking, Bucky" . . . Ibid.

through a railing and into a vat of acid . . . *Detective Comics* #27 (May 1939).

flip a goon over the edge of a roof . . . *Detective Comics* #28 (June 1939).

strong kick to stop a gun-toting villain . . . *Detective Comics* #30 (August 1939).

gas pellet thrown into the cockpit . . . *Detective Comics* #33 (November 1939).

William Moulton Marston and the Origins of Wonder Woman

Background information on Marston, Peter, and the creation of Wonder Woman comes from Geoffrey C. Bunn's "The Lie Detector, *Wonder Woman* and Liberty: The Life and Work of William Moulton Marston" in *History of the Human Sciences* 10, no. 1 (1997); and Les Daniels's *Wonder Woman: The Complete History*.

parlaying their work into a "real" job . . . Charles Brownstein, *Eisner/Miller* (Milwaukee: Dark Horse Books, 2005), 188.

ads for Gillette razors . . . These ads appeared in the October 24, November 21, and December 19 editions of *LIFE* magazine in 1938.

women made only slight gains in the workforce . . . Claudia Dale Goldin, *Understanding the Gender Gap: An Economic History of American Women* (New York: Oxford University Press, 1990), 17.

often in jobs with little opportunity for advancement . . . Ibid., vii–viii.

Although they could now vote . . . S. J. Kleinberg, *Women in the United States, 1830–1945* (New Brunswick: Rutgers University Press, 1999), 288.

Those interested in higher education . . . Nancy F. Cott, *The Grounding of Modern Feminism* (New Haven: Yale University Press, 1987), 221.

"take over the rule of the country . . ." "Marston Advises 3 L's for Success," *New York Times*, November 11, 1937.

Elizabeth, his wife . . . Marguerite Lamb, "Who Was Wonder Woman? Long-ago LAW Alumna Elizabeth Marston Was the Muse Who Gave Us a Superheroine," *Boston University Alumni Magazine*, Fall 2001.

Her mother, Ethel Higgins Byrne . . . "Byrne, Ethel Higgins (1883–1955)," The Margaret Sanger Papers, http://wyatt.elasticbeanstalk.com/mep/MS /xml/bbyrnee.html.

"Don't Laugh at the Comics" . . . Interview with William Moulton Marston in Olive Richard, "Don't Laugh at the Comics," *Family Circle*, October 25, 1940.

"it seemed to me, from a psychological angle . . ." William Moulton Marston, "Why 100,000,000 Americans Read Comics," *American Scholar* 13 (January 1944): 42.

"America, the last citadel of democracy . . ." *All Star Comics* #8 (December 1941/January 1942).

"a double dose of pleasantness . . ." William Moulton Marston, *Emotions of Normal People* (New York: Harcourt, Brace, and Company, 1928), 280.

"women, as a sex . . ." Ibid., 258–259.

"there isn't love enough. . ." William Moulton Marston, letter to Coulton Waugh, March 5, 1945; all letters cited are from the Smithsonian's collection of Marston's papers.

"only when the control of self . . ." William Moulton Marston, letter to Max Gaines, March 20, 1943.

"the future is woman's . . ." William Moulton Marston, "Women: Servants of Civilization," *Tomorrow*, February 1942, 44–45.

"the next one hundred years will see . . ." "Marston Advises 3 L's for Success," *New York Times*.

"was writing a feminist book . . ." Sheldon Mayer, quoted in Les Daniels, *Wonder Woman: The Complete History* (San Francisco: Chronicle Books, 2000), 33.

"these simple, highly imaginative picture . . ." Interview with William Moulton Marston in Olive Richard, "The Women Are Our Future," *Family Circle*, August 14, 1942.

Wonder Woman outsold *Superman* at times . . . Ibid.

The Women of Wonder Woman

"Come on, let's have a Superwoman . . ." "Elizabeth H. Marston, Inspiration for Wonder Woman, 100" (obituary), *New York Times*, April 3, 1993.

Olive is often credited as the inspiration . . . Daniels, *Wonder Woman*, 31.

Roubicek was the first female assistant editor . . . Norman Tippens, "Dorothy Woolfolk, Superman Editor," *Daily Press*, December 6, 2000.

the only name we know is Helen Schpens . . . Roy Thomas, foreword to *Wonder Woman Archives Volume*, vol. 6, by William Moulton Marston and H. G. Peter (New York: DC Comics, 2010), 6.

Several issues were also lettered by Louise Marston . . . Ibid., 6.

Utopian Genesis and a New Approach to Crime Fighting

"With its fertile soil, its marvelous vegetation . . ." *All Star Comics* #8 (December 1941/January 1942).

"we do not permit ourselves . . ." Ibid.

"the beauty of Aphrodite . . ." *Sensation Comics* #3 (March 1942).

"a race of Wonder Women!" . . . *All Star Comics* #8 (December 1941/January 1942).

"You girls can develop strength . . ." *Wonder Woman* #23 (May/June 1947).

took their marching band to distract . . . *Sensation Comics* #2 (February 1942).

FN a *zoster,* a belt that represented . . . Michael J. Bennett, *Belted Heroes and Bound Women: The Myth of the Homeric War King* (Lanham, MD: Rowman & Littlefield, 1997), 171.

"Submitting to a cruel husband's domination . . ." *Wonder Woman* #5 (June/July 1943).

"get strong! Earn your own living . . ." Ibid.

"Wonder Woman made me work like you . . ." *Sensation Comics* #8 (August 1942).

"You're a born dancer . . ." *Sensation Comics* #22 (October 1943).

Rather than merely recapturing . . . *Wonder Woman* #3 (February/March 1943).

2. Damsels in Distress

Information concerning the role of women in 1940s popular culture came primarily from Linda Christian-Smith's "Gender, Popular Culture, and Curriculum: Adolescent Romance Novels as Gender Text" in *Curriculum Inquiry* 17, no. 4 (Winter 1987); Rita C. Hubbard's "Relationship Styles in Popular Romance Novels, 1950 to 1983" in *Communication Quarterly* 33, no. 2

(Spring 1985); Justine Larbalestier's *Battle of the Sexes in Science Fiction*; and Leerom Medovoi's *Rebels: Youth and the Cold War Origins of Identity*.

Robbins found that the earliest costumed heroine . . . Trina Robbins, *The Great Women Superheroes* (New York: Kitchen Sink Press, 1996), 3.

Timely Comics' Black Widow . . . *Mystic Comics* #4, August 1940.

Quality Comics' Phantom Lady . . . *Police Comics* #1, August 1941.

Miss America . . . *Military Comics* #1, August 1941.

the comic strip heroine Miss Fury . . . Trina Robbins, "Miss Fury," *Comics Journal* 288 (2007): 110–111.

"the perseverance of classical Hollywood . . ." Harry M. Benshoff and Sean Griffin, *America on Film: Representing Race, Class, Sexuality, and Gender at the Movies* (Oxford: Blackwell Publishing, 2004), 203.

"her value was acquired through . . ." Linda K. Christian-Smith, "Gender, Popular Culture, and Curriculum: Adolescent Romance Novels as Gender Text," *Curriculum Inquiry* 17, no. 4 (Winter 1987): 375–376.

"this literature was chockfull of cruel . . ." Joanna Russ, "The Image of Women in Science Fiction," in *Images of Women in Fiction: Feminist Perspectives*, ed. Susan Koppelman Cornillon (Bowling Green: Bowling Green University Popular Press, 1973), 83.

Wonder Woman

Superman rode a missile alongside fighter jets . . . *Superman* #18 (September/October 1942).

Batman and Robin delivered a gun to a soldier . . . *Batman* #30 (August/September 1945).

"Wonder Woman says do your duty . . ." *Sensation Comics* #8 (August 1942).

shut down Japanese bases all over the world, from Mexico . . . *Wonder Woman* #1 (Summer 1942).

to South America . . . *Sensation Comics* #18 (June 1943).

to China . . . *Wonder Woman* #4 (April/May 1943).

seized a German U-boat . . . *Sensation Comics* #6 (June 1942).

overturned a Japanese dreadnought . . . *Wonder Woman* #6 (Fall 1943).

captured an entire fleet of Nazi battleships . . . *Sensation Comics* #15 (March 1943).

a plot to poison the water supply . . . *Sensation Comics* #2 (February 1942).

disrupt American industry . . . *Sensation Comics* #16 (April 1943).

a Nazi spy impersonating an American general . . . *Sensation Comics* #20 (August 1943).

the hands of subterranean molemen . . . *Wonder Woman* #4 (April/May 1943).

an invading army from Saturn . . . *Wonder Woman* #10 (Fall 1944).

bullying was important to Wonder Woman . . . *Sensation Comics* #23 (November 1943).

When Steve was taken by Nazi gangsters . . . *Sensation Comics* #3 (March 1942).

about to shoot Steve . . . *Sensation Comics* #7 (July 1942).

"Tearing off door after door . . ." *Sensation Comics* #12 (December 1942).

"Wonder Woman is the most gorgeous . . ." *Sensation Comics* #2 (February 1942).

"Wonder Woman—my beautiful angel . . ." *Wonder Woman* #1 (Summer 1942).

"Steve, overjoyed at having the case . . ." *Sensation Comics* #13 (January 1943).

"Oh, my beautiful angel . . ." *Sensation Comics* #13 (January 1943).

"Look, angel—this plane . . ." *Sensation Comics* #24 (December 1943).

"Oh, Steve is going . . ." *Sensation Comics* #3 (March 1942).

"Will—(sob) you—(sob) . . ." Ibid.

"Ha! Ha! Diana the sleuth . . ." *Sensation Comics* #10 (October 1942).

"I'm almost jealous of myself . . ." *Sensation Comics* #7 (July 1942).

"Superman didn't become Superman . . ." Soliloquy by Bill (David Carradine), in *Kill Bill: Volume 2*, written and directed by Quentin Tarantino (Miramax, 2004).

"[Diana] will have to go on mooning . . ." *Sensation Comics* #6 (June 1942).

"the man Diana loves . . ." *Sensation Comics* #2 (February 1942).

FN "Diana Prince" was literally someone else . . . *Sensation Comics* #1 (January 1942).

Lois Lane

rescuing her from kidnappers . . . *Action Comics* #1 (June 1938).

catching her as she plummeted . . . *Action Comics* #6 (November 1938).

faster than a speeding bullet . . . *New York World's Fair* #1 (June 1939), in *The Superman Chronicles*, vol. 1, by Jerry Siegel and Joe Shuster (New York: DC Comics, 2006), 176.

"He's grand! He's glorious . . ." *Action Comics* #9 (February 1939).

"Don't go! Stay with me . . ." *Action Comics* #5 (October 1938).

"I'd advise you not to print . . ." *Action Comics* #1 (June 1938).

"Save the questions!" . . . *Action Comics* #2 (July 1938).

"too important!—This is no . . ." *Action Comics* #5 (October 1938).

the lovelorn column . . . *Superman* #3 (Winter 1939).

Clark often knocked Lois unconscious with a nerve pinch . . . See *Superman* #4 (Spring 1940) and *Superman* #7 (November/December 1940) for examples.

"Oh, how I hate Clark Kent . . ." *Superman* #3 (Winter 1939).

only to steal her big revelation . . . Ibid.

recommended for the Distinguished Service Cross . . . *Sensation Comics* #18 (June 1943).

Robin, the Boy Wonder

Batman saved her from the clutches . . . *Detective Comics* #32 (October 1939).

called off the engagement . . . *Detective Comics* #49 (March 1941).

stop chasing the villain to tend to . . . *Batman* #8 (December 1941/January 1942).

dispatch a group of thugs . . . *Batman* #5 (Spring 1941).

allow himself to be captured . . . *Batman* #7 (October/November 1941).

"You reckless young squirt . . ." *Detective Comics* #38 (April 1940).

"Well doggone! All I can say . . ." *Detective Comics* #39 (May 1940).

Catwoman

Information concerning femme fatales came from Jack Boozer's "The Lethal Femme Fatale in the Noir Tradition" in *Journal of Film and Video* 51, no. 3/4 (Fall 1999); and Elisabeth Bronfen's "Femme Fatale—Negotiations of Tragic Desire" in *New Literary History* 35, no. 1 (Winter 2004).

Catwoman first appeared as the Cat . . . *Batman* #1 (Spring 1940).

she was called Cat-woman or Cat Woman . . . *Batman* #10 (April/May 1942).

a beautician named Elva Barr . . . *Batman* #15 (February/March 1943).

she became Selina Kyle in 1952 . . . *Batman* #62 (December 1950/January 1951).

"I'll bet you bumped into me . . ." *Batman* #1 (Spring 1940).

"What a night! A night for . . ." *Batman* #3 (Fall 1940).
Catwoman's kiss left Batman . . . *Batman* #10 (April/May 1942).
"It's too bad she has to be a crook!" . . . *Batman* #3 (Fall 1940).

The Inverted World of Wonder Woman

"not even girls want to be girls . . ." Marston, "Why 100,000,000 Americans
   Read Comics," 42.

3. Amazon Princess, Bondage Queen

A Note on Charts and Numbers

Starting in this chapter, and throughout the rest of the book, I use a lot of
charts and numbers to talk about things. The full, raw data for any number I
use in the book is available online somewhere at http://thanley.wordpress.com,
and you can see how I arrived at my various percentages and figures there.

A Staggering Amount of Bondage

Robbins points out that because Billy . . . Robbins, *The Great Women Superheroes*, 13.

Bondage and the Coming Matriarchy

"Will war ever end in this world . . ." Richard, "The Women Are Our Future."
"as the greatest—no, even more . . ." Ibid.
"nature-endowed soldiers of Aphrodite . . ." Ibid.
"boys, young and old, satisfy their wish thoughts . . ." Ibid.
"the subconscious, elaborately disguised desire of males . . ." Ibid.
"The only hope for peace is to teach people . . ." William Moulton Marston,
   letter to Max Gaines, February 20, 1943.
At Christmastime, the Amazons celebrated Diana's Day . . . *Wonder Woman*
   #3 (February/March 1943).
"Oh yes, we love it!" . . . *Wonder Woman* #6 (Fall 1943).
"Bind me as tight as you can . . ." *Wonder Woman* #13 (Summer 1945).

"On Paradise Island where we play . . ." *Sensation Comics* #35 (November 1944).

"You weel regret zis . . ." *Wonder Woman* #26 (November/December 1947).

"Horsefeathers! You'll end up loving . . ." Ibid.

"These bonds feel wonderful! Keep me here . . ." *Sensation Comics* #22 (October 1943).

"I shall make you tell the truth . . ." *Sensation Comics* #20 (August 1943).

"dramatized symbol of her sex . . ." Richard, "The Women Are Our Future."

"woman's charm is the one bond that can be . . ." Ibid.

"Daughter, if any man welds chains . . ." *Sensation Comics* #4 (April 1942).

"Aye weep, captive girl . . ." *Wonder Woman* #2 (Fall 1942).

rip her spirit from her body . . . *Wonder Woman* #5 (June/July 1943).

"My Wonder Woman often lets . . ." Richard, "The Women Are Our Future."

The Bondage Battle

This section owes a great deal to Les Daniels's *Wonder Woman: The Complete History* as well as the collection of Marston's papers available via the Smithsonian Institution.

"this feature does lay you open . . ." Josette Frank, letter to Max Gaines, February 17, 1943.

"My impressions confirmed those of . . ." W. W. D. Sones, letter to Max Gaines, March 15, 1943.

"I am one of those odd, perhaps unfortunate . . ." US Army sergeant, letter to Max Gaines, September 1943.

"this is one of the things I've . . ." Max Gaines, letter to William Moulton Marston, September 14, 1943.

"Miss Roubicek hastily dashed off . . ." Ibid.

"I have the good Sergeant's letter in which . . ." William Moulton Marston, letter to Max Gaines, September 1943.

"the fact is, it was a runaway best-seller" . . . Sheldon Mayer, quoted in Daniels, *Wonder Woman*, 61.

"the strip is full of significant sex . . ." Josette Frank, letter to Max Gaines, January 29, 1944.

"normal men retain their childish longing . . ." Richard, "The Women Are Our Future."

"was writing a feminist book, but not for . . ." Mayer, quoted in Daniels, *Wonder Woman*, 33.

"the unique appeal of the erotic actress" . . . William Moulton Marston, "Sex Films Great Moral Aid," *Indiana Weekly Messenger*, September 26, 1929, along with several other newspapers across the country.

Sex with Marston

"the husband is sometimes like an orang-outang . . ." Havelock Ellis, *The Psychology of Sex: A Manual for Students* (New York: Emerson Books, 1938), 284.

these manuals espoused sexual harmony for married couples . . . See Michael Gordon, "From an Unfortunate Necessity to a Cult of Mutual Orgasm: Sex in American Marital Education Literature, 1830–1940," in *Studies in the Sociology of Sex*, ed. James M. Henslin (New York: Appleton-Century-Crofts, 1971), 53–80; and M. E. Melody and Linda M. Peterson, *Teaching America About Sex: Marriage Guides and Sex Manuals from the Late Victorians to Dr. Ruth* (New York: New York University Press, 1999).

repressive ideas about women and sex . . . For critiques of early sexologists, see Margaret Jackson, " 'Facts of Life' or the Eroticization of Women's Oppression? Sexology and the Social Construction of Heterosexuality," in *The Cultural Construction of Sexuality*, ed. Pat Caplan (London: Tavistock Publications, 1987), 52–81; Kathleen Barry, *Female Sexual Slavery* (Englewood Cliffs: Prentice-Hall, 1979); Margaret Jackson, "Sexual Liberation or Social Control? Some Aspects of the Relationship Between Feminism and the Social Construction of Knowledge in the Early Twentieth Century," in *Women's Studies International Forum* 6, no. 1 (1983): 1–17; and Ruth Bleier, *Science and Gender: A Critique of Biology and Its Theories on Women* (New York: Pergamon Press, 1984).

so researchers looked to the animal kingdom . . . Havelock Ellis, *Studies in the Psychology of Sex, Volume III: Analysis of the Sexual Impulse* (New York: Random House, 1942; orig. publ. 1903), 69.

her unconscious self had actually consented to the act . . . See Susan Brownmiller, *Against Our Will: Men, Women and Rape* (New York: Fawcett Columbine, 1975), 315.

"compatible with a high degree of general . . ." Havelock Ellis, *Studies in the Psychology of Sex, Volume I: The Evolution of Modesty, the Phenomena of Sexual Periodicity, and Auto-Erotism* (New York: Random House, 1942; orig. publ. 1900), 166.

"however much dominant resistance the . . ." Marston, *Emotions*, 337.

"the male becomes a constant attendant . . ." Ibid., 332.

the woman should initiate all of the movements . . . Ibid., 335.

"normal males get the maximum of love . . ." Marston to Gaines, March 20, 1943.

"abnormal extreme" and arguing . . . Marston, *Emotions*, 385.

"the enjoyment of other people's actual . . ." Marston to Gaines, February 20, 1943.

Venus with Us, Marston's Ancient Roman Sex Romp

"The title is from the Latin 'Venus nobiscum' . . ." William Moulton Marston, *Venus with Us*, (New York: Sears Publishing Company, 1932), inside flap, via the Book Collector's Library, www.tbclrarebooks.com.

"Here is the whole panorama of Roman times . . ." William Moulton Marston, *The Private Life of Julius Caesar (Venus with Us)* (New York: Universal, 1953), 1953, back cover.

"Is it possible that you do not understand . . ." Ibid., 65.

"love without pleasure is a dreary occupation . . ." Ibid., 66.

"I have a notion it's really rather good . . ." Ibid., 39.

Ursula lost, and much tickling and spanking . . . Ibid., 266–267.

"I *love* to call you Mistress . . ." Ibid., 135.

"it was the girl who ruled . . ." Ibid., 19.

"She made him boast himself her slave . . ." Ibid., 20.

Metala kept her as a slave . . . Ibid., 76–82.

"but Caesar, with a natural gift for psychology . . ." Ibid., 15.

"Julius glanced about the room and laughed . . ." Ibid., 45.

"the prettiest sight I have ever seen" . . . Ibid., 231.

"the most marvelous spectacle . . ." Ibid., 242.

"Caesar had not felt so well for twenty years . . ." Ibid., 236.

William Moulton Marston, Bondage Connoisseur

"This is the famous 'brank' . . ." *Wonder Woman* #6 (Fall 1943).

In certain areas of Europe from the sixteenth . . . See "The Brank," Medieval Times & Castles, www.medievality.com/brank.html.

"As the Fabulous French Women's Prison Falls . . ." Carl De Vidal Hunt, "As the Fabulous French Women's Prison Falls After 14 Years, Comes the First Look-In on Its Million Secrets," *Miami News*, June 19, 1932, and several other newspapers across the country, with further reports in the weeks that followed.

embedding Wonder Woman in a three-inch-thick statue . . . *Wonder Woman* #8 (Spring 1944).

freezing her in a block of ice . . . *Wonder Woman* #13 (Summer 1945).

turning her into a being of pure color . . . *Wonder Woman* #16 (March/April 1946).

The Interconnectedness of All Things

call Marston a quack or a pervert . . . See David Hadju, *The Ten-Cent Plague: The Great Comic-Book Scare and How It Changed America* (New York: Farar, Straus, and Giroux, 2008), 77–78; and Douglas Wolk, *Reading Comics: How Graphic Novels Work and What They Mean* (Cambridge, MA: Da Capo Press, 2008), 98, for dismissive treatments of Marston.

pretend that the bondage is inconsequential . . . See Robbins, *The Great Women Superheroes*, 12–13.

Interlude 1: *Wonder Woman*'s Extra Features

The Golden Age

"what a large part comics and comic books . . ." *Wonder Woman* #1 (Summer 1942).

"women still have many problems and have not yet . . ." Alice Marble, letter to Miss Nila Frances Allen, July 23, 1942, available at http://scoop.diamondgalleries.com/public/default.asp?t=1&m=1&c=34&s=259&ai=53962&ssd=9/16/2006&arch=y.

In 1944, the newly married Marble suffered . . . See Alice Marble and Dale
Leatherman, *Courting Danger: My Adventures in World-Class Tennis,
Golden-Age Hollywood, and High-Stakes Spying* (New York: St. Martin's Press, 1991), 192–239.

The Interregnum

"Race to the Top of the World" . . . *Wonder Woman* #30 (July/August 1948).
"You Name It" . . . *Wonder Woman* #31 (September/October 1948).
the calendar . . . "Our Amazing Calendar," in *Wonder Woman* #32 (November/
December 1948).
the Colossus of Rhodes . . . "The Majestic Giant," in *Wonder Woman* #33
(February 1949).
pineapples . . . "The Friendly Fruit," in *Wonder Woman* #37 (October 1949).
unique headdresses . . . "Where'd You Get That Hat?" in *Wonder Woman* #41
(May/June 1950).
"can wear her hair in bangs or a chignon . . ." "Those Lovely Liberty Belles,"
in *Wonder Woman* #58 (March/April 1953).

4. A Herculean Task

Wonder Woman comics from the Silver Age are collected in four black-and-
white *Showcase Presents: Wonder Woman* volumes comprising *Wonder
Woman* #98 through *Wonder Woman* #177. All other DC series mentioned
are collected in either *Showcase* or *Archive* volumes, occasionally both, with
varying degrees of completeness. Typically, the more well-known the character, the more collections there will be.

surveys showed that 80 percent of female wartime workers . . . Maureen
Honey, *Creating Rosie the Riveter: Class, Gender, and Propaganda During World War II* (Amherst: University of Massachusetts Press, 1984), 24.

Prelude to the Silver Age

For information on Wertham, the Senate hearings, and the Comics Code
Authority, see Bart Beaty's *Fredric Wertham and the Critique of Mass Culture*;

David Hadju's *The Ten-Cent Plague: The Great Comic-Book Scare and How It Changed America*; Amy Kiste Nyberg's *Seal of Approval: The History of the Comics Code*; and pretty much every book written on the history of comics ever. Information about William Gaines came from Frank Jacobs's *The Mad World of William M. Gaines.*

He argued against Ethel Rosenberg's solitary . . . Bart Beaty, *Fredric Wertham and the Critique of Mass Culture* (Jackson: University Press of Mississippi, 2005), 85.

he gave testimony during the landmark . . . Ibid., 95.

several articles about the dangers of comic books . . . See Fredric Wertham, "The Comics . . . Very Funny," *Saturday Review of Literature*, May 29, 1948, 6–7, 27–29; Wertham, "The Curse of Comic Books: The Value Patterns and Effects of Comic Books," *Religious Education* 49 (1954) : 394–406.

"1) The comic-book format . . ." Fredric Wertham, *Seduction of the Innocent* (New York: Rinehart & Company, 1954), 118.

"Hitler was a beginner compared to . . ." "Testimony of Dr. Fredric Wertham, Psychiatrist, Director, Lafargue Clinic, New York, N.Y.," April 21, 1954, available at www.thecomicbooks.com/wertham.html.

"My only limits are the bounds of good taste . . ." "Testimony of William S. Gaines, Publisher, Entertaining Comics Group, New York, N.Y.," April 21, 1954, available at www.thecomicbooks.com/gaines.html.

NO HARM IN HORROR, COMICS ISSUE SAYS . . . Peter Khiss, "No Harm in Horror, Comics Issuer Says; Comics Publisher Sees No Harm in Horror, Discounts 'Good Taste,' " *New York Times*, April 22, 1954.

"in every instance shall good triumph . . ." 1955 Comic Code, in Amy Kiste Nyberg, *Seal of Approval: The History of the Comics Code* (Jackson: University Press of Mississippi, 1998), 166.

"terror" and "horror" . . . Ibid., 167.

The Dawn of the Silver Age

For information concerning the Silver Age, see *Superhero: The Secret Origin of a Genre* by Peter Coogan, *Men of Tomorrow: Geeks, Gangsters and the Birth of the Comic Book* by Gerard Jones, and *Comic Book Nation: The Transformation of Youth Culture in America* by Bradford Wright, though again, any book on this period will cover similar ground.

Hal Jordan, who appeared as the new Green Lantern . . . First appeared in
   Showcase #22 (October 1959), created by John Broome and Gil Kane.

The new Hawkman, Katar Hol . . . First appeared in *The Brave and the Bold*
   #34 (February/March 1961), created by Gardner Fox and Joe Kubert.

Ray Palmer, was a physicist . . . First appeared in *Showcase* #34 (September/
   October 1961), created by Gardner Fox and Gil Kane.

Martian Manhunter . . . First appeared in *Detective Comics* #225 (November
   1955), created by Joseph Samachson and Joe Certa.

Supergirl . . . First appeared in *Action Comics* #252 (May 1959), created by
   Otto Binder and Curt Swan.

Fantastic Four gained superpowers . . . First appeared in *The Fantastic Four*
   #1 (November 1961), created by Stan Lee and Jack Kirby.

Peter Parker became Spider-Man . . . First appeared in *Amazing Fantasy* #15
   (August 1962), created by Stan Lee and Steve Ditko.

Bruce Banner into the raging Hulk . . . First appeared in *The Incredible Hulk*
   #1 (May 1962), created by Stan Lee and Jack Kirby.

Kathy Kane became Batwoman . . . First appeared in *Detective Comics* #233
   (July 1956), created by Bob Kane and Sheldon Moldoff.

Betty Kane joined her as Bat-Girl . . . First appeared in *Batman* #139 (April
   1961), created by Bob Kane and Sheldon Moldoff.

turned into an alien . . . *Batman* #140 (June 1961).

sent back to ancient Babylon . . . *Batman* #102 (September 1956).

battling gods, dragons . . . *Batman* #153 (May 1963).

Robert Kanigher Revises Wonder Woman

baby Diana was visited by four . . . *Wonder Woman* #105 (April 1959).

"Woe is us . . . we are alone . . ." Ibid.

"man's world to battle crime and injustice . . ." *Wonder Woman* #98 (May
   1958).

she could manipulate updrafts . . . Ibid.

There were men in a few Amazon myths . . . Of the ancient sources, only
   Herodotus, Hippocrates, Xenophon, and Diodorus Siculus mention the
   Amazons living with men, and only Herodotus has them doing so without
   maiming and mangling the male children.

Apollodorus's ancient account . . . Apollodorus, *The Library*, vol. 1, trans. Sir James George Frazier (Cambridge, MA: Harvard University Press, 1967), 203.

a few screwball romance stories with Hippolyta . . . See *Wonder Woman* #130 (May 1962) and *Wonder Woman* #132 (August 1962).

"Kanigher's plots hurtled from event to event . . ." Will Jacobs and Gerard Jones, *The Comic Book Heroes: The First History of Modern Comic Books—from the Silver Age to the Present* (Rocklin, CA: Prima, 1997), 56.

"I'm an instinctual writer . . ." Robin Snyder, "The Golden Age Gladiator: Robert Kanigher," in *Comics Journal* 85 (October 1983): 64.

"Impossible! She never had a father" . . . Ibid.: 62.

"strong influence" on how Wonder Woman . . . Ibid.: 65.

Kanigher's new story appeared for Wonder Woman . . . *Secret Origins* #1 (Summer 1961).

5. Focus on the Family, or Superman Is a Jackass

"would create a feeling of warmth . . ." Elaine Tyler May, *Homeward Bound: American Families in the Cold War Era* (New York: Basic Books, 1988), 23.

"the treatment of love-romance stories . . ." 1955 Comic Code, in Nyberg, *Seal of Approval*, 168.

Wonder Woman

a clam was a gateway to travel through time . . . *Wonder Woman* #131 (July 1962).

battled a cannibal clam . . . *Wonder Woman* #107 (July 1959).

giants from different dimensions . . . *Wonder Woman* #100 (August 1958).

planets . . . *Wonder Woman* #102 (November 1958) and *Wonder Woman* #120 (February 1961).

time periods . . . *Wonder Woman* #109 (October 1959).

pterodactyls . . . *Wonder Woman* #101 (October 1958).

rocs . . . *Wonder Woman* #113 (April 1960).

dimorphodons . . . *Wonder Woman* #121 (April 1961).

a space eagle . . . *Wonder Woman* #105 (April 1959).

Steve gave Wonder Woman perfume . . . *Wonder Woman* #102 (November 1958).

"I'd love to, Steve! You know I like . . ." *Wonder Woman* #137 (April 1963).

"I can't marry you—until my services . . ." *Wonder Woman* #99 (July 1958).

"How can I become your wife 100% . . ." *Wonder Woman* #137 (April 1963).

"It would be unfair to marry you . . ." *Wonder Woman* #133 (October 1962).

seashell fraternity pin . . . *Wonder Woman* #115 (July 1960).

sea dances . . . *Wonder Woman* #111 (January 1960).

"I've had enough! And to think . . ." *Wonder Woman* #116 (August 1960).

out of a group of Wonder Woman robots . . . *Wonder Woman* #103 (January 1959).

Wonder Woman disguised herself as a movie star . . . *Wonder Woman* #133 (October 1962).

she called him two-faced . . . *Wonder Woman* #126 (November 1961).

"The nerve of Steve! Always praising . . ." *Wonder Woman* #130 (May 1962).

"Angel—if you really cared for me . . ." *Wonder Woman* #122 (May 1961).

"I don't care whether you think it's fair . . ." *Wonder Woman* #127 (January 1962).

"I'm getting sick and tired . . ." *Wonder Woman* #133 (October 1962).

"I'm tired of waiting around for you . . ." Ibid.

"If you really loved me . . ." *Wonder Woman* #137 (April 1963).

if Steve picked Wonder Woman out . . . *Wonder Woman* #99 (July 1958).

if Wonder Woman had to save Steve . . . *Wonder Woman* #101 (October 1958).

Steve tried to show her that he was braver . . . *Wonder Woman* #118 (November 1960).

"Now you're trying to make a fool . . ." *Wonder Woman* #132 (August 1962).

Lois Lane

"It seems you owe your career to Superman . . ." *Superman's Girl Friend Lois Lane* #17 (May 1960).

"AMBITION: To become Mrs. Superman" . . . For example, in *Wonder Woman* #98 (May 1958).

took a leave of absence . . . *Superman's Girl Friend Lois Lane* #1 (March/ April 1958).

wore a new, exotic outfit every day . . . *Superman's Girl Friend Lois Lane* #5 (November/December 1958).

an experimental youth ray . . . *Superman's Girl Friend Lois Lane* #10 (July 1959).

"the fattest girl in Metropolis" . . . *Superman's Girl Friend Lois Lane* #5 (November/ December 1958).

encasing her entire head in a lead box . . . *Superman's Girl Friend Lois Lane* #13 (November 1959).

a local hero named Samson . . . *Superman's Girl Friend Lois Lane* #19 (August 1960).

then with Robin Hood . . . *Superman's Girl Friend Lois Lane* #22 (January 1961).

an alien named Astounding Man . . . *Superman's Girl Friend Lois Lane* #18 (July 1960).

"Whatever got into Clark . . ." *Superman's Girl Friend Lois Lane* #3 (July/ August 1958).

"I'll have to teach her lesson for using . . ." *Superman's Girl Friend Lois Lane* #1 (March/April 1958).

pretended that Lois had developed Kryptonite . . . *Superman's Girl Friend Lois Lane* #16 (April 1960).

"Now she's stuck in a revolving door . . ." Ibid.

Supergirl

"No, Supergirl! I have many cunning . . ." *Action Comics* #258 (November 1959).

"I won't get any headlines . . ." *Action Comics* #253 (June 1959).

used her heat vision to burn a roast . . . *Action Comics* #254 (July 1959).

helping Timmy Tate . . . *Action Comics* #253 (June 1959).

proving that Paul was not lying . . . *Action Comics* #266 (July 1960).

help Frank Cullen shoot several . . . *Action Comics* #270 (November 1960).

Nancy could iron her dress . . . *Adventure Comics* #278 (November 1960).

to help Eddie Moran rescue. . . *Action Comics* #274 (March 1961).

Tommy Tomorrow find parents . . . *Action Comics* #255 (August 1959).

found a home for a Bizarro baby . . . *Superman* #140 (October 1960).

"Jeepers! If . . . if cousin Superman . . ." *Superman's Girl Friend Lois Lane* #14 (January 1960).

"H-how long will I have to wait . . ." *Adventure Comics* #278 (November 1960).

Supergirl was finally adopted . . . *Action Comics* #279 (August 1961).

"You must be taught a lesson . . ." *Action Comics* #258 (November 1959).

FN "Now that she's superior to me . . ." *Action Comics* #282 (November 1961).

Star Sapphire

"Mr. Jordan, *puh-lease!* From now on . . ." *Showcase* #22 (September/ October 1959).

"Night and day . . . day and night . . ." *Green Lantern* #1 (July/August 1960).

the two sporadically went out on the town . . . *Green Lantern* #6 (May/June 1961).

"Carol Ferris, in the absence of her father . . ." *Green Lantern* #7 (July/August 1961).

"the young and pretty 'boss' . . ." *Green Lantern* #18 (January 1963).

"from a world tremendously in advance . . ." *Green Lantern* #16 (October 1962).

"As our future queen you must be made . . ." Ibid.

"She doesn't seem to realize that men . . ." Ibid.

"She acts as if a man could be . . ." Ibid.

"I feel so weak . . . so helpless . . ." Ibid.

Using her impressive powers . . . *Green Lantern* #26 (January 1964).

6. Conforming to the Code

Fredric Wertham and the Seduction of the Innocent

"Superman (with the big S on his uniform . . ." Wertham, *Seduction of the Innocent*, 34.

"they live in sumptuous quarters . . ." Ibid., 190.

"the lesbian counterpart of Batman . . ." Wertham, *Seduction of the Innocent*, 192.

"the homosexual connotation . . ." Ibid., 192.

FN Recent research by Carol Tilley shows . . . Carol L. Tilley, "Seducing the Innocent: Fredric Wertham and the Falsifications That Helped Condemn Comics," *Information & Culture* 47, no. 4 (2012): 383–413.

"extremely sadistic hatred of all males . . ." Ibid., 193.

"for boys, Wonder Woman is a frightening image" . . . Ibid., 193.

"Her followers are the 'Holliday . . ." Ibid., 193.

"even when Wonder Woman adopts . . ." Ibid., 234.

"They do not work. They are not homemakers . . ." Ibid., 234.

"Wonder Woman is not the natural daughter . . ." Ibid., 234.

"if it were possible to translate a cardboard figure . . ." Ibid., 235.

Suffering Sappho!! Was Wonder Woman a Lesbian?

"that nearly half of the female love relationships . . ." Marston, *Emotions*, 338.

"in several cases, well-adapted love . . ." Ibid., 338.

"the pick of the women who the average man . . ." Havelock Ellis, *Studies in the Psychology of Sex, Volume II: Sexual Inversion* (New York: Random House, 1942, orig. publ. 1897), 222.

male homosexuality was a purely dominant . . . Marston, *Emotions*, 252–253.

"with regard to the possibly deleterious . . ." Ibid., 339.

FN "the excessive amount of passion response . . ." Ibid., 339.

"girls and women who indulge in this . . ." Ibid., 338.

"with the invaluable aid of my collaborators" . . . Ibid., 338.

one of the most, if not *the* most, detailed . . . Ibid., 299–313.

"excited pleasantness of captivation . . ." Ibid., 300.

"about three-fourths of the girls . . ." Ibid., 311.

"it seems undoubtedly to be the fact . . ." Ibid., 313.

"Bona Dea is a woman's goddess exclusively . . ." Marston, *Private Life of Julius Caesar*, 114.

"very young girls, some of them still . . ." Ibid., 123.

"Cassandra felt the hands of several women . . ." Ibid., 124.

Etta swinging a piece of candy . . . *Sensation Comics* #3 (March 1942).

paddled by a hooded girl . . . *Sensation Comics* #4 (April 1942).

bound, blindfolded, and left in the middle . . . *Wonder Woman* #12 (Spring 1945).

"grand mistress of spanks and slams" . . . *Wonder Woman* #22 (March/April 1947).

"By Sappho's stylus . . ." *Wonder Woman* #6 (Fall 1943).

watch a movie in Sappho Hall . . . *Comic Cavalcade* #12 (Fall 1945).

he stated outright that all of the Amazons were lesbians . . . Trina Robbins, "Wonder Woman: Lesbian or Dyke? Paradise Island as a Woman's Community," paper presented at WisCon 2006, available at www.girl-wonder .org/papers/robbins.html.

Steve carrying Wonder Woman across a brook . . . *Sensation Comics* #94 (November/December 1949).

bringing her flowers . . . *Sensation Comics* #97 (May/June 1950).

The Changing Content of Wonder Woman

"suggestive and salacious illustration . . ." 1955 Comic Code, in Nyberg, *Seal of Approval*, 168.

"sex perversion or any inference to same . . ." Ibid.

The Real World Carries On

For the social activism of women in the 1950s, see *Not June Cleaver: Women and Gender in Postwar America, 1945–1960*, ed. Joanne Meyerowitz, specifically: Susan Rimby Leighow's "An 'Obligation to Participate,' " Dorothy Sue Cobble's "Recapturing Working-Class Feminism," Ruth Feldstein's "I Wanted the Whole World to See," Dee Garrison's "Our Skirts Gave Them Courage," and Margaret Rose's "Gender and Civic Activism in Mexican Barrios in California"; and Lynne Olson's *Freedom's Daughters: The Unsung Heroines of the Civil Rights Movement from 1830 to 1970*. For information concerning women and sexuality in the 1950s, see Wini Breines's *Young, White, and Miserable: Growing Up Female in the Fifties*, David Halberstam's *The Fifties*, and Brett Harvey's *The Fifties: A Women's Oral History*.

"All you have to do is perform a few feats . . ." *Wonder Woman* #136 (February 1963).

Interlude 2: Letters and Advertisements

Advertisements

Jewelry ads featuring smiling women . . . See National Diamond Sales in *Wonder Woman* #192 (January/February 1971); and Woodstock-inspired jewelry in *Wonder Woman* #193 (March/April 1971).

a model "especially for girls" . . . This ad first appeared in *Wonder Woman* #183 (July/August 1969).

Iverson cut any mention of their girls' bicycle . . . *Wonder Woman* #186 (January/February 1970).

In *Fantastic Four,* the ad showed a young man . . . *Fantastic Four* #47 (February 1966).

young man was replaced by a young woman . . . *Millie the Model* #147 (March 1967).

7. Wonder Woman No More

Wonder Woman comics from the Bronze Age are collected in four full-color, softcover *Diana Prince: Wonder Woman* volumes, comprising her mod adventures from *Wonder Woman* #178 through *Wonder Woman* #203. A brief portion of her later adventures as the Amazon Wonder Woman are collected in *Wonder Woman: The Twelve Labors,* comprising *Wonder Woman* #212 through *Wonder Woman* #222. DC comics from this era are collected primarily in *Showcase* volumes, with special volumes for specific, famous story lines. Marvel comics from this era are collected in *Essential* and *Omnibus* volumes.

The Marvel Age

For information on Marvel Comics in the 1960s, see *Tales to Astonish: Jack Kirby, Stan Lee, and the American Comic Book Revolution* by Ronin Ro, *Stan Lee and the Rise and Fall of the American Comic Book* by Jordan Raphael and Tom Spurgeon, as well as any book about comic history that mentions the 1960s at all . . . Marvel will come up.

Marvel's first new series, *Fantastic Four* . . . First appeared in *Fantastic Four* #1 (November 1961), created by Stan Lee and Jack Kirby.

soon followed by *The Incredible Hulk* . . . First appeared in *The Incredible Hulk* #1 (May 1942), created by Stan Lee and Jack Kirby.

Lee and Ditko created Spider-Man . . . First appeared in *Amazing Fantasy* #15 (August 1962), created by Stan Lee and Steve Ditko.

the X-Men, a group of powerful . . . First appeared in *The X-Men* #1 (September 1963), created by Stan Lee and Jack Kirby.

Iron Man, a millionaire . . . First appeared in *Tales of Suspense* #39 (March 1963), created by Stan Lee, Larry Lieber, Don Heck, and Jack Kirby.

Doctor Strange, master of the occult . . . First appeared in *Strange Tales* #110 (July 1963), created by Stan Lee and Steve Ditko.

Thor, the Norse god . . . First appeared in *Journey into Mystery* #83 (August 1962), created by Stan Lee, Larry Lieber, and Jack Kirby.

Daredevil, a blind man . . . First appeared in *Daredevil* #1 (April 1964), created by Stan Lee and Bill Everett.

"ranked Spider-Man and the Hulk alongside . . ." Bradford W. Wright, *Comic Book Nation: The Transformation of Youth Culture in America* (Baltimore: Johns Hopkins University Press, 2001), 223.

The Bronze Age

As always, see *Superhero: The Secret Origin of a Genre* by Peter Coogan, *Men of Tomorrow: Geeks, Gangsters and the Birth of the Comic Book* by Gerard Jones, and *Comic Book Nation: The Transformation of Youth Culture in America* by Bradford Wright for discussion of the emergence of this age, and any comics history book that discusses this period. For changes to Batman, see Les Daniels's *Batman: The Complete History* and Will Brooker's *Batman Unmasked*.

Marvel ultimately surpassed DC in total sales . . . See Chris Tolworthy, "Marvel and DC Sales Figures," Enter the Story, www.zak-site.com/Great-American-Novel/comic_sales.html.

"I been readin' about you . . ." *Green Lantern/Green Arrow* #76 (April 1970).

"My ward is a JUNKIE" . . . *Green Lantern/Green Arrow* #85 (August/September 1971).

The End of Wonder Woman

"I didn't see how a kid, male or female . . ." Mike Sekowksy, quoted in Daniels, *Wonder Woman*, 125.

"Girls! If you dig romance, and we know . . ." This ad appeared in *Superman's Girl Friend Lois Lane* #92 (May 1969), along with several other series.

Steve went on a secret mission to infiltrate . . . *Wonder Woman* #179 (November/December 1968).

"For ten thousand years, we have . . ." Ibid.

"I love you, mother . . . you and my . . ." Ibid.

Steve's arrest for murder . . . *Wonder Woman* #178 (September/October 1968).

"She's so much more than what I thought . . ." Ibid.

Diana saw an old, blind man being attacked . . . *Wonder Woman* #179 (November/December 1968).

"I've lost everything! Without family . . ." *Wonder Woman* #180 (January/ February 1969).

8. Doin' It for Themselves

"films of the late 1960s and early . . ." Benshoff and Griffin, *America on Film*, 276.

female lead characters wanted some control . . . Linda K. Christian-Smith, "Gender, Popular Culture, and Curriculum: Adolescent Romance Novels as Gender Text," *Curriculum Inquiry* 17, no. 4 (Winter 1987): 389–390.

letter columns and editorials in pulp magazines . . . Justine Larbalestier, *Battle of the Sexes in Science Fiction* (Middletown: Wesleyan University Press, 2002), 106.

one of the most popular subgenres . . . Ibid., 148–149.

made Sue the most powerful member . . . See Laura Mattoon D'Amore, "Invisible Girl's Quest for Visibility: Early Second Wave Feminism and the Comic Book Superheroine," *Americana: The Journal of American Popular Culture* 7, no. 2 (Fall 2008), www.americanpopularculture.com /journal/articles/fall_2008/d'amore.htm.

"Face it, Tiger . . . you just hit the jackpot" . . . *Amazing Spider-Man* #42 (November 1966)

Diana Prince as the New Wonder Woman

"I'm no more than an ordinary mortal . . ." *Justice League of America* #69 (February 1969).

"As Don Rickles might say, 'YOU DUMMY!'" . . . *Justice League of America* #72 (June 1969).

"Then—there is fury . . ." *Wonder Woman* #180 (January/February 1969).

strafing Chinese fighter jets . . . *Wonder Woman* #189 (July/August 1970).

killed at least twenty men . . . *Wonder Woman* #190 (September/October 1970).

shot down the enemy's airships . . . *Wonder Woman* #192 (January/February 1971).

"Happiness for any healthy, red-blooded . . ." *Wonder Woman* #182 (May/June 1969).

"Imagine me in the same room . . ." Ibid.

"on her quest for a new self . . ." Janice Radway, *Reading the Romance: Women, Patriarchy, and Popular Literature* (Chapel Hill: University of North Carolina Press, 1991), 138.

"a passive, expectant, trembling creature . . ." Ibid., 145.

"I'm becoming fond of Tim . . ." *Wonder Woman* #181 (March/April 1969).

"in the few hours since we met . . ." *Wonder Woman* #182 (May/June 1969).

Patrick McGuire, a pilot . . . *Wonder Woman* #187 (March/April 1970) through *Wonder Woman* #189 (July/August 1970).

Ranagor, leader of the rebels . . . *Wonder Woman* #190 (September/October 1970) through *Wonder Woman* #192 (January/February 1971).

Baron Anatole Karoli . . . *Wonder Woman* #196 (September/October 1971).

Jonny Double, a private detective . . . *Wonder Woman* #199 (March/April 1972) through *Wonder Woman* #202 (September/October 1972).

Diana almost kissed Superman . . . *World's Finest* #204 (August 1971).

"You lied to me! You said . . ." *Wonder Woman* #182 (May/June 1969).

"Diana (Wonder Woman) Prince, hurt . . ." *Wonder Woman* #183 (July/August 1969).

"Karate . . . judo . . . kung fu . . ." *Wonder Woman* #181 (March/April 1969).

"Still, Ching fights better even . . ." Ibid.

"I tried to tell you, Diana, I could . . ." *Wonder Woman* #186 (January/February 1970).

"You can't pay less than minimum . . ." *Wonder Woman* #203 (November/December 1972).

"I'm for equal wages, too! But I'm . . ." Ibid.

"Perhaps I'm incompetent and unsure . . ." Ibid.

"Now I feel I've really accomplished . . ." Ibid.

Lois Lane

Lois had won the Pulitzer Prize . . . *Superman's Girl Friend Lois Lane* #80 (January 1968).

"You've ignored me, hurt me . . ." Ibid.

"You've had me on the string for years . . ." *Superman's Girl Friend Lois Lane* #90 (February 1969).

transform herself into a black woman . . . *Superman's Girl Friend Lois Lane* #106 (November 1970).

"It's you who are blind! My heart . . ." *Superman's Girl Friend Lois Lane* #110 (May 1971).

"Por dios, señorita! We all want to . . ." *Superman's Girl Friend Lois Lane* #111 (July 1971).

"You don't want to be down-graded . . ." *Superman's Girl Friend Lois Lane* #114 (September 1971).

"Now that my sister's gone, I'm going to live . . ." *Superman's Girl Friend Lois Lane* #121 (April 1972).

"You're only being twice as stupid!" . . . *Superman's Girl Friend Lois Lane* #122 (May 1972).

"Be a good girl . . . oooo! Sometimes he is . . ." *Superman's Girl Friend Lois Lane* #127 (October 1972).

"I'm tired of your super-interfering . . ." *Superman's Girl Friend Lois Lane* #129 (February 1973).

"I-I'm sorry, Diana! But Superman's . . ." *Superman's Girl Friend Lois Lane* #93 (July 1969).

Batgirl

"Everybody thinks of me as a 'Plain Jane' . . ." *Detective Comics* #363 (May 1967).

"Holy interference! She's ruining . . ." *Detective Comics* #359 (January 1967).

"That suits me fine! Nabbing crooks . . ." *Batman* #197 (December 1967).

"I'll welcome her aid, Commissioner . . ." *Detective Comics* #359 (January 1967).

"Batgirl sure is tops in my book!" . . . Ibid.

she'd actually infiltrated the organization . . . *Batman* #214 (August 1969).

"My vanity betrayed me!" . . . *Detective Comics* #371 (January 1968).

"It's the only way I can really fight crime . . ." *Detective Comics* #422 (April 1972).

"Will they clean up the slums? Create . . ." *Detective Comics* #423 (May 1972).

Emerald Empress

"the most wanted female criminal . . ." *Adventure Comics* #352 (January 1967).

the Empress blasted him out of the room . . . *Adventure Comics* #353 (February 1967).

the Empress separated the two . . . Ibid.

the Empress handled Brainiac 5 . . . *Superboy and the Legion of Super-Heroes* #231 (September 1977).

hammered the Boy of Steel . . . *Superboy* #198 (October 1973).

encased him in a force field . . . Ibid.

carried around a piece of Kryptonite . . . *Adventure Comics* #352 (January 1967).

9. Restoration and Re-creation

"return our heroine to the feminism . . ." Joanne Edgar, "Wonder Woman Revisited," *Ms.* 1, no. 1 (1972): 55.

"the feminism and strength of the original Wonder Woman . . ." Gloria Steinem, introduction to *Wonder Woman* (New York: Holt, Rinehart and Winston, 1972), 5.

The Liberal Feminism of *Ms.* Magazine

"the most widely recognized publication . . ." Rosemarie Tong, *Feminist Thought: A More Comprehensive Introduction*, 3rd ed. (Boulder: Westview Press, 2009), 46.

"The purpose of NOW is to take . . ." Betty Friedan, "The National Organization for Women's 1966 Statement of Purpose," available at National Organization for Women official website, www.now.org/history/purpos 66.html.

"self-esteem and independence" . . . Mary Peacock, quoted in Amy Erdman Farrell, *Yours in Sisterhood: Ms. Magazine and the Promise of Popular Feminism* (Chapel Hill: University of North Carolina Press, 1998), 42.

based on the editors' belief that . . . Mary Thom, *Inside Ms.: 25 Years of the Magazine and the Feminist Movement* (New York: Henry Holt and Company, 1997), 46.

Originary Matriarchy

"is defined and differentiated with reference . . ." Simone de Beauvoir, *The Second Sex*, trans. H. M. Parshley (New York: Alfred A. Knopf, 1957), xx.

"the first males were mutants, freaks . . ." Elizabeth Gould Davis, *The First Sex* (New York: G. P. Putnam's Sons, 1971), 35.

"the previous age of peace and . . ." Ibid., 135.

"in the beginning, there was woman" . . . Berta Eckstein-Diener [Helen Diner, pseud.], *Mothers and Amazons: The First Feminine History of Culture*, trans. John Philip Lundin (New York: The Julian Press, 1965) 1.

what he called "mother right" . . . See J. J. Bachofen, *Myth, Religion, and Mother Right: Selected Writings of J. J. Bachofen*, trans. Ralph Manheim (Princeton, NJ: Princeton University Press, 1967).

the many inaccuracies behind originary matriarchy . . . See Ti-Grace Atkinson, quoted in Judy Antonelli, "Atkinson Re-evaluates Feminism," *Off Our Backs* 5, no. 5 (June 1975): 19; or Sarah B. Pomeroy, "A Classical Scholar's Perspective on Matriarchy," in *Liberating Women's History: Theoretical and Critical Essays*, ed. Berenice A. Carroll (Chicago: University of Chicago Press, 1976), 223.

"The true history of woman was rewritten . . ." Rhoda Lerman, "In Memoriam: Elizabeth Gould Davis," in *Ms.* 3, no. 6 (December 1974): 74.

Alpert believed that the maternal nature of women . . . Jane Alpert, "Mother Right: A New Feminist Theory," *Ms.* 2, no. 2 (August 1973): 92.

The Amazon Connection

"just one small, isolated outcropping . . ." Steinem, introduction to *Wonder Woman*, 6.

an imagined meeting between herself, Diner . . . Phyllis Chesler, "The Amazon Legacy," in *Wonder Woman* (New York: Holt, Rinehart and Winston, 1972), 1–2.

a battle over whether patriarchy . . . Eckstein-Diener, *Mothers and Amazons*, 105.

"a step forward to a purer form of life" . . . Bachofen, *Myth, Religion, and Mother Right*, 105.

"many genuine Amazon and matriarchal . . ." Chesler, "The Amazon Legacy," 13.

"Wonder Woman is an important symbol . . ." Letter from Ann Forfreedom, *Wonder Woman* #212 (June/July 1974).

Revising Wonder Woman

"her creator had also seen straight . . ." Steinem, introduction to *Wonder Woman*, 1.

"a glorified image of woman on which . . ." Joanne H. Wright, *Origin Stories in Political Thought: Discourses on Gender, Power, and Citizenship* (Toronto: University of Toronto Press, 2004), 149.

"The new identity being forged has little . . ." Ibid., 149.

"So the gr-reat Wonder Woman is-ss . . ." *Wonder Woman* #6 (Fall 1943).

"the distorted and villainized Nazis . . ." Edgar, "Wonder Woman Revisited," 55.

"highly jingoistic and even racist overtones" . . . Steinem, introduction to *Wonder Woman*, 4.

"Wonder Woman's artists sometimes . . ." Steinem, "Politics," in *Wonder Woman* (New York: Holt, Rinehart and Winston, 1972).

"compared to the other comic book characters . . ." Steinem, introduction to *Wonder Woman*, 4.

"some of the Wonder Woman stories preach . . ." Ibid., 3.

"much of the blame rests with history . . ." Ibid., 3.

She regularly ousted local leaders . . . See *Sensation Comics* #18 (June 1943) and *Sensation Comics* #62 (February 1947).

"all these doubts paled beside the relief . . ." Steinem, introduction to *Wonder Woman*, 4.

"Give them an alluring woman stronger . . ." Marston, "Why 100,000,000 Americans Read Comics," 43.

"females were sometimes romanticized . . ." Steinem, introduction to *Wonder Woman*, 3.

"Is the reader supposed to conclude women . . ." Ibid., 3.

"rarely has the leisure to hint at what . . ." Ibid., 3.

"Who could resist a role model like that?" . . . Edgar, "Wonder Woman Revisited," 52.

"the comic also underlines the importance . . ." Chesler, "The Amazon Legacy," 14.

"a version of the truisms that women . . ." Steinem, introduction to *Wonder Woman*, 2.

"Strength and self-reliance for . . ." Ibid., 3.

"Wonder Woman's final message to . . ." Steinem, "Sisterhood," in *Wonder Woman* (New York: Holt, Rinehart and Winston, 1972).

"With my speculum, I am strong . . ." The cover of *Sister: The Newspaper of the Los Angeles Women's Center*, July 1973.

Epic Comic Book Fail

"like many of us, she went into a decline . . ." Edgar, "Wonder Woman Revisited," 52.

"Dottie Cottonman, women's magazine . . ." *Wonder Woman* #204 (February 1973).

FN reports that Woolfolk's outspoken feminism . . . See interview with Jeff Rovin by Jon B. Cooke, "Rise & Fall of Rovin's Empire," www.twomorrows.com/comicbookartist/articles/16rovin.html; and Alan Kupperberg, "Dorothy Woolfolk Remembered," www.alankupperberg.com/woolfolk.html.

In Her Satin Tights, Fighting for Her Rights

"a modern-day Lynda Carter" . . . Inside cover of *Playboy* 55, no. 2 (February 2008).

"What bothered me more then . . ." Heidi Meeley, "Lynda Carter She Ain't! The Reaction Starts," *Comics Fairplay* blog, January 11, 2008, http://comicsfairplay.blogspot.com/2008/01/lynda-carter-she-ain.html.

"How exactly did Tiffany Fallon earn . . ." Commenter "borrowedwings," in response to Rachel Edidin, "No, It Really Is That Simple," *Rachel* blog, January 16, 2008, http://rachel-edidin.livejournal.com/72684.html.

"when [Carter] put on that uniform . . ." Lisa Fortuner, "Just Past the Horizon: That's Not Power," *Newsarama*, January 11, 2008, http://blog.newsarama.com/2008/01/11/just-past-the-horizon-thats-not-power/.

"I grew up watching the TV show . . ." George Khoury, "Beautiful Girl: An Interview with Tiffany Fallon," *Comic Book Resources*, February 18, 2008, www.comicbookresources.com/?page=article&id=15771.

"If the Nazis win, the whole world would be . . ." "The Feminum Mystique Part One," in *Wonder Woman: The Complete First Season* (Warner Video, 2004), DVD.

"I named this island 'Paradise' . . ." "The New Original Wonder Woman," in *Wonder Woman: The Complete First Season.*

"Fraulein Grabel, you are a woman of great . . ." "Fausta: The Nazi Wonder Woman," in *Wonder Woman: The Complete First Season.*

"Women are the wave of the future . . ." "The New Original Wonder Woman," in *Wonder Woman: The Complete First Season.*

"STEVE: She is a wonder. Strong and fearless . . ." "Last of the Two-Dollar Bills," in *Wonder Woman: The Complete First Season.*

"We needed a large woman, a statuesque . . ." Douglas Cramer, interviewed in "Beauty, Brawn, and Bulletproof Bracelets: A Wonder Woman Retrospective," in *Wonder Woman: The Complete First Season.*

10. The Mundane Modern Age

Comics from the Modern Age are collected by story line, with the vast majority of them currently out of print. The early years of the Pérez era were collected in four volumes, now out of print, and subsequent stories were collected sporadically. Only the newest arcs and bestselling titles remain available for any character, and there are few for Wonder Woman.

In 1970, its average monthly circulation . . . Chris Tolworthy, "Marvel and DC Sales Figures," www.zak-site.com/Great-American-Novel/comic_sales.html.

The George Pérez Era

Wonder Woman was hit by the Anti-Monitor's antimatter blast . . . *Crisis on Infinite Earths* #12 (March 1986).

Knowing the book was having trouble . . . George Pérez, introduction to *Wonder Woman Volume One: Gods and Mortals* (New York: DC Comics, 2004).

"strong . . . brave . . . compassionate . . ." *Wonder Woman* #1 (February 1987).

"chosen race—born to lead humanity . . ." Ibid.

"open yourself to fair Artemis . . ." Ibid.

they became part of the world again . . . *Wonder Woman* #22 (November 1988).

Myndi Mayer died of a drug overdose . . . *Wonder Woman* #20 (September 1988).

Vanessa's cheery friend Lucy Spears committed suicide . . . *Wonder Woman* #46 (September 1990).

Vanessa was concerned her boyfriend wouldn't like her . . . *Wonder Woman* #16 (May 1988).

made Etta Candy feel sensitive about her weight . . . *Wonder Woman* #15 (April 1988).

Background Player

She became a space pirate . . . Starting in *Wonder Woman* #69 (December 1992).

got a job at the Mexican fast food restaurant . . . *Wonder Woman* #73 (April 1993).

John Byrne took over as writer and artist . . . *Wonder Woman* #101 (September 1995).

even killed her for a few issues . . . Starting in *Wonder Woman* #127 (November 1997).

Batman had eighty-four titles listed and . . . DC Comics, *DC Entertainment Essential Graphic Novels and Chronology 2013* (New York: DC Comics, 2013), 97–104.

Wonder Woman died twice . . . *War of the Gods* #3 (November 1991); and *Wonder Woman* #127.

lost the title of Wonder Woman . . . Starting in *Wonder Woman* #92 (December 1994).

The Fridged Women of DC Comics

they eventually got married . . . *Superman: The Wedding Album* (December 1996).

she was shot while embedded with troops . . . *Adventures of Superman* #631 (October 2004).

First coined by Gail Simone . . . See the website Women in Refrigerators, www.lby3.com/wir/.

One of the most famous fridgings involved Barbara Gordon . . . *Batman: The Killing Joke* (1988).

"I may never be as good as he is, but Kal . . ." *Crisis on Infinite Earths* #7 (October 1985).

Steph was promoted when the current Robin . . . *Robin* #126 (July 2004).

brutally tortured and killed by Black Mask . . . *Batman* #633 (December 2004).

The second issue revealed that years before . . . *Identity Crisis* #2 (September 2004).

The culprit was actually Jean Loring . . . *Identity Crisis* #7 (February 2005).

So Wonder Woman snapped his neck . . . *Wonder Woman* #219 (September 2005).

Conclusion

SPIDER-MAN AND BARACK OBAMA . . . http://splashpage.mtv.com/2009/02/02 /spider-man-and-barack-obama-comic-book-team-up-hits-fifth-printing/.

THE AVENGERS SHATTERS BOX OFFICE RECORDS . . . www.rollingstone.com /movies/news/the-avengers-shatters-box-office-records-for-opening -weekend-20120507.

WONDER WOMAN'S NEW HAIRDO CAUSES A STIR . . . http://web.kitsapsun.com /redesign/2003-04-09/nationworld/118111.shtml.

JOSS WHEDON DISCUSSES HIS DEFUNCT "WONDER WOMAN" MOVIE . . . www .screenrant.com/joss-whedon-wonder-woman-sandy-139177/.

WONDER WOMAN FINALLY GETS A PAIR OF PANTS . . . www.disgrasian.com/2010 /06/wonder-woman-finally-gets-a-pair-of-pants/.

DC REVEALS SUPERMAN'S NEW LEADING LADY . . . AND IT'S A DOOZY . . . http:// shelf-life.ew.com/2012/08/22/justice-league-12-exclusive/.

On *The Big Bang Theory* . . . "The Wheaton Recurrence," *The Big Bang Theory*, season 3, episode 19.

On *30 Rock*, Liz Lemon sang part . . . "Lee Marvin vs. Derek Jeter," *30 Rock*, season 4, episode 17.

On *The Simpsons*, Homer mentioned that . . . "Three Men and a Comic Book," *The Simpsons*, season 2, episode 21.

Bibliography

Alpert, Jane. "Mother Right: A New Feminist Theory." *Ms.* 2, no. 2 (August 1973): 52–55, 88–94.

Antonelli, Judy. "Atkinson Re-evaluates Feminism." *Off Our Backs* 5, no. 5 (June 1975): 19.

Apollodorus. *The Library.* Vol. 1. Translated by Sir James George Frazier. Cambridge, MA: Harvard University Press, 1967.

Atkinson, Ti-Grace. *Amazon Odyssey.* New York: Link Books, 1974.

Bachofen, J. J. *Myth, Religion, and Mother Right: Selected Writings of J. J. Bachofen.* Translated by Ralph Manheim. Princeton, NJ: Princeton University Press, 1967.

Barry, Kathleen. *Female Sexual Slavery.* Englewood Cliffs: Prentice-Hall, 1979.

Beaty, Bart. *Fredric Wertham and the Critique of Mass Culture.* Jackson: University Press of Mississippi, 2005.

"Beauty, Brawn, and Bulletproof Bracelets: A Wonder Woman Retrospective." In *Wonder Woman: The Complete First Season.* Warner Video, 2004.

Beauvoir, Simone de. *The Second Sex.* Translated by H. M. Parshley. New York: Alfred A. Knopf, 1957.

Bennett, Michael J. *Belted Heroes and Bound Women: The Myth of the Homeric War King.* Lanham, MD: Rowman & Littlefield, 1997.

Benshoff, Harry M., and Sean Griffin. *America on Film: Representing Race, Class, Sexuality, and Gender at the Movies*. Oxford: Blackwell Publishing, 2004.

Benton, Mike. *Superhero Comics of the Silver Age: An Illustrated History*. Dallas: Taylor Publishing Company, 1991.

Binder, Otto, Jerry Siegel, et al. *Showcase Presents: Supergirl*. Vol. 1. New York: DC Comics, 2007.

Binder, Otto, Jerry Coleman, et al. *Showcase Presents: The Superman Family*. Vol. 2. New York: DC Comics, 2008.

Binder, Otto, Robert Bernstein, et al. *Showcase Presents: The Superman Family*. Vol. 3. New York: DC Comics, 2009.

Bleier, Ruth. *Science and Gender: A Critique of Biology and Its Theories on Women*. New York: Pergamon Press, 1984.

Boozer, Jack. "The Lethal Femme Fatale in the Noir Tradition." *Journal of Film and Video* 51, no. 3/4 (Fall 1999): 20–35.

Breines, Wini. *Young, White, and Miserable: Growing Up Female in the Fifties*. Boston: Beacon Press, 1992.

Bronfen, Elisabeth. "Femme Fatale—Negotiations of Tragic Desire." *New Literary History* 35, no. 1 (Winter 2004): 103–116.

Brooker, Will. *Batman Unmasked: Analyzing a Cultural Icon*. New York: Continuum, 2001.

Broome, John, Carmine Infantino, et al. *Showcase Presents: Batgirl*. Vol. 1. New York: DC Comics, 2007.

Broome, John, Gardner Fox, et al. *Showcase Presents: Green Lantern*. Vol. 1. New York: DC Comics, 2005.

Broome, John, Gardner Fox, et al. *Showcase Presents: Green Lantern*. Vol. 2. New York: DC Comics, 2007.

Brownmiller, Susan. *Against Our Will: Men, Women and Rape*. New York: Fawcett Columbine, 1975.

Brownstein, Charles. *Eisner/Miller*. Milwaukee: Dark Horse Books, 2005.

Bunn, Geoffrey C. "The Lie Detector, *Wonder Woman* and Liberty: The Life and Work of William Moulton Marston." *History of the Human Sciences* 10, no. 1 (1997): 91–119.

Chesler, Phyllis. "The Amazon Legacy." In *Wonder Woman*. New York: Holt, Rinehart and Winston, 1972.

Christian-Smith, Linda K. "Gender, Popular Culture, and Curriculum: Adolescent Romance Novels as Gender Text." *Curriculum Inquiry* 17, no. 4 (Winter 1987): 365–406.

Coogan, Peter. *Superhero: The Secret Origin of a Genre*. Austin: Monkey-Brain Books, 2006.

Cott, Nancy F. *The Grounding of Modern Feminism*. New Haven: Yale University Press, 1987.

D'Amore, Laura Mattoon. "Invisible Girl's Quest for Visibility: Early Second Wave Feminism and the Comic Book Superheroine." *Americana: The Journal of American Popular Culture* 7, no. 2 (Fall 2008). www.american popularculture.com/journal/articles/fall_2008/d'amore.htm.

Daniels, Les. *Batman: The Complete History*. San Francisco: Chronicle Books, 1999.

———. *DC Comics: Sixty Years of the World's Favorite Comic Book Heroes*. New York: Bulfinch Press, 1995.

———. *Superman: The Complete History*. San Francisco: Chronicle Books, 1998.

———. *Wonder Woman: The Complete History*. San Francisco: Chronicle Books, 2000.

Davis, Elizabeth Gould. *The First Sex*. New York: G. P. Putnam's Sons, 1971.

DC Comics. *DC Entertainment Essential Graphic Novels and Chronology 2013*. New York: DC Comics, 2013.

Deckard, Barbara Sinclair. *The Women's Movement: Political, Socioeconomic, and Psychological Issues*. New York: Harper & Row, 1979.

Douglas, Susan J. *Where the Girls Are: Growing Up Female with the Mass Media*. New York: Time Books, 1994.

Echols, Alice. *Daring to Be Bad: Radical Feminism in America, 1967–1975*. Minneapolis: University of Minnesota Press, 1989.

Eckstein-Diener, Berta [Helen Diner, pseud.]. *Mothers and Amazons: The First Feminine History of Culture*. Translated by John Philip Lundin. New York: The Julian Press, 1965.

Edgar, Joanne. "Wonder Woman Revisited." *Ms.* 1, no. 1 (1972): 52–55.

Edidin, Rachel. "No, It Really Is That Simple." *Rachel* blog, January 16, 2008. http://rachel-edidin.livejournal.com/72684.html.

Eller, Cynthia. *The Myth of Matriarchal Prehistory: Why an Invented Past Won't Give Women a Future*. Boston: Beacon Press, 2000.

Ellis, Havelock. *The Psychology of Sex: A Manual for Students*. New York: Emerson Books, 1938.

———. *Studies in the Psychology of Sex, Volume I: The Evolution of Modesty, the Phenomena of Sexual Periodicity, and Auto-Erotism*. New York: Random House, 1942; orig. publ. 1900.

————. *Studies in the Psychology of Sex, Volume II: Sexual Inversion*. New York: Random House, 1942, orig. publ. 1897.

————. *Studies in the Psychology of Sex, Volume III: Analysis of the Sexual Impulse*. New York: Random House, 1942; orig. publ. 1903.

Farrell, Amy Erdman. *Yours in Sisterhood: Ms. Magazine and the Promise of Popular Feminism*. Chapel Hill: University of North Carolina Press, 1998.

Fingeroth, Danny. *Disguised as Clark Kent: Jews, Comics, and the Creation of the Superhero*. New York: Continuum, 2008.

Firestone, Shulamith. *The Dialectic of Sex: The Case for Feminist Revolution*. New York: Bantam Books, 1970.

Fortuner, Lisa. "Just Past the Horizon: That's Not Power." *Newsarama*, January 11, 2008. http://blog.newsarama.com/2008/01/11/just-past-the-horizon-thats-not-power/.

Freedman, Estelle B. *No Turning Back: The History of Feminism and the Future of Women*. New York: Ballantine Books, 2002.

Friedan, Betty. *The Feminine Mystique*. New York: Norton, 1963.

————. "The National Organization for Women's 1966 Statement of Purpose." Available at National Organization for Women official website. www.now.org/history/purpos66.html.

Gilbert, James. *A Cycle of Outrage. America's Reaction to the Juvenile Delinquent in the 1950s*. Oxford: Oxford University Press, 1986.

Goldin, Claudia Dale. *Understanding the Gender Gap: An Economic History of American Women*. New York: Oxford University Press, 1990.

Gordon, Michael. "From an Unfortunate Necessity to a Cult of Mutual Orgasm: Sex in American Marital Education Literature, 1830–1940." *Studies in the Sociology of Sex*. Edited by James M. Henslin. New York: Appleton-Century-Crofts, 1971, 53–80.

Hadju, David. *The Ten-Cent Plague: The Great Comic-Book Scare and How It Changed America*. New York: Farar, Straus, and Giroux, 2008.

Halberstam, David. *The Fifties*. New York: Fawcett Books, 1993.

Haraway, Donna. "The Virtual Speculum in the New World Order." In *Revisioning Women, Health, and Healing: Feminist, Cultural, and Technoscience Perspectives*. Edited by Adele E. Clarke and Virginia L. Oleson. New York: Routledge, 1999, 49–96.

Harvey, Brett. *The Fifties: A Women's Oral History*. New York: Harper Collins, 1993.

Heggs, Dan. "Cyberpsychology and Cyborgs." *Cyberpsychology.* Edited by Ángel J. Gordo-López and Ian Parker. New York: Taylor & Francis, 1999, 184–201.

Heinecken, Dawn. *The Women Warrior of Television: A Feminist Cultural Analysis of the New Female Body in Popular Media.* New York: Peter Lang, 2003.

Honey, Maureen. *Creating Rosie the Riveter: Class, Gender, and Propaganda During World War II.* Amherst: University of Massachusetts Press, 1984.

Hubbard, Rita C. "Relationship Styles in Popular Romance Novels, 1950 to 1983." *Communication Quarterly* 33, no. 2 (Spring 1985): 113–125.

Jackson, Margaret. " 'Facts of Life' or the Eroticization of Women's Oppression? Sexology and the Social Construction of Heterosexuality." *The Cultural Construction of Sexuality.* Edited by Pat Caplan. London: Tavistock Publications, 1987, 52–81.

———. "Sexual Liberation of Social Control? Some Aspects of the Relationship Between Feminism and the Social Construction of Knowledge in the Early Twentieth Century." *Women's Studies International Forum* 6, no. 1 (1983): 1–17.

Jacobs, Frank. *The Mad World of William M. Gaines.* Secaucus: Lyle Stuart, 1972.

Jacobs, Will, and Gerard Jones. *The Comic Book Heroes: The First History of Modern Comic Books—from the Silver Age to the Present.* Rocklin, CA: Prima, 1997.

Johnston, Jill. *Lesbian Nation: The Feminist Solution.* New York: Simon and Schuster, 1973.

Jones, Gerard. *Men of Tomorrow: Geeks, Gangsters and the Birth of the Comic Book.* New York: Basic Books, 2004.

Kane, Bob, and Bill Finger. *The Batman Chronicles.* Vols. 1–9. New York: DC Comics, 2005–2010.

Kanigher, Robert, Ross Andru, et al. *Showcase Presents: Wonder Woman.* Vols. 1–4. New York: DC Comics, 2007–2011.

Kaplan, Arie. *From Krakow to Krypton: Jews and Comic Books.* Philadelphia: Jewish Publication Society, 2008.

Khiss, Peter. "No Harm in Horror, Comics Issuer Says; Comics Publisher Sees No Harm In Horror, Discounts 'Good Taste.' " *New York Times.* April 22, 1954.

Khoury, George. "Beautiful Girl: An Interview with Tiffany Fallon." *Comic Book Resources*. February 18, 2008. www.comicbookresources.com /?page=article&id=15771.

Kill Bill: Volume 2. Written and directed by Quentin Tarantino. Miramax, 2004.

Kleinberg, S. J. *Women in the United States, 1830–1945*. New Brunswick: Rutgers University Press, 1999.

Lamb, Marguerite. "Who Was Wonder Woman? Long-Ago LAW Alumna Elizabeth Marston Was the Muse Who Gave Us a Superheroine." *Boston University Alumni Magazine*, Fall 2001.

Lang, Jeffrey S., and Patrick Trimble. "Whatever Happened to the Man of Tomorrow? An Examination of the American Monomyth and the Comic Book Superhero." *The Journal of Popular Culture* 22, no. 3 (1988): 157–173.

Larbalestier, Justine. *Battle of the Sexes in Science Fiction*. Middletown: Wesleyan University Press, 2002.

Lerman, Rhoda. "In Memoriam: Elizabeth Gould Davis." *Ms.* 3, no. 6 (December 1974).

Marble, Alice, and Dale Leatherman. *Courting Danger: My Adventures in World-Class Tennis, Golden-Age Hollywood, and High-Stakes Spying*. New York: St. Martin's Press, 1991.

Marston, William Moulton. *Emotions of Normal People*. New York: Harcourt, Brace, and Company, 1928.

———. *The Private Life of Julius Caesar (Venus with Us)*. New York: Universal, 1953.

———. "Why 100,000,000 Americans Read Comics." *American Scholar* 13 (January 1944): 35–44.

———. "Women: Servants of Civilization." *Tomorrow*, February 1942, 42–45.

Marston, William Moulton, and H. G. Peter. *Wonder Woman Archives*. Vols. 1–7. New York: DC Comics, 1998–2012.

May, Elaine Tyler. *Homeward Bound: American Families in the Cold War Era*. New York: Basic Books, 1988.

Medovoi, Leerom. *Rebels: Youth and the Cold War Origins of Identity*. Durham: Duke University Press, 2005.

Meeley, Heidi. "Lynda Carter She Ain't! The Reaction Starts." *Comics Fairplay* blog, January 11, 2008. http://comicsfairplay.blogspot.com/2008/01 /lynda-carter-she-ain.html.

Melody, M. E., and Linda M. Peterson. *Teaching America About Sex: Marriage Guides and Sex Manuals from the Late Victorians to Dr. Ruth.* New York: New York University Press, 1999.

Meyerowitz, Joanne, ed. *Not June Cleaver: Women and Gender in Postwar America, 1945–1960.* Philadelphia: Temple University Press, 1994.

Miller, John Jackson. "Comic Book Sales by Month." The Comic Chronicles: A Resource for Comics Research. www.comichron.com/monthlycomics sales.html.

———. "Comic Book Sales by Year." The Comic Chronicles: A Resource for Comics Research. www.comichron.com/yearlycomicssales.html.

Morse, Ben. "Thunderstruck." *Wizard Magazine* 179 (September 2006).

New York Times. "Marston Advises 3 L's for Success." November 11, 1937.

Nyberg, Amy Kiste. *Seal of Approval: The History of the Comics Code.* Jackson: University Press of Mississippi, 1998.

Olson, Lynne. *Freedom's Daughters: The Unsung Heroines of the Civil Rights Movement from 1830 to 1970.* New York: Scribner, 2001.

O'Neil, Denny, Mike Sekowsky, et al. *Diana Prince: Wonder Woman.* Vols. 1–4. New York: DC Comics, 2008–2009.

Playboy 55, no. 2 (February 2008).

Pomeroy, Sarah B. "A Classical Scholar's Perspective on Matriarchy." In *Liberating Women's History: Theoretical and Critical Essays.* Edited by Berenice A. Carroll. Chicago: University of Chicago Press, 1976, 217–223.

Radway, Janice. *Reading the Romance: Women, Patriarchy, and Popular Literature.* Chapel Hill: University of North Carolina Press, 1991.

Raphael, Jordan, and Tom Spurgeon. *Stan Lee and the Rise and Fall of the American Comic Book.* Chicago: Chicago Review Press, 2003.

Redstockings of the Women's Liberation Movement. *Feminist Revolution: An Abridged Edition with Additional Writings.* New York: Random House, 1975.

Richard, Olive. "Don't Laugh at the Comics." *Family Circle*, October 25, 1940.

———. "The Women Are Our Future." *Family Circle*, August 14, 1942.

Ro, Ronin. *Tales to Astonish: Jack Kirby, Stan Lee, and the American Comic Book Revolution.* New York: Bloomsbury, 2004.

Robbins, Trina. *The Great Women Superheroes.* New York: Kitchen Sink Press, 1996.

———. "Miss Fury." *Comics Journal* 288 (2007): 110–111.

———. "Wonder Woman: Lesbian or Dyke? Paradise Island as a Woman's Community." Paper presented at WisCon 2006. Available at www.girl-wonder.org/papers/robbins.html.

Robinson, Lillian S. *Wonder Women: Feminisms and Superheroes*. New York: Routledge, 2004.

Russ, Joanna. "The Image of Women in Science Fiction." In *Images of Women in Fiction: Feminist Perspectives*. Edited by Susan Koppelman Cornillon. Bowling Green: Bowling Green University Popular Press, 1973, 79–94.

Siegel, Jerry, and Joe Shuster. "How Would Superman End World War II?" In *Superman Sunday Classics: Strips 1–183, 1939–1943*. New York: Sterling Publishing, 1999, 187–190.

———. *The Superman Chronicles*. Vols. 1–10. New York: DC Comics, 2006–2012.

Snyder, Robin. "The Golden Age Gladiator: Robert Kanigher." *Comics Journal* 85 (October 1983).

———. "The Golden Age Gladiator: Robert Kanigher, Part II." *Comics Journal* 86 (November 1983).

Steinem, Gloria. Introduction to *Wonder Woman*. New York: Holt, Rinehart and Winston, 1972.

Thom, Mary. *Inside Ms.: 25 Years of the Magazine and the Feminist Movement*. New York: Henry Holt and Company, 1997.

Tilley, Carol L. "Seducing the Innocent: Fredric Wertham and the Falsifications That Helped Condemn Comics." *Information & Culture* 47, no. 4 (2012): 383–413.

Tolworthy, Chris. "Marvel and DC Sales Figures." Enter the Story. www.zak-site.com/Great-American-Novel/comic_sales.html.

Tong, Rosemarie. *Feminist Thought: A More Comprehensive Introduction*. 3rd ed. Boulder: Westview Press, 2009.

Weeks, Jeffrey. "Havelock Ellis and the Politics of Sex Reform." In *Socialism and the New Life: The Personal and Sexual Politics of Edward Carpenter and Havelock Ellis*. London: Pluto Press, 1977, 139–185.

Weinstein, Simcha. *Up, Up, and Oy Vey! How Jewish History, Culture, and Values Shaped the Comic Book Superhero*. Baltimore: Leviathan Press, 2006.

Wertham, Fredric. "The Comics . . . Very Funny." *Saturday Review of Literature*, May 29, 1948, 6–7, 27–29.

———. "The Curse of Comic Books: The Value Patterns and Effects of Comic Books." *Religious Education* 49 (1954): 394–406.

————. *Seduction of the Innocent*. New York: Rinehart & Company, 1954.

Willis, Ellen. *No More Nice Girls: Countercultural Essays*. Hanover: Wesleyan University Press, 1992.

Wolk, Douglas. *Reading Comics: How Graphic Novels Work and What They Mean*. Cambridge, MA: Da Capo Press, 2008.

Wonder Woman: The Complete First Season. Warner Video, 2004. DVD.

Wright, Bradford W. *Comic Book Nation: The Transformation of Youth Culture in America*. Baltimore: Johns Hopkins University Press, 2001.

Wright, Joanne H. *Origin Stories in Political Thought: Discourses on Gender, Power, and Citizenship*. Toronto: University of Toronto Press, 2004.

Index

civil rights advocates, 77, 148
clams, as villains, 110
Cleopatra (character), 67
"Clothing of Fortune!" strip, 81
codes, 74
Comic Book Heroes, The (Jacobs & Jones), 105
comic book industry
  birth of, 4–5
  CCA rules, 95–96, 99, 108, 127, 145–46, 162
  horror and crime genre, 91–92, 95–96
  1970s slump, 168, 225–26
  superhero popularity, 91, 97
  Wertham's influence, 93–94, 142
  women in, 18, 231
Comic Book Nation (Wright), 165
comic books, as a product, 166, 225–27, 231
Comic Cavalcade, 91
Comics Code Authority (CCA), 95–96, 99, 108, 127, 145–46, 162, 166
Comics Journal, 105
contests, 112–13
Cramer, Douglas, 219, 223
Crime SuspenStories, 94–95
Crisis on Infinite Earths (miniseries), 3n, 227–28, 239
Crosby, Cathy Lee, 218

damsel in distress roles, 26, 34–35, 36
Danvers, Carol (character), 7n
Danvers, Linda Lee (Supergirl), 120
Daredevil (character), 164, 165
Dark Knight Returns, The (Miller), 235
Dark Knight Rises, The, 236, 238
Davis, Elizabeth Gould, 202
"Dazzling Dolls, The" strip, 82
DC Comics, 3n, 92, 96, 166, 168, 226
DC Entertainment Essential Graphic Novels and Chronology 2013, 235
DC Explosion campaign, 226
DC Implosion, 226
DeConnick, Kelly Sue, 7n

Delany, Dana, 238
Delany, Samuel, 183, 184–85
Deodato, Mike, Jr., 232
Detective Comics, debut of, 4–5
Detective Comics Inc., founding of, 4–5
DeWitt, Alex (character), 238
Diana. *See* Prince, Diana
Diana Prince: Wonder Woman, 168–73
Dibny, Sue (character), 241
DiDio, Dan, 240
Diner, Helen, 203, 205
DISC theory, 11, 15, 135
Ditko, Steve, 162
Doctor Strange, 163–64
domestic containment, 108
Donenfeld, Harry, 4–5, 92
"Don't Laugh at the Comics" (Marston), 12–13
Doomsday (character), 236
Doran, Colleen, 231
Double, Jonny (character), 181
drug use, depicted in comics, 166, 167–68, 231
Dunst, Kirsten, 238
Durance, Erica, 238

EC Comics (Education Comics), 92
Eckstein-Diener, Bertha, 203
Edgar, Joanne, 198, 209, 215
Edidin, Rachel, 218
Education Comics (EC Comics), 92
Eisner Awards, 232, 233n
Ellis, Havelock, 56–57, 134
Emerald Empress (character), 193–96
Emotions of Normal People (Marston), 15, 57–58, 133, 135–37
Equal Rights Amendment, 200
Esposito, Mike, 90, 161
ethnicity, stereotypes about, 129
Evanier, Mark, 152n

Fader, Scott, 178–79
Fallon, Tiffany, 217–18
families, depiction of, 98–99, 107–9, 120–22, 126, 144
Family Circle magazine, 12, 47–48

Also from Chicago Review Press

Superman vs. Hollywood
How Fiendish Producers, Devious Directors, and Warring Writers Grounded an American Icon
Jake Rossen
978-1-55652-731-9
$16.95 (CAN $18.95)
Also available in e-book formats

For the first time, one book unearths all the details of Superman's turbulent adventures in Tinseltown, from his radio serial through the 2006 film *Superman Returns*. Based on extensive interviews with producers, screenwriters, cast members, and crew, *Superman vs. Hollywood* spills the beans on Marlon Brando's eccentricities; the challenges of making Superman appear to fly; the casting process that at various points had Superman being played by Sylvester Stallone, Neil Diamond, Nicolas Cage, Ashton Kutcher, and even Muhammad Ali; and the Superman movies, fashioned by such maverick filmmakers as Kevin Smith and Tim Burton, that never made it to the screen.

Stan Lee and the Rise and Fall of the American Comic Book
Jordan Raphael and Tom Spurgeon
978-1-55652-541-4
$16.95 (CAN $25.95)
Also available in e-book formats

The face of Marvel Comics and the cocreator of Spider-Man, the X-Men, the Fantastic Four, and hundreds of other colorful heroes, Stan Lee is known as a dazzling writer, a skilled editor, a relentless self-promoter, a credit hog, and a huckster—a man equal parts P. T. Barnum and Walt Disney. This book, based on interviews with Stan Lee and dozens of his colleagues and contemporaries, as well as extensive archival research, is at once a professional history, an appreciation, and a critical exploration of Stan Lee and his many accomplishments.

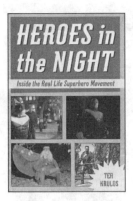

Heroes in the Night
Inside the Real Life Superhero Movement
Tea Krulos
978-1-61374-775-9
$16.95 (CAN $18.95)
Also available in e-book formats

Heroes in the Night traces journalist Tea Krulos's journey into the strange subculture of Real Life Superheroes, random citizens who have adopted comic book–style personas and hit the streets to fight injustice. Some concentrate on humanitarian or activist missions—helping the homeless, gathering donations for food banks, or delivering toys to children—while others actively patrol their neighborhoods looking for crime to fight. By day, these modern Clark Kents work as dishwashers, pencil pushers, and executives in Fortune 500 companies. But by night they become heroes for the people. Through historic research and extensive interviews, Krulos shares not only their shining, triumphant moments, but also some of their ill-advised, terrifying disasters.

Leaving Mundania
Inside the Transformative World of Live Action Role-Playing Games
Lizzie Stark
978-1-56976-605-7
$16.95 (CAN $18.95)
Also available in e-book formats

"With humor, intelligence, and more than a little bravery, Lizzie Stark guides us into the vast subculture of larping, where lawyers become vampire hunters and systems analysts turn into knights. Hilarious, honest, and enlightening, *Leaving Mundania* reminds us how thin the boundaries are between the roles we play and the selves we believe ourselves to be." —Stacey Richter, Pushcart Prize–winning author of *My Date with Satan* and *Twin Study: Stories*

Afrofuturism
The World of Black Sci-Fi and Fantasy Culture
Ytasha L. Womack
978-1-61374-796-4
$16.95 (CAN $18.95)
Also available in e-book formats

In this hip, accessible primer to the music, literature, and art of Afrofuturism, author Ytasha Womack introduces readers to the burgeoning community of artists creating Afrofuturist works, the innovators from the past, and the wide range of subjects they explore. From the sci-fi literature of Samuel Delany, Octavia Butler, and N. K. Jemisin to the musical cosmos of Sun Ra, George Clinton, and the Black Eyed Peas' will.i.am, to the visual and multimedia artists inspired by African Dogon myths and Egyptian deities, the book's topics range from the "allen" experience of blacks in America to the "wake up" cry that peppers sci-fi literature, sermons, and activism.

The Cartoon Music Book
Daniel Goldmark and Yuval Taylor, editors
978-1-55652-473-8
$18.95 (CAN $28.95)
Also available in e-book formats

The popularity of cartoon music, from Carl Stalling's work for Warner Bros. to Disney sound tracks and *The Simpsons'* song parodies, has never been greater. This lively and fascinating look at cartoon music's past and present collects contributions from well-known music critics and cartoonists, and interviews with the principal cartoon composers. Here Mark Mothersbaugh talks about his music for *Rugrats*, Alf Clausen about composing for *The Simpsons*, Carl Stalling about his work for Walt Disney and Warner Bros., Irwin Chusid about Raymond Scott's work, Will Friedwald about *Casper the Friendly Ghost*, Richard Stone about his music for *Animaniacs*, Joseph Lanza about *Ren and Stimpy*, and much, much more.

WONDER WOMAN UNBOUND